OTHER BOOKS BY DAVID CHANOFF AND DOAN VAN TOAI

A Vietcong Memoir (with Truong Nhu Tang)
The Vietnamese Gulag

'Vietnam'
A Portrait of
Its People at War

DAVID CHANOFF

AND

DOAN VAN TOAI

I.B.Tauris Publishers
LONDON · NEW YORK

First published in paperback in 1996 by
I.B.Tauris & Co Ltd
Victoria House, Bloomsbury Square, London WC1B 4DZ

In the United States of America
and Canada distributed by
St Martin's Press
175 Fifth Avenue
New York
NY 10010

First published in the UK by I.B.Tauris in 1987 in hardback as *Portrait of the Enemy*

Grateful acknowledgment is made to the following for permission to reprint from previously published material:
Doubleday & Company, Inc.: Excerpt from *Prisoner at War: The Survival of Commander Richard Stratton* by Scott Blakey. Copyright © 1978 by Scott Blakey. Reprinted by permission of Doubleday & Company, Inc.

Harcourt Brace Jovanovich, Inc.: Excerpt adapted from *A Vietcong Memoir,*
copyright © 1985 by Truong Nhu Tang, David Chanoff, and Doan Van Toai.
Reprinted by permission of Harcourt Brace Jovanovich, Inc.

Presidio Press: Excerpt from *Silence Was a Weapon*. Reprinted with permission, copyright © 1982 by Presidio Press; published by Presidio Press,
31 Pamaron Way, Novato, CA 94947.

A full CIP record for this book is available from the British Library

A full CIP record for this book is available from the Library of Congress
Library of Congress catalog card number: available

ISBN 1 86064 076 1

Printed and bound in Great Britain by
WBC Ltd, Bridgend, Mid Glamorgan

We dedicate this book with love to our wives—Yvonne and Liisa, and to our children—Dinh, Binh, Huy; Sasha, Olli and Molly.

ACKNOWLEDGMENTS

THIS BOOK WOULD NOT EXIST WERE IT NOT FOR THE COUR-age of those who chose to speak. To the ones whose names appear and to the ones whose names don't, we owe an unrepayable debt. In truth, this is their book as much as ours. Special thanks are also due to the people who put their own faith on the line and assisted in making the essential contacts, among them: Nguyen Quang Manh, Nguyen Van Phuc, Colonel Hoang Song Liem, Colonel Stuart Herrington, and Orrin Deforest. Of the people who helped us over the many unexpected difficulties we encountered, we would like to extend our appreciation especially to Ambassador Eugene Douglas and Mrs. Jane Sloat. Our thanks go also to Douglas Pike, who generously made available the rich collection of material at the Indochina Archives, and to Steven Denney, the competent and gracious librarian at the Archives.

The Historical Research Foundation and the Earhart Foundation both provided grants which enabled us to do much of the traveling *Portrait of the Enemy* required. Their assistance is gratefully acknowledged, as is that of Pham Van Cong, who made available his considerable talents as a translator.

In this book as in our previous efforts, Doan Minh Trung, Duong Thi Mai, and Doan Trang have given us the constant spiritual support, friendship, and counsel which facilitated our work and sustained us during the difficult times—as have Mai Phuong, Tuan Phuong, Da Thao, Ngan Khanh, Minh Duy, Phu Sy, Da Huong, and Huu Chung. Finally, Nguyen Van Dat has been a friend and companion who made the road easier at every turn.

CONTENTS

PART TWO: STRUGGLE

Part Three: Resolution

INTRODUCTION

THE ART OF PROPAGANDA DURING THE WAR
WAS TO PAINT THE SOCIETY
AS HAVING A SINGLE WILL.

HAN VI, POLITICAL OFFICER, HANOI CONSERVATORY OF MUSIC

A GREAT DEAL IS KNOWN ABOUT WHAT HAPPENED TO AMERICANS during the Vietnam War: the brutalization of the men who fought it, the racism, the drug use, the posttraumatic stress that grew out of it. Yet the general impression throughout the West, among both those who believed the war was justified and those who thought it immoral, is that revolutionary Vietnam was a land inhabited by a supremely dedicated, single-minded people, either heroic or fanatic, depending on the observer's politics.

The truth is different, and far more human. Revolutionary Vietnam was no monolith. It was peopled by different political, social, and ethnic groups and by individuals who thought and cared about the war in very different ways. Disillusionment, cynicism, family conflicts, and deep psychological trauma were as pervasive on the other side as on our own. They went hand in hand with the idealism, courage, and relentless tenacity that composed the image the revolution sought constantly to project. In the spectrum of human emotions that spring from war, the Vietnamese were as varied as Americans. In this book we have tried to convey something of the complexity and variety—as well as the drama—that marked their lives. We have done it by letting the Vietnamese speak for themselves. First-person histories have their problems—some interviewees have a need to embellish, others to cover up; memories are fuzzy and variable. Yet there's often an immediacy about the firsthand account that gives it unusual impact. In the middle of the Romantic era William Wordsworth said he thought a poet should be "a man speaking to other men." When people talk to you about what's been important in their lives, you can often feel the texture of their experience in a way you couldn't through a third person's interpretation. You get that direct illumination Wordsworth was thinking of with his "man speaking to men." And when they are trying to convey the most vivid kinds of experiences people can undergo—and at the same time reach across a cultural chasm as wide as the Pacific—the results can be striking.

At least that has been our experience during the two years it has taken to put this book together. Initially, our thought was to collect an oral history of the Vietcong and North Vietnamese Army at war. What we wanted were first-person accounts of the Vietnam War as seen from the other side, eyewitness reports that would focus on battles and scenes already familiar to us: Khe Sanh, the Tet Offensive, the Cambodia invasion, B-52 attacks, the Ho Chi Minh Trail. A number of books get across a gut impression of what Vietnam was like for Americans who fought there. You couldn't read Al Santoli's *Everything We Had* or Wallace Terry's *Bloods* without your bones feeling the grind of slogging and fighting through Vietnam's paddies and jungles and your mind reeling from the psychic aberrations that particular war produced. We believed we could do the same thing for the people who fought on the other side.

We guessed that the dehumanization, the psychic darkness, and the sudden, unexpected human triumphs could be found on that side as well as on ours. But the revolutionary soldiers' (the Vietnamese call them *bo doi*) experiences would, of course, be molded by the circumstances of Vietnamese life. The *bo doi* and the GI would have a lot in common when it came to the concrete details of fighting and dying. But how they perceived what they were doing might show, along with the similarities, remarkable differences. And both differences and similarities would throw light on the hearts and minds of an enemy Americans had never understood, though they needed desperately to do so. Learning how the situation looked to the other side would be a way of bridging the two cultures, of making the Vietnamese experience comprehensible to Americans.

But as we began tracking down sources and doing initial interviews, we realized that whatever came of our efforts would be both more and less than we had initially planned. We had decided right off that we would limit ourselves to talking with Vietcong and People's Army veterans who were living outside Vietnam. Even if we were able to get permission to interview inside the Socialist Republic, we knew it would mean working with government translators or other officials present. And that would effectively eliminate the possibility of getting the kind of candor and revealing introspection that burns through in the accounts of so many American veterans. But revolutionary veterans living outside their former country compose a fairly small fraternity. Leaving aside the problem of access, there simply are not enough of them to put together a thorough, multiperspective military account of the war.

On the other hand, we quickly became aware that the flood of Vietnamese refugees has included many individuals who, though they might not have worn uniforms, had in one way or another been on the other side during the war. Fighters and Party officials had indeed come out, but so had opposition politicians, militant Buddhist monks, North Vietnamese peasants, craftspeople, nurses, engineers, factory workers, and artists. Every Vietnamese refugee community has its former Party members (though they will most often keep that past hidden) and its former anti-American nationalists who had made common cause with the Communist-led Front and with their "brothers" from the North. Families that escaped often were composed of several generations. Youngsters and oldsters alike had arrived bearing their own memories, as distinct and varied as those of the warriors.

Interviews with such people could not counterpoint the American soldier's war experience exactly, but in place of that, we saw the makings of a composite portrait of life on the other side. Given the limitations of time and money, it wouldn't be a vast canvas, but we believed we could at least trace the outlines of what it was like to come of age in revolutionary Vietnam, to live in the web of one of the most provocative, lengthy, and least understood social dramas of our era. "It was a time," reflected a former Vietcong minister, smiling wistfully in his Paris apartment, "to nourish the most sublime hopes." "None of us would have minded," said a Haiphong worker, still angry after a decade at the government he fled from, "if the Saigon army had invaded the North and liberated us from them. If the Americans were helping Saigon, then we thought maybe they would come some day." Between revolutionary fervor and a bitter cynicism about life under the revolution ran a continuum of feelings. And beneath the feelings were the events in individuals' lives that gave rise to them.

Like all personal accounts, those included in this book are not objective in any scientific way. It is a commonplace that personal perspectives color events, that the ten blind men are feeling the same elephant. It is also human to talk about oneself so that others will see you as you wish to be seen. We stayed away from Vietnam itself because beyond the standard rememberer's foibles is the officially inspired (and enforced) requirement that the nation's war experience be portrayed in the colors of epic poetry. *Nhan Dan (The Party Daily)* and the published autobiographies, memoirs, and reminiscences about the war focus almost exclusively on the inspirational—bravery, endurance, determination, suffering, and sacrifice—a Vietnamese Communist version of heroic song and legend.

But that is not to say that the overseas Vietnamese do not have their own prejudices. The individuals who speak from these pages come from different backgrounds: some were accomplished Party propagandists, others uneducated and apolitical peasants. But everyone we interviewed had one thing in common: they had escaped. Each one had his story—of an unendurable life in Vietnam, of a risky, often terror-filled flight, of the need to build new lives in strange countries. Many of them had tried to escape more than once. (One former secretary we talked to made nine attempts before she finally succeeded. She was caught each time and had spent over six years in jail.) Most have left family behind, and almost all feel an intense physical attachment to the land they are separated from. Many still harbor violence in their hearts toward those they consider responsible for the losses that have marked their lives. This is background. It is impossible to say to what extent it colors any particular individual's memory of events. But our hope is that this book will contribute toward an understanding of a previously unexamined dimension of the war. If it is to do that effectively, readers should be aware of the salient features of the material they are dealing with. The greater part of this material has been gathered from refugees, and that should be kept firmly in mind.

Having said that, it is also necessary to say that the political points of view of people whose stories make up this book vary widely. Vietnamese are political animals to a greater degree than Americans; their recent history has forced them to be. Yet in revolutionary Vietnam, as everywhere, the need to earn a living, to support families and raise children, absorbed most of the attention and energy of most of the people. The propaganda picture of militant village associations devoting themselves to revolutionary "struggle" had some truth to it. But the larger truth is that most Vietnamese paid outward allegiance to whoever held the whip hand and kept their inner allegiance for themselves, their families, and their work. "You play the game according to the rules of the country you live in" was the way one middle-aged North Vietnamese Army veteran put it. Many of our interviewees would have agreed.

Others, particularly those from "bad" class backgrounds, grew up with an instinctive distrust of the revolution. Middle and upper peasants, sons and daughters of the petit bourgeois, and scions of former aristocrats often resigned themselves with distaste to the social reorganization that had brought harder times or perhaps tragedy to their families. Even fear and hatred for the Americans who were bombing their homes didn't necessarily foster any affection for the Party or the system the Party had imposed.

Still others had been ardent Communists, imbued with the vision of egalitarian social justice the Party promised. One of our great surprises was to find that some of those we interviewed still were. Though circumstances had forced them out of Vietnam, they had in no way forsaken the ideals they had fought for. They repented nothing and regretted nothing.

THE bulk of the material in this book was gathered in interviews done over a period of two years in the United States, Europe, and Southeast Asia. Because we were asking people to talk about subjects that were not only personal but also delicate and potentially dangerous for them and their families, we encountered a number of special problems. We have touched on some of these in the afterword.

Another complicating factor was that David Chanoff, who conducted most of the interviews, is an American. This enabled us to ask the kinds of questions that no Vietnamese could ask another Vietnamese—questions about daily affairs, growing up, personal lives, and making decisions that could come only from someone outside the respondent's cultural universe. But it also meant that we had to find ways to overcome significant cultural barriers to communication. We have also used the afterword to discuss some of the more challenging difficulties involved in interpreting one culture to the other.

In addition to live interviews, we have gone to several other sources for material. Recorded military interrogations of Vietcong and North Vietnamese POWs and ralliers enabled us to present accounts of subjects we had become especially interested in, but did not have sufficient material for among our respondents. We used these reports to provide readers with a fuller idea of such subjects as how revolutionary soldiers felt about volunteering or being drafted, about infiltration into the South, and about sapper tactics that were one of the chief weapons in the Liberation Army's effort against fortified American positions.

Our technique in live interviews was to encourage people to talk freely about their lives, at times guiding them toward areas we wanted to hear about or asking them to elaborate on or give details about subjects they had described generally. Ideally, we wanted wide-ranging personal narratives, autobiographies as complete as we were able to get in the time available. But military interrogation reports often present the reader with a different style. Sometimes replies to interrogators' questions come in narrative chunks; other times in short bursts of speech. Interrogators will pursue certain subjects, then pick up a different trail, then come back to the first interest after the new trail is played out. The result can easily be a disconnected and difficult-to-read report whose awkwardness has likely been compounded by the unidiomatic English of the original Vietnamese translator. In such cases we have drawn together stories that have been fragmented, and edited the language into conversational English.

A few accounts have been taken from Vietnamese sources, interviews and memoirs that have appeared in *Nhan Dan* (*The Party Daily*) or other publications. We have chosen to use these because they describe events of particular interest (the capture of an American pilot, the first trek down the Ho Chi Minh Trail, the first Vietcong attempt to fight a conventional battle). They also provide a small taste of the heroic style that is common among Vietnamese revolutionaries when they are addressing their own. To the Western ear, some of this may sound turgid and stylized, but the fact is that Vietnamese often do view themselves as heroic people, leading precisely the same sort of lives as the heroes who liberated the country from the Mongols in 1287 or from the Chinese in 1789. Westerners, used to self-doubt and introspection, may not find this Vietnamese trait endearing, or even particularly human. But it is no less real for that.

A number of American soldiers and government workers were in Vietnam for the entire eight years the United States kept land forces in the South. A very few found themselves involved in Vietnam even longer; in one way or another the United States supported South Vietnam for slightly more than two decades. But for most Americans, the war meant a one-year hitch—in and out (if you were lucky) in 365 days.

That kind of time frame meant nothing to any Vietnamese. They were there for the duration, until one side or the other called it quits. And after that they'd have to live with the consequences. The American-style short-term view was especially alien to the Vietcong and North Vietnamese *bo doi*. Ho Chi Minh had informed Lyndon Johnson that the war might take five, ten, or fifteen years, but eventually Vietnam would win. Ho Chi Minh's government told its young men when they were drafted or volunteered that they would fight for as long as it took, "The battlefield couldn't be controlled."

By the time the marines landed at Danang, war had become a way of life for the Vietnamese. Many revolutionary soldiers who were in their forties when the war ended had been fighting almost continuously for thirty years. Some older Party officials had spent long lifetimes in the struggle movement. Open war against the French began on August 22, 1945, a week after Japan's surrender in World War II threw Vietnam up for grabs. After a half year of fighting a truce was arranged that lasted until Ho Chi Minh called the nation to arms on December 19, 1946. The war cry he raised then was not finally stilled until April 30, 1975.

For the Vietnamese, this was a struggle that didn't simply punctuate lives, it embraced them. To get at the root of why a given individual fought, it is often necessary to reach deep into childhood memories. Ask an American Vietnam veteran why he fought and chances are he'll tell you about being drafted after high school or joining up from college. Ask a Vietnamese, and you may well find yourself on a journey back through time to a native village pillaged by the French or to a home raided at midnight by the special police and a father suddenly gone. "Before the Americans came there were the French," began the former chief of propaganda for Ben Tre Province. "I was fifteen when war broke out with them, in tenth grade." "My earliest clear memories," reminisced a leading anti-Thieu assemblyman, "go back to when I was about eight or nine, in the middle of the French war." "In 1942, I joined the resistance movement against the Japanese invaders. I was twelve years old. I joined because the Japanese had killed my father," said the ethnic Chinese village secretary whose career as a revolutionary spanned forty years.

Time is one key to understanding the Vietnamese experience. Choice is another. Vietnam was not a "good war" for Americans. From many it demanded a moral decision: to support it or not, to fight in it or not. For Vietnamese the war was vastly more complex—a maelstrom in which the contending tides of colonialism and liberation, communism and nationalism, reform and revolution, Northern revanchism and Southern regionalism clashed violently and mixed treacherously. Some Vietnamese found a fixed moral star to guide their actions; others switched allegiance more than once as the war shifted from one phase to another. More were simply pawns of their times. But even the pawns often made decisions. Droves of Southern soldiers deserted at the same time Saigon's *Chieu Hoi* (Open Arms) program for ralliers processed more than 200,000 North Vietnamese and Vietcong.

Nor did the war's end relieve the Vietnamese from the burden of choice. The unquiet history of Vietnam since 1975 has for many forced resolutions to a lifetime of conflict that they never anticipated. For some of the older militants especially, it has brought their lives full circle. Decisions they made early on that determined how they were to spend the prime of their lives, balanced now by decisions that have determined how their later years will go. As interviewers, we have seen a pattern emerge from these stories: choice leading to struggle leading to resolution. In our own thinking this schema has helped make sense of the war's convolutions.

Generally speaking, this pattern—choice, struggle, resolution—has governed the organization of the book. In the first section individuals talk about how and why they became involved. In the second they relate their wartime experiences. In the third they describe the conclusions to their personal struggles.

Some individuals appear only briefly, some at length and more than once. But all the accounts are clustered around the stories of three men whose stories run throughout the book. Each of these amounts to a separate mini-autobiography that can, if the reader wishes, be followed continuously from beginning to end.

XUAN VU was a combat reporter and propaganda chief, a writer who has the distinction of having won both the revolution's Cuu Long Prize for Literature (in 1952) and South Vietnam's National Prize for Literature and Art (1972). His career as a revolutionary covered twenty-five years, from the August insurrection of 1945 to the day in 1969 when he decided he had had enough fighting.

NGUYEN CONG HOAN was a South Vietnamese student militant who in 1971 was elected to the National Assembly from his home province of Phu Yen. As one of the small bloc of opposition politicians, he fought the regime from the inside until the last days of Saigon. After the war he was chosen by the Fatherland Front to represent his province in the unified National Assembly that met in Hanoi in July 1976, making him the only person to serve in both the Saigon and Hanoi assemblies.

TRINH DUC was born on Hainan Island, where he joined the Communist resistance during World War II. In 1948 he fled Hainan for Saigon, where he worked as an urban organizer for the Vietminh. In 1954 he stayed on as a member of the secret infrastructure the Party left in the South after the regrouping of forces ordered by the Geneva agreement. Eventually identified and arrested, Duc was in prison ten years before the first American troops came ashore in Vietnam. Released under an amnesty, he made his way to COSVN (the Party headquarters for most of South Vietnam) and spent the rest of the war fighting Americans and their Saigon army allies as a village secretary in Long Khanh.

None of these three—Vu, Hoan, or Duc—is necessarily typical of those who opposed the American presence in Vietnam. Yet among them they give a sense of the diversity of motives and experiences of our former adversaries. Around their stories are clustered the accounts of others, some of whom were fighters, some of whom simply tried to survive. Taken together, we hope their stories will provide a glimpse at a world we should have known better.

PART ONE

CHOICE

HOW DID VIETNAMESE FIND THEMSELVES IN THE REVOLUTIONARY Army? It depended on place and time. For the Party, the war against France and the war against the United States were continuous, two phases of the same fight. (After 1954 the enemy was *"My-Diem"*—America-Diem; then *"My Nguy"*—America-Puppet.) Vietnamese born early enough to get into the French war often found themselves fighting right through.

For most of the veterans there was a layover between July 1954, when the Geneva Agreement put an end to the first phase, and 1959–60 when the Party felt strong enough to resume battle. But not for all: despite the mandated regrouping of forces north of the 17th parallel, some resistance people stayed behind, secretly preparing the ground for the unification elections that were supposed to come, or—failing that—for war. But for both groups, those who went North and those who went underground, the decision to fight the French led to an automatic decision to fight Diem and his American backers.

Although the first revolutionary forces from the North didn't begin coming down the Ho Chi Minh Trail until 1959, the homegrown Southern resistance made itself known from the mid-1950s on—volunteers for the most part, villagers and city dwellers who disappeared into the old resistance zones to link up with small wandering groups of anti-Diem guerrillas.

Meanwhile, for most Northerners the Southern struggle didn't reach center stage until 1960. After that some joined up; others waited for their draft notices or for their school deferments to run out. It was like the United States.

There were other similarities, too. As the conflict grew more violent and deaths mounted, zeal for the war faded, melting into resignation and fear. Some refused to go, faking their way through physicals or hiding from authorities. Powerful officials did everything they could to secure precious foreign scholarships for their children that would keep them from the bloodletting. It wasn't like the low-technology French war where the chances for survival were good. "Born in the North to die in the South" became the motto of a generation of North Vietnamese boys. For some it was a matter of pride, for others an unwelcome inevitability.

Not all those on the other side were soldiers; some were monks, politicians, and journalists. Often such people thought of themselves as "Third Force"—not Communists and not anti-Communists, but advocates of democracy and Vietnam for the Vietnamese. At times their impact was immense, as effective in undermining Saigon's stability and blackening its image as anything that happened on the battlefield or propaganda front. The anger of Buddhist monks and nuns helped pull to pieces the nine-year-old regime of Ngo Dinh Diem, and militant students and opposition politicians kept Diem's successors shaky on their thrones.

Most often, opposition of this sort matured over years, though occasionally it was some compelling event that made the difference. For these people, choosing a side was almost always a matter of careful reflection. They knew they were walking a narrow and dangerous path, perhaps the least tenable of any the Vietnamese wartime horizon offered.

XUAN VU

WAR REPORTER, PROPAGANDA CHIEF, NOVELIST

A handsome man in his mid-fifties, he came to meet me at my hotel in the red pickup truck he uses in the painting business that keeps him alive while he writes for half a dozen Vietnamese-language magazines. The move to the United States hasn't been kind to him. You sense the pain that leaving Vietnam has caused. He is a wordsmith deprived of his audience. But when he gets into his story, the air of resignation disappears and he comes alive. He has a vivid memory and a sharp sense for detail and drama. It is easy to see why he was one of Vietnam's most talented writers.

XUAN VU'S STORY: *The French War*

BEFORE THE AMERICANS CAME THERE WERE THE FRENCH. I WAS fifteen when war broke out with them, in tenth grade. The high school I went to was in My Tho, a city in the Mekong Delta about fifty miles from my home village. By the time the school year started in 1945 My Tho was blockaded, cut off from the countryside. Inside the city were the French soldiers, outside were the Vietminh guerrillas. My village and all the other villages were controlled by the Vietminh—actually they belonged to the Vietminh, heart and soul. Everyone was part of the movement, everyone supported it. There was this great rush of patriotic feeling. To struggle for independence, to be proud of the nation—that was what everybody wanted. We had been slaves of the Chinese for a thousand years, slaves of the French for a hundred. Now we were going to be *free*. The feeling was everywhere—an outpouring—in all the villages, all the farms. It was unstoppable.

Anyway, I was fifteen, and I was right in the middle of it. I had to join, it was such an exciting time. Besides, I couldn't get back to school because of the blockade. So there was no chance of getting on with my studies. Also I had an uncle who was a university man—where I came from that was a rare thing (I was the only one from my village who had even gone to high school)—and this uncle was one of the leaders of the local Vietminh Youth League. So he took me to help out in the Youth League office. I like to write, and as I said, I was the only one in the village who had gone past elementary school. With such magnificent credentials, very soon I was in charge of the office.

Before long they started sending me and some other guys around to organize. We'd go into a village and just walk around, talking to all of the teenagers we could find, telling them to come to our meeting tonight, say at eight o'clock. When eight o'clock came everyone would be there. It was a little bit of excitement that nobody wanted to miss. The three or four of us would have a routine prepared. I played the guitar, someone else played the mandolin, all of us knew how to sing. We'd start off with some patriotic songs. Everybody would respond to the words and the sentiment (we would always feel it). Then we'd talk to them, telling stories about the Chinese domination and the French domination, stories of all the great Vietnamese heroes who had resisted the invaders or rebelled against them. We'd mix the stories with more songs and with poems.

These were things that everyone knew by heart, words and music they had inside them. The crowd would join in and clap as we played. As part

of our preparation we would be given articles to read that we could use
in our talks. For example, we would tell them that the French had enslaved the country, that they had built more jails than schools. We told
them that the French had spent much more on giving alcohol and drugs
to the people than they ever had on medicine. Of course we needed these
articles ourselves in order to know what to talk about. Because aside from
the popular history that came through the stories and poems, we hardly
had any facts at all.

But nobody else did either. And we used that, too. We'd talk about
the fact that there were no schools, that the French had built hardly any.
And we'd point to people in the audience. "Look, you can't read, you
can't write. You are ignorant. Do you know why? You're ignorant because
of the French, because of their colonialism. They've kept you like animals—do you like that?" And it was true too. Because maybe only one
or two people in the audience had had any significant schooling at all.

Then we'd go around with a sign-up list, for people who wanted to
volunteer to join the Youth League. They'd all join. There would be
tremendous enthusiasm. Of course no one wanted to be accused of being
pro-French either, so there was a lot of unspoken social pressure. But
they also wanted to organize. They knew that the chances of their actually
becoming real fighters wasn't very good. At that time it was a great
honor just to be accepted into the Vietminh army. But at least they could
join the Youth League and pay their ten cents dues every month and be
part of what was going on.

I traveled all around Ben Tre Province like this for two or three years.
I was fifteen, sixteen, seventeen years old. I found out I was an effective
speaker, that I could get people to do what I wanted them to. I was
proud of it. I felt I was leading them in the right way. We traveled
constantly from one village to another. We got no pay for any of this, no
food rations, nothing. Our families would do whatever they could to help
us. But mainly we relied on the people in the villages. They'd offer us
their homes to sleep in, feed us, give us whatever we needed. We didn't
even have mosquito nets of our own. Instead we carried woven straw
sleeping mats, a little bit like a sleeping bag, except made out of dried
grass fiber. We'd carry these mats around rolled up on our backs like a
badge of honor. They identified us as revolutionaries. But sleeping in
them wasn't quite so rewarding. They were hot as hell—so hot you'd
have to stick your head out every once in a while for a breath of fresh air,
mosquitoes or not. There was even a famous song called "The Mat Song
of the Resistance" that people sang right through the French war and the
American war, too—right up to 1975.

Last August on the twenty-third
We answered our nation's call.
Everywhere the people cheered
As we marched to the front
Our mats and machetes across our backs.

It was an exhilarating time. I even got to fight in a battle that took place in my home village in 1947. There was a blockhouse there that sat next to the road—a big square building that had originally been a rice storehouse and was barricaded by thick bales of paddy rice. At that time the French had managed to garrison the blockhouse with about thirty soldiers. Since they could control the traffic on the provincial road, the local Vietminh commander decided to try and take the blockhouse, even though it was so well fortified.

The road at that point was built up above ground level and the Vietminh fighters—maybe sixty of them—took up positions behind the embankment. Then they began firing at the blockhouse. But the only guns they had were old French musquetons that must have gone back to the nineteenth century. They were worthless for this kind of attack. While the shooting was going on, crowds of villagers gathered behind the embankment to watch what was happening and to help the fighters. They had bamboo stakes, knives, hoes—anything they could get their hands on. I was part of the crowd.

As we watched, the guerrilla commander—his name was Phan Van Phai—and two men ran out from behind the embankment toward the blockhouse to try to set it on fire. Somehow they managed to get to the front without being shot—to a place where they were safe from the firing coming out of the windows. Then a grenade came flying out. One of Phai's men grabbed it and threw it away before it could explode. Two others followed—big potato masher–type grenades. Phai's men also managed to grab those and get rid of them. The fourth exploded just as it was being picked up. Phai and both men were killed.

When this happened the peasants went wild. They practically tore apart a couple of nearby houses to get flammable material—wood, straw, piles of coconut palm leaves. They ran out and began throwing this stuff all around the blockhouse, despite the shooting. I was throwing things too. I hardly knew where I was. We were all in a frenzy. Some people were shot down, but others began heaving Molotov cocktails. The palm leaves caught fire first. Before long the whole building was billowing fire and clouds of smoke. One French soldier came running out on fire. Phai's men shot him down. The rest of them were trapped inside. We barbecued them all. Once the paddy rice bales started burning, they never went out. They smoldered for months. You could see the bones of the French soldiers in the charred ruins of their blockhouse.

It was no surprise to anyone that the Huong My peasants were daring enough to expose themselves to French fire and burn the blockhouse. Everywhere you turned there was the same kind of passion. Ben Tre Province was one of the centers of revolution. People would listen for hours to the Vietminh speakers, hanging on every word. They'd lean out of windows or perch in trees to get a view of them over the heads of the crowd. The speakers would keep coming back to the revolutionary slogans that by now everyone knew by heart. "Freedom or Death" they would chant. And the crowd would shout back "Freedom or Death, Freedom or Death." *"Muon doc lap phai do mau!"* — "For freedom you have to spend your blood!" And the crowd would yell *"Do mau, Do mau!"* — "Yes! Spend blood! Spend blood!"

For a while I became secretary at a camp my uncle had opened to train propagandists and speakers. It was next to a beautiful beach area in Ben Tre and every district sent people to the training sessions, which lasted about a month. My uncle and the other trainers gave them painstaking instruction. They taught them how to stand up and walk to the front of the crowd or to the stage after they were introduced. "So and so will now talk to us about Tran Hung Dao" [a great hero of the anti-Chinese wars of the thirteenth century]. And the student speaker would learn how to get up from the middle of the crowd where he was squatting, smile, bow, then walk slowly to the front, never turning his back completely on the people. He'd learn how to keep eye contact with the audience, how to modulate his voice and vary the speed of his speech. He'd learn how to gesture, and how to coordinate gestures with intonation. He'd learn when to stop his speech for music or maybe a poem from someone else on his agit-prop team, then how to take it up again smoothly building on the heightened mood.

The trainees would be given topics for practice speeches that they'd spend all day preparing. Then at night the whole school would gather to listen, and the speaker would go through the entire routine: "We fight for *independence*!" — coming to a crescendo using big, expansive hand gestures; "We fight for the *nation*!" — shouting out "nation." The trainers and other students would respond and clap, playing their own role to create a realistic setting. Afterwards would come the criticism, first from the other students then from the instructors.

Then there'd be discussion groups. Trainees would be taught how to lead discussions, how to get responses from people, what topics to concentrate on. In all this there was never a mention of communism. Patriotism and independence were the great themes—though of course a certain amount of politics came through too. For example, one topic was "Men and Women Are Equal." That was great, always good for a lively discussion. Up till then nobody had ever heard of the idea.

After a while I decided to go back to school to finish my studies. I had been an itinerant propagandist and secretary, et cetera, for several years already when I heard the Vietminh had opened up a school in the resistance zone. I spent a year there. But the level of instruction wasn't anywhere near what I had expected, certainly nothing like my old French high school in My Tho. So I quit again, this time to become a war reporter for the famous Vietminh army newspaper in Military Zone 9—the Ca Mau Peninsula.

For a while I covered Battalion 410, which was commanded by Albert Pham Ngoc Thao. Thao was a fascinating character who later was sent to Saigon as a special agent. Still later—in the American war—he convinced Diem and his brother Nhu that he had broken all his ties with the resistance. Eventually, Thao became chief of military security for South Vietnam's army and was involved in several military coups, including the one that got rid of the Diem family in 1963. After 1975 it came out that he had been a resistance officer all along, right up to the time he was killed [in 1965]. When the war was over the Communist government gave him a posthumous medal and made him a national hero.

When I was covering his battalion in Ca Mau, Thao had a crazy fearlessness. He wasn't afraid of anything. Everybody would be dug in like hell, and he'd be walking around as if he were taking a stroll in the country. Sometimes his soldiers would try to pull him down into cover. But he'd always push them away. At one point I asked him about it. He told me, "Maybe if I weren't in charge I'd be able to hide. But as things are, if I hid, what would my men do?"

For me, I loved covering the war. I was in the middle of everything, I saw everything—and I could write about it. Although I wasn't a fighter, I couldn't have been closer to the fighting. And occasionally I got to take part in it. Near Can Tho City in 1952 I was with a unit that was attacking a French fort, another one of these blockhouses. Inside, one of the Vietnamese auxiliaries was an agent of ours. The plan was that while he was on guard duty at night he would open the door, so that our unit could slip inside when the garrison was asleep. As insurance against his having any second thoughts, the unit was holding his family hostage.

As we moved in on the blockhouse, cutting through the barbed wire protecting it, we could hear a regular knocking sound coming from inside. Every few minutes the sentry was supposed to knock on a block of wood to indicate to the post duty officer that everything was clear and that he was still making his rounds. We were already through the wire when we began to suspect it was a trap. But then the door swung open from inside and the entire section slipped through. We followed the agent to the French sleeping quarters. We just shot the soldiers through their mosquito netting while they slept. When one of the fighters' rifle jammed, the French soldier he was about to shoot jumped up and grabbed the gun. I rushed to help and the three of us staggered around in the dark wrestling for the rifle. Another French soldier got off a shot that hit me in the thigh. I fell down and was carried out to one of the boats we had waiting on the canal. When we got back to camp, they managed to dig the bullet out. It took me a month before I could get back to work.

But I hardly needed to do any fighting myself to get a taste of what it was like. I understood what the fighters were thinking and what their motivations were—how they could stand up to the French, who were all professional soldiers with firepower the guerrillas could never match. I wrote reports, stories, poetry about what they were doing, about the bravery and comradeship I saw everywhere. And my work was getting to be known. I was eventually put in charge of propaganda and literature for Can Tho Province. I was putting out magazines and coordinating all the artists, writers, and composers, as well as doing my own writing. In 1952 I won the Cuu Long Prize for Literature, for my stories and poetry. I was twenty-two years old, the youngest prizewinner. I was on top of the world.

My career was opening out in front of me. I was already a writer. And I was intent on becoming a great writer, as great as Balzac, my hero from French literature. Balzac had said, "In literature I am not seeking a marshal's baton, but an emperor's crown." I liked that. I thought. Okay, I'll try. I took that as my private motto. Balzac had also once said to Napoleon, "You started your career with your sword. I'll finish it with my pen." I saw myself the same way. I'd be the chronicler of the revolution and of the martial virtues of the Vietnamese people.

About the political realities behind the fighting I knew very little. There was a struggle going on between the Communists and the Vietnamese Democratic Party. But what had caused it or what its results might be I didn't know. Nor was I particularly interested. I knew the people—the soldiers and the peasants. And I practically worshipped Ho Chi Minh. That was enough for me.

When the war was finally ended by the Geneva Agreement in 1954, I had mixed feelings. The whole period—from 1945 on—had been a beautiful time. I was happy that it was over. But I also had to make a major decision: to stay in the South with my family, or go North with my comrades. [The Geneva Agreement called for Vietminh troops to regroup north of the 17th parallel.] My father told me, "Look, you've been away for nine years. That's enough. Come home and get married. Give me grandchildren."

On the other hand, I really wanted to go. I had writers' blood. I wanted to travel, to see new things and new places—and then write about them. New experiences were like life's blood. So finally I told my father that I was going. It would only be two years. [Unification elections were supposed to take place in two years.] Then I'd be back. My mother was crying. But I didn't listen to her. I told her, "Look Mom, it's not that long. Don't worry." I believed it too. Two years of peace, then I'd come home and settle down. In the meantime, this was an opportunity I couldn't miss.

So I left for North Vietnam on a Russian ship, along with all my friends. We waved goodbye to our families at Chac Bang harbor. People on the dock were crying when the ship pulled out and we were giving them the victory sign, holding up two fingers—for the two years we'd be gone. When they saw us doing this, the French soldiers who were sitting on the dock took off their shoes and waved their hands and feet at us— wiggling their fingers and toes in the air. They were saying that we would be up there twenty years, not two years. But I didn't care what they were saying. I was excited as hell to be making the trip. I could see new horizons opening up before my eyes.

Xuan Vu's story continues on page 74.

NGUYEN CONG HOAN

OPPOSITION ASSEMBLY DEPUTY

The first impression is fierce. High cheekbones and a thick black mustache give him the look of a warrior. By contrast, the living room of his suburban house has an unusual serenity to it. A magnificent carved rosewood relief of Buddha looks down from the long wall as if giving its blessing to those in the room. Palm fronds set off the burnished wood. It's a little like being in a temple.

Spending time with him, you come to feel that the gentleness of the Buddha relief reflects his personality more faithfully than the warrior's face. He talks passionately about "my people"—by which he means the poor peasants of Phu Yen Province whom he represented as an opposition leader in Saigon's National Assembly and then in the first two Communist assemblies in Hanoi.

He was a child during the French war. A frightful scar running diagonally across his back is a memento. ("I had to lie on my stomach for two months.") Now he is a printer and publisher, specializing in Vietnamese Buddhist literature. During the days that we talked, several monks came by on business. In their saffron robes they looked right at home under the gaze of the rosewood Buddha.

Hoan's wife, Ty, works with him, constantly busy. It was not until the third time I visited that she consented to join the discussion. Up to that point I had the impression of passivity and obedience. Not at all. "We were there for six months after they sentenced Hoan to death," she said of the period following her husband's defection. A remarkably strong and composed individual emerges from her description of life as wife of the only person to have served in both national assemblies.

NGUYEN CONG HOAN'S STORY: *Coming of Age in the South*

I'M FROM PHU YEN, A COASTAL PROVINCE IN THE CENTER OF VIET-nam. My earliest clear memories go back to when I was about eight or nine, in the middle of the French war. Our village wasn't a center of opposition, but it was outside French control. So the French soldiers and the mercenaries would come in on sweep operations, to arrest people or round them up for labor. My father had been killed during one of these sweeps before I was born. When I was about five my mother remarried. I remember that quite often they would arrive by ship in the fishing harbor. When that happened we would all scramble to get out of the village, running toward the mountains or at least to the bunkers beyond the houses. Of course I didn't know why any of this was happening, only that we hated them. I thought they just wanted to take everything— pigs, chickens, rice—and that they loved smashing things.

One morning when we were going out to work, word spread that a French ship was coming into the harbor. It was panic, people running around to gather up kids and grab whatever rice they could. I had a sack of rice and some clothes. My older sister was carrying my baby half sister. In the confusion we were separated. Somehow my sister didn't get to the mountain with us. I didn't see her for the two days we were there, before people thought it was safe to go back down.

When we came back the village was wrecked. Most of the houses were burned down, but our house was still standing. In front of it we found my baby sister, crawling around next to my older sister's body. Her chest was a mass of dried blood. My parents were crying over her. I remember them picking her up very gently.

That's my first clear memory. Some time later the villagers of Phu Lac decided to abandon the village. Right on the sea like it was, it was too vulnerable. The French came too often and there was nothing we could do to keep them out. So the village scattered. There wasn't much to take. If a family had a sampan they put their chickens in it, their pig, a few pieces of furniture. We walked away, carrying our things. We went to Phuoc Giang, about three miles away and closer to the mountain.

Phuoc Giang was safe from attack by sea, but it was closer to the national highway, which was also controlled by the French. From the highway the French artillery would sometimes pound the village. And once in a while the planes would come, bombing and strafing.

One of these times—I must have been about twelve—the guns began sounding and we heard the planes droning in the distance. It sounded like a big attack. The whole village was running toward the bunkers which were dug along the line of the jungle. The roar of the planes and the explosions were terrifying. I was curled up in a bunker with my eyes shut tight, praying that it would be over.

When the planes went away we came out. I was looking at the bodies of people who hadn't gotten into the bunkers. My best friend, Huu, was lying on the ground, burned by napalm. She wasn't dead, but she was dying. We sat around her at night watching her. Her body glowed with phosphorus.

The attacks were like an epidemic. I didn't escape from them myself either. A couple of months after Huu was killed I was in my house when the guns began. I ran toward the jungle when suddenly there was a huge noise and I fell down. I knew I had been hit, but I didn't feel anything. I tried to get up but I couldn't move. People were standing over me and saying things, but I couldn't hear them. I wondered why I couldn't hear anything.

Later I woke up in my house. My parents were there and others, looking at me and crying. I still didn't feel anything, any pain—not at first, though it began later. My mother used a towel and salt water to treat the wounds in my back, but they became infected. No one in the village had any medicine for them.

It must have been about two months that I had to lie on my stomach, facedown, looking at the floor. What I thought about I don't know, except killing the French. I thought about that a lot. But everybody thought about that, all the young people at least. That's what we'd do when we grew up—kill the French.

Aside from the artillery and the planes that flew over us once in a while, the war didn't come to the village. There was no actual fighting around us. We never saw any guerrillas in Phuoc Giang, or any French troops either. So it was better than Phu Lac, my home village. Sometimes one of the villagers would disappear, and people would say that he had gone to join the revolution.

But life went on pretty much as normal. I did exactly the same things every other village child did. I helped the fishermen bring in their catches. I took care of the buffalo, carried water, chopped wood, foraged for food in the jungle. It was the same for all of us.

My favorite job was taking care of our buffalo. His name was Phao and he lived in a shed with a little corral next to our house. A giant strong animal, but very nice, very gentle. I'd take him out in the morning, open the gate, and tap him with my stick. He understood four words: "Right," "Left," "Forward," and "Stop." Of course I wasn't afraid of him at all. None of the children were afraid of their buffalos. But if a buffalo got mad at a stranger, he could be terrible.

I'd take Phao out to the field where he'd just graze and pull the plow that my father would hook up to him. If I was in a happy mood I'd grab the buffalo's tail and jump up onto his back. Sometimes I'd stand on top there as he walked along, balancing on his back muscles. There were songs we'd all sing riding on a buffalo, like the one that went: "Yesterday I followed you down the road / Today I cut a flower for your grave." The words sounded sad if you thought about them. But it was a happy song anyway, the one we sang for riding.

A child growing up in Phuoc Giang did not think about the future—not like a child in the West who wonders what he's going to be. You grow up doing what you're doing, that's all. You don't have dreams about doing anything else. I did go to school, though. A teacher opened up a classroom in one of the village huts. He taught the ABCs, arithmetic, spelling, and reading. So I learned to read and I loved it.

I was thirteen years old in 1954, the year the Geneva Agreement was signed. People in the village were full of joy that the war was over. I heard that over and over, "No more war." On the other hand, nobody thought much at all about the division of the country into North and South. In Phuoc Giang, no one ever talked about Hanoi or Saigon, the two great cities. They never even talked about Hue, which was the old capital in the center. As far as I was concerned, Tuy Hoa was the biggest city that had any reality. People talked a lot about Tuy Hoa, but who ever went there? It was fifteen miles away, a long day's walk.

But in 1958 I went there myself, to go to high school. After Geneva, a few of the families in Phuoc Giang sent their sons to study in Tuy Hoa. That was one of the blessings of peace. I was one of the lucky ones. I had an aunt who worked in a hospital in the city, so there was a place for me to live. I was excited about going, especially since I loved to study.

At the beginning of the school year of 1958 I walked to Tuy Hoa together with a friend who was also being sent to high school. Actually, we only walked about halfway, down the national highway. In a village some way outside the city we rented bicycles for the rest of the trip. The bicycle owner told me about bike regulations in Tuy Hoa, about who has priority, cars or bikes. He told me explicitly that bikes had priority—he was very sure of that.

But when we got into Tuy Hoa, a car almost hit me, and I fell off. Apparently the bike owner was wrong. It looked to me like it was the strongest who had the right of way. Anyway, cars were unbelievable. It never occurred to me that I might ride in one one day. Photographs were another wonder. My friend and I saw them spread out in the window of a photography shop and we stopped to stare at them.

But it didn't take long to get used to the modern wonders of Tuy Hoa. And school was like heaven. I made friends with a lot of the other boys. And I studied—history, geography, math, physics, chemistry, French, and English. I really liked studying, I was avid about it and I did it well. Back in the village I had seen what prestige the teacher had. Sometimes I thought that I'd like to become like him. In Tuy Hoa the teachers had the same tremendous respect from everyone. I'm sure some of that rubbed off on me, the idea that I might get to enjoy the same stature.

I also got the idea that maybe I could learn to build things, roads and bridges, which would help the people in my village. At the least, I knew that if I did a good job in school I'd have a better future. My parents certainly wanted that badly. And I wanted to do everything I could to please them.

At some point, maybe a year or two after I started high school, I began to hear something about the government and war. My friends and I would get news from our relatives that people were being arrested in the villages because they had been Vietminh guerrillas. We also heard about men from the villages who just disappeared. That made me think about the French war when someone's father or older brother disappeared and rumors would go around that they had joined the underground.

I can't say that I was becoming aware of things politically. I didn't put the news in a context of who was right and who was wrong. I certainly didn't have the vaguest understanding of communism or of what Ngo Dinh Diem [the president] stood for. But I did know that things were happening that disturbed me because they reminded me of the French times.

Then, starting around 1960, conflicts began between Catholics and Buddhists. It wasn't really between Catholics and Buddhists. Actually, it was discrimination against the Buddhists by the government—and that caused a lot of problems in the villages.

The discrimination took the form of government aid. [Ngo Dinh Diem and his family were Catholic (the president's eldest brother was bishop of Vinh Long) and much of their support came from the Catholic community.] Many new Catholic churches were being built in the countryside with money from Saigon. And Catholic believers were receiving rice, clothes, corrugated tin for roofs, and other supplies. Buddhists weren't getting any of this, and a lot of them were angry. Other people who didn't care much about any religion were even becoming Catholics so they could get some of the government aid.

I say that the Buddhists were angry, but actually most of the peasants weren't really Buddhist. They understood Buddhism and followed some of the Buddhist customs. But underneath they were *Ong Ba*, the traditional religion of Vietnam's countryside. *Ong Ba* is mainly ancestor worship, celebrating death anniversaries and sacrificing to the spirits of the ancestors. Catholics weren't allowed to do any of that.

As a result there was a lot of popular feeling against Catholics. You know, for *Ong Ba*, Catholics were almost anathema. What would happen was that the villagers' lives would revolve around the death anniversaries of their ancestors—the whole ritual of feasts and prayers and celebrations. That's what gave them their feelings of being a family. The fact that everybody did it gave a village the sense that it was a big family.

But Catholic families wouldn't come to the feasts because they didn't believe in the whole thing. Not only didn't they believe in it, but they disdained the ceremonies because they thought they were pagan. So the *Ong Ba* were insulted. It wasn't that they cared what the Catholics believed or didn't believe. For example, it didn't get them angry if the Catholics believed in Jesus Christ. They were completely tolerant about things like that. But they felt the Catholics' disdain for their own beliefs was an insult to them personally and an insult to their families. And all of a sudden the government in Saigon was appointing these Catholics as local chiefs and officials, and was giving them special favors.

The villagers were angry about this, and I was too. It wasn't the kind of anger that leads to violence. But everybody knew that the government and Catholicism were one and the same. When you added this to the arrests of the former Vietminh guerrillas, it created bad feelings about the regime in Saigon.

Although I shared these feelings, what I thought about most were my studies. I liked schoolwork so much that in 1961 I decided to take the baccalaureate examination. This was a nationwide exam given to all high school students who wanted to go to the university. It was a leftover from the French system of education. If you passed, it was the most prestigious thing that could happen to you.

I passed. As soon as word got around, I became a village hero. For my parents it was the most wonderful thing they could imagine. They killed a pig and invited everyone in Phuoc Giang to a grand celebration. The idea that the village was sending one of its children to Saigon to study brought glory to everyone.

In September 1961 I enrolled in the school of science at Saigon University. My earlier attraction for math, physics, and chemistry had matured, and now I had my sights set on a Ph.D. in science. The original idea of becoming an engineer and building things had changed into plans for a career in chemistry. That was my real love. I was amazed at the constant change and interaction among elements. I thought I could never get tired of observing and analyzing the world on this level. I thought about developing foods, or doing something else practical with the knowledge I'd have—although exactly what I wasn't quite sure. But chemistry could solve so many real problems. It could be so helpful to people.

So I started my studies in Saigon with the same enthusiasm I had before. Even more, if that was possible. I felt strongly that I had to be worthy of the village's pride in me. I was also stimulated by the openness and freedom at the university. As much as I liked it, high school was like the army. The teachers kept strict discipline and constantly told you what to do. But at the university I lived an open free life. I decided which lectures I wanted to attend and which professors were the best. Nobody checked on anything. They didn't care if you attended or where you sat if you did attend. All they cared about was that you took the exams. I was on my own for the first time in my life. I felt, Okay, now I'm becoming an adult. This is what it's like, making your own decisions.

But even though I was so involved in my studies, I was also learning other things in Saigon. I started to come alive politically. I started with a critical view of Ngo Dinh Diem's government because of the arrests and religious favoritism that I knew about in my home province. Now I saw that Saigon had two faces. In one way it was exactly the rich fairyland I had dreamed about, a city of magnificent buildings, luxurious cars, and wealth. But it was also a place where people lived in the most miserable shanties, or just out on the street. Beggars were all over the place. So were the prostitutes, in their short skirts and tight blouses and lots of makeup. They'd grab you as you were walking along, actually grab you and try to pull you with them.

I saw that this second face of Saigon was poverty stricken and humiliated—and that was the city's real face. Of course my village was very poor. But the village always took care of its own. As long as people had food they shared it. Nobody went without a roof over his head. As far as I was concerned, it was the government's business to take care of Saigon's poor. But it didn't.

When I began to see what the relationship was between politics and economics, I liked Diem even less than I had before. At this point I didn't see myself becoming involved personally in anything. I was still completely innocent about the world of power politics. But I was angry. I also didn't have the basic sense to keep my opinions to myself. So of course I talked about my feelings with my friends, many of them were making the same observations that I was.

But during this time—my first two years in Saigon—I was mainly concerned with my personal life. My studies were going along very well. I also met a girl whom I fell in love with and married. She was from Nha Trang, in the middle of the country, next to my home province of Phu Yen. In August 1963 we went back to Nha Trang to visit her family. It was during this trip that I had my real political enlightenment.

The summer of 1963 was when the conflict between Catholics and Buddhists was most intense. In May and June, Buddhists were rioting against the government. In June the first monk burned himself to death in Saigon.

In Nha Trang there is a famous Buddhist pagoda called Hai Duc. One day during our visit to my wife's parents, I went down to Hai Duc with a friend of mine to see what was happening. I thought maybe there would be some demonstrations or speeches, or something else interesting. But when we got there, nothing was going on. The only thing in front of the pagoda was a public bulletin board. We read the notices, then we turned around to leave. Just as we did, three men grabbed us and threw us into a car. It took me a minute to realize that these guys were police, but I was too shocked by the assault to do anything anyway. It only took a couple of minutes to get to the police station. They searched me and took my wallet and ID. Then they shoved me into a cell by myself.

In a little while an officer and two police came into the cell. The officer told me I had to admit everything. He said he wanted to know all about why I was working for the Buddhists and what my methods were. When I couldn't answer anything he began beating me with a stick. He'd beat me, then ask me again to tell him. But there was nothing I could say. I didn't have any idea what he was talking about. After a while he stopped hitting me and gave me a pencil and some pieces of paper for me to write out my autobiography. While I was writing I was thinking to myself that I belonged to the police the same way the villagers belonged to the French during the war. The French could just come in and do whatever they wanted. Nobody could stop them. It was a fact of life that you just accepted, like the weather.

This is a hard thing to explain to Americans, because Americans are used to the idea of justice. In the United States, if the police arrest you falsely and beat you, you get a lawyer and sue the police and try to have them arrested. But justice like this was not a part of life in Vietnam. If you were arrested, you didn't have anyone to appeal to. You just belonged to the police—period. If they got you, you were unlucky, as if you had been struck by a disease. They had gotten others, and some of them had disappeared and some of them had been killed. Now it was my turn, so I accepted it, because there was nothing I could do about it anyway.

After I finished the autobiography, they were even angrier. They still thought I was working for the Buddhists and refusing to tell them about it. So they kept hitting me and asking me questions. They kept me in that cell for three days and three nights without any food or sleep, with constant questions and hitting. I was sure that they would kill me. The police who were there were wearing guns, but I couldn't figure out how I could get my hands on one and shoot them. And there was no way of getting out.

Finally they stopped and brought me to another room where they gave me some rice soup to eat. When I was finished, the officer said that now if I didn't tell them what they wanted to know they were going to torture me. I thought that if I hadn't been tortured up to now, what could they do to me? I was so scared. The only thing that kept me from breaking down was that the room was empty—it didn't look anything like a place where they would torture somebody—so I thought that if they kept me there I'd be all right.

While they talked to me in this room, I found out that my friend, the one I had been arrested with, was a police informer. He had denounced me because I had told him about all the things I didn't like in Saigon and about what I thought of the government. But after they interrogated me for three days, they apparently didn't think that I knew anything specific about the Buddhist movement because they stopped beating me.

Instead they sent me from the police station to the Nha Trang prison, where I was put in a collective cell with about fifty others. As far as I could make out, most of the other prisoners were suspects, like I was. The cell was about twenty feet wide by forty feet long, with wooden sleeping platforms on each side. Food was brought in twice a day in containers. Rice and vegetables, which we'd divide up. Also, twice a day they would let us out of the cell, to walk around in the courtyard and to go to the bathroom and wash ourselves. Each prisoner was allowed to have visitors once a week, so I was able to get word out to my wife where I was. After the first two weeks she came to visit regularly. I was in the Nha Trang prison for almost two months. They released me after the first week in October, just three weeks before Diem was overthrown on November 1. I was happy as hell to get out, and even happier when Diem was killed.

NGUYEN THI TY (NGUYEN CONG HOAN'S WIFE):
Hoan in Prison

WHEN HOAN WAS ARRESTED IT WAS DURING THE TROUBLES BETWEEN the government and the Buddhists. He left the house, then he just didn't come back. I was worried of course. A lot of students were being arrested at that time. My grandfather said that maybe they'd killed him and thrown his body in the river. I thought that maybe they had. The Buddhist movement was very strong, and the police were kidnapping and killing people.

Every day I went down to the prison to see if I could find out any information about him. I was part of a crowd of people that gathered there every day, wandering around in front of the main gate. They were all relatives of people who had been arrested. I hoped I could find out something, but I was too frightened to ask directly. I didn't know how I could get through the guard at the front gate. If I said something to him I was sure he would just shout at me to go away.

When the gate was opened you could see a kind of fenced area in the courtyard. People who were allowed to visit could go in and talk to their relatives through the fence. One day I was standing in front of the open gate trying to see if I could recognize any of the prisoners in the courtyard. While I was looking I heard someone yell out, "Ty, your husband's here with me! Bring some liniment with you when you visit!"

It was a student I knew who had been arrested. He had recognized me through the fence. I was so happy! At least Hoan was still alive, even if he was hurt. I knew he must be hurt, that's why he needed the liniment. But he was alive.

The next day I got to see him. He looked sick and weak, but he pretended that he was all right. I gave him the package I had brought with me—clothes, oranges, bananas, cooked meat—and the liniment. After that I came to see him every week. I had no idea how long he might be there, but I thought it might be a long time.

Nguyen Cong Hoan and Nguyen Thi Ty's stories continue on page 84.

TRINH DUC

URBAN ORGANIZER, PRISONER, VILLAGE SECRETARY

He speaks no French or English, only Chinese and Vietnamese. "My two countries," he says. In one he "learned how to be patient and sacrifice." In the other, "how to die for a cause." Although fifty-five years old, he hasn't an ounce of fat. Trim, muscular, and quick in his movements. When he describes the difference between the Russian AK-47 and the M-16 he jumps up and demonstrates: BAM-BAM-BAM-BAM! The M-16 is lighter and fires faster, but he likes the AK better. It has more penetrating power.

Although a fighter most of his life, he has a good grasp of politics and likes to talk about the subject. When he does, you see the trained Marxist cadre. He punctuates his speech with waves of the hand or a finger thrusting upward toward the hot sky of the French Midi, where he lives. At the end of an eight-hour session I'm exhausted, but he hasn't even slowed down. "Any more questions?" An iron will and concentration. This is a hard man. One session with him tells a lot about how he survived for ten years in South Vietnam's worst prisons.

At dinner I met his wife and children. Mrs. Trinh Duc was a Communist agent at the age of fifteen. Later, after she served her own time in jail, she became a health cadre in the liberated zone. Her face is strikingly beautiful. She is broad, intelligent, quick to smile. A photograph of her would melt American hearts. We should never have gotten into a war with people as photogenic as this.

TRINH DUC'S STORY: *In the Underground*

I WAS BORN ON HAINAN ISLAND, THE SON OF A PEASANT. [HAINAN Island lies off the southern coast of China and the eastern coast of Vietnam. Politically and ethnically, it is part of China.] In 1942, I joined the resistance movement against the Japanese invaders. I was twelve years old. I joined because the Japanese killed my father. They also killed one of my older brothers, who was fighting in the resistance against them. So I joined as soon as I was old enough to do something.

All of the people in Hainan hated the Japanese and fought against them in every way they could. In the cities the resistance was organized by Chiang Kai-shek's Kuomintang government. In the countryside the resistance belonged to the Communists. I lived in the countryside, so I joined the Communists. First I was guide and messenger boy, then after a couple of years I became a fighter.

The Communist youth organization that I was part of—the Mao Zedung Youth Union—gave me military training and political training. The political lessons were not usually about Marxism, but about things like how to treat the peasants and about the atrocities of the Japanese. The lessons were meant to make us hate the Japanese even more than we already did and to want to kill them.

By 1945, when the Japanese surrendered, I was a full-time soldier. After they left I stayed in the Youth Union, but I also went back to live with my family and help them. We were able to buy two oxen and we used them to haul a wagon, transporting things for people. That's how we made our living. It was a happy time of my life, after the war.

But my happiness didn't last long. During the fighting the Kuomintang and the Communists were unified against the Japanese. But afterward things changed. The Communists had always controlled the peasants, but now the Kuomintang officials and soldiers came into the villages and began to arrest and kill people they accused of being Communists. They brought terror and atrocities everywhere they went.

At this time I was about sixteen or seventeen years old. Even though I had been a member of the Mao Zedung Youth for many years, I was not a Communist in an ideological way. At least I didn't think of myself like that. I was a fighter, then I was an oxcart driver. But when the Kuomintang came to my area they arrested or killed the entire Communist resistance network that I belonged to. The Party boss for the region had rallied to them, and they just rolled us up. They overwhelmed us.

When this started happening, the Party couldn't respond. We weren't strong enough to fight them. In my immediate unit there were five people. When the Party finally told us to save ourselves, only two of us were still alive. The directive said to scatter, each man for himself. Everybody who was left tried to find some way to escape Hainan. Some went to Thailand, some to Vietnam, and some tried to get to safe areas in China.

I decided to try and escape to Vietnam. My oldest brother had emigrated there a long time ago and was living in Cholon [Saigon's Chinese quarter], where he owned a restaurant. I knew he would take care of me. I was able to buy a boat ticket as part of a large group that was being organized, mainly people who were going to visit relatives or to look for work and settle there.

Of course my first thought was just to escape. I also had the vague idea that I could go to school in Saigon, and that I could make contact with the Party in Vietnam. Even though we had all been told to get out, we were still Party members. No matter where we went, as long as there was a Chinese community we would be able to link up with the local Party organization. We were expected to do that. As far as what was happening in Vietnam was concerned—in Vietnam's revolution—I hardly had any knowledge at all. I had heard of Ho Chi Minh. I knew that he and some other Vietnamese leaders had been in China. But in the Hainan countryside that was all we knew. So I didn't really have any idea of what to expect when I got to Saigon.

My first sight of the city was tremendously exciting. It was the biggest place I had ever seen. The Cholon Chinese guy who organized the trip brought me to meet my brother, whom I hadn't seen since I was four. I felt at home immediately—my brother's family was very kind to me and Cholon was full of Chinese. The atmosphere was very very Chinese—everybody there spoke Chinese, though many didn't know the Hainan dialect. Anyway, life in Saigon was a combination of new things and homelike things.

Soon after I arrived I began to help my brother in his restaurant. Since the restaurant was near a military post, a lot of his customers were French soldiers. They were the first Europeans I had seen. I can't say I was prejudiced against them, but I already had the beginnings of hatred for them from my Party training, which had taught us something about French colonialism.

My brother and most of the workers in his restaurant also had very strong views. I found out quickly that there was heavy fighting going on between the French and the Vietminh, and that my brother and others in the restaurant were revolutionaries. They were in the Vietminh system, organizing for the Communists in the Chinese community. They educated the Chinese people to support the Vietnamese Revolution and also to love China and the Chinese Revolution. They distributed literature, conducted meetings, and ran different kinds of clandestine groups.

I was living in the middle of this from the moment I arrived in Saigon. The Vietnamese and ethnic Chinese revolutionaries had a single purpose, but the Chinese had all their own organizations: women, labor, youth, intellectuals, also their own security teams. Occasionally Kuomintang Chinese would try to infiltrate the groups, but by and large there weren't many of them and they weren't very successful. The Vietnamese police who worked for the French were much more dangerous. Many people were arrested and imprisoned, some in Con Son [a maximum security prison island located in the South China Sea about seventy-five miles off Vietnam's southern coastline]. The stories that came back from the prisons about torture and starvation were hair-raising. They didn't stop anyone, but all the revolutionaries knew what to expect if they were caught.

Several months after I got to Cholon I enrolled in school, in the third grade. I was by far the oldest in the class. All the rest of them were ten or eleven and I was seventeen. Even though I was small for my age, it still looked funny. Besides that, even though it was a Chinese school, the language of the school was Mandarin, not Hainan dialect, and at first I couldn't understand a word. In the mornings I would get up around four and go to help start the day in the restaurant. Afterwards I'd go to school, put in another stint at the restaurant, then come home at night.

By 1950 I had already been working as a political proselytizer for some time. But it wasn't until that year that I was officially nominated as a member of the student group. My job was mainly to talk, to spread information about China and the revolution, and to arouse the students' anger against the French.

There were three steps to follow in proselytizing work. First I would just talk generally, to find out who was sympathetic, or at least partly sympathetic. Once I was sure someone would be receptive, I'd start giving him literature to read and I'd talk to him specifically about the literature and about questions he had. Finally, if a person seemed like he was strong and ardent, I'd recruit him for the youth organization.

I also distributed leaflets on the streets. Every Party directive or announcement was circulated by leaflet as well as by word of mouth at meetings. So was other important news. The leaflets were printed in Chinese, and an elaborate plan was set up to make sure they got distributed. Each person would be assigned a district and street, and we'd blanket Cholon with them, usually early in the morning, while it was still dark.

I was scared, but I did it anyway. I was ready to be arrested at any time.

I was prepared for it. If you were a revolutionary you had to be ready to sacrifice, that's the beginning and the end of it. I was a revolutionary. When I was young I had witnessed a lot of killing, a lot of terrible things that had happened to innocent people. I hated injustice and I wanted to help the victims and to defend them. When I came to Vietnam I still had those ideals, to achieve justice—that was my motivation. In Saigon I found myself working on the political side of the revolution instead of the fighting side, and I found that I preferred that. But the danger was just as great. I accepted it completely.

After I officially joined the student organizing group, I began to learn more about politics and about revolutions. In our classes I studied the French and American revolutions as well as the Russian Revolution—even the Japanese Revolution under Meiji. Among other things, we were taught that some of the French sympathized with us. The Americans we considered to be in the same camp as the French. We knew that we had to distinguish between the leaders of these countries and the people. At least some of the people might become allies, but their governments were colonialist. We hated the capitalists and colonialists—not with much understanding perhaps, but with powerful feelings.

In 1952 I was accepted as a member of the Communist Party. Actually I was recruited for the *Dang Lao Dong* [the Vietnamese Communist Party]. Since 1951 a resolution had been in effect directing ethnic Chinese to join the local Communist Party—the Thai Party, the Vietnamese Party—wherever you lived, instead of the CCP [Chinese Communist Party]. But although I was a member of the *Dang Lao Dong* all my responsibilities were among the ethnic Chinese, not in the Vietnamese community. My duty was to organize, educate, and train the ethnic Chinese to support Vietnam's revolution. We were taught that it was as glorious to struggle for Vietnam as to struggle for China. The policy was that Vietnam and China were "like lips and teeth." If the lips don't close, the teeth get cold.

Shortly after I joined the Party I was appointed to control activities in three local high schools—Truong Phap, Chi Thanh, and Hoa Hoa, where I was still a student. Each school had a leadership unit, and I directed the units. One of my jobs was to make sure that they received all the documents and booklets for prospective members, material that was either printed in China and smuggled in or reprinted in Cholon from an original sent from the mainland.

This was primarily propaganda material, reporting in glowing terms the glorious victories of the Chinese Communists, and also the horrible crimes the Nationalists had committed. They described what the great victory in China meant to the Vietnamese Revolution, and how communism was an invincible historical force, the only movement that could defeat foreign domination and restore true freedom and independence to underdeveloped countries like China and Vietnam.

In 1953 I joined the Intellectual Association staff for Saigon/Cholon and was given more responsibilities. Now I started to broaden my activities, proselytizing among teachers as well as students, and starting to move into labor organizing.

When the Geneva Agreement was signed in July of 1954, we distributed the text in Chinese and more information describing how essential China's help had been in achieving the great victory. [In fact, the Vietnamese prime minister, Pham Van Dong, was incensed at China for having acquiesced to a division of the country. Privately he felt that Zhou Enlai, the Chinese representative in Geneva, had double-crossed the Vietnamese Revolution.]

After Geneva I was put on the list of those to be transferred North. This was the greatest honor I had ever received. I was elated about being chosen to go. My embarkation point was Camau, at the tip of the Delta. Gathering there was a joyous occasion. Thousands and thousands of fighters were there and thousands more who had been released from Con Son and other horrible jails. Sons and daughters had come along to see their fathers off. There were even about a hundred French who had fought with the Vietminh.

We all camped out, waiting for the ships that would take us North. But after four or five days, I was taken aside by a cadre who led me to an isolated house on a large sugarcane farm and told me to wait. Later that day a Chinese-speaking cadre came to the house to stay with me, to teach me and give me instructions. He told me that I would not be going North after all. The Party analysis was that Diem would not hold elections after two years, as the Agreement had stipulated. Because of this, some cadres would have to stay behind, to maintain the organizations and attempt to force the elections through. I had proven myself an effective organizer and my identity had never been compromised, so I was to stay.

When I first heard this I was dismayed. But as the cadre explained things I began to reconcile myself to the idea of not seeing the North. After hearing what he had to say, I agreed that keeping the structures alive in the South was necessary. It was the correct decision and I resolved to carry it out.

The main guideline for the people who were to stay was that there was to be no public violation of the Agreement. We were supposed to maintain our legal identities as ordinary citizens. Organizations were to be maintained at the most minimal levels; no written communications or papers were to be utilized in any way. The object was complete, total secrecy.

Aside from keeping our basic networks alive, we also cached weapons and ammunition, buried for the most part in tombs and graves. These were simply left; they were not to be used in any way. But we would have them whenever the Party felt it was necessary to renew the war.

The overt Party line was that reunification elections would take place on schedule, exactly as the Agreement said they would. There would be a two-year waiting period, then the nation would be unified again, this time under Ho Chi Minh and the government of the Democratic Republic of Vietnam. This is what all the departing fighters and cadres were told. But inside the Party the understanding was different. Those of us who stayed were told, "If you want the Agreement carried out, you have to be strong, you have to maintain strength in the South."

We were told that Diem might honor the Agreement or he might not. But in either case we had to continue the movement, keep people warmed up and keep the organizations going. If there really were elections, then we would be able to capitalize on the situation more quickly if the networks were in place. And if there weren't, we would be better prepared to resume the struggle. In any event, the Party could never sleep on its victories.

I received instruction on these things for more than two weeks. Then I went back to Saigon to finish my last year of high school and to continue building.

Trinh Duc's story continues on page 94.

LE VAN TRA

VIETMINH MESSENGER BOY

Some had a different choice made for them. Tra's whole family fought with the Vietminh against the French. But in 1954 he stayed home instead of going North. His older brother had told him it was his duty to stay, to take care of their elderly parents. "Besides," he said, "you can serve the people here, too." Tra did, by becoming an engineer, then an upper-level provincial administrator for the Saigon government.

Shortly before the Tet Offensive, Tra met his brother secretly in a safe area in Cu Chi. It was the first time they had seen each other in fourteen years.

A week later the attack broke. Tra's brother was among the casualties, killed leading his unit in the assault on Saigon.

LE VAN TRA: *Leave-taking*

IN 1945 I WAS NINE YEARS OLD. MY BROTHER HAD GRADUATED FROM high school that year and had joined the Vietminh city commando in Binh Duong, where we lived. My job was to steal ammunition, grenades, anything I could get. I say it was my job, but all the kids did it. We'd hang around at the marketplace and watch the French soldiers as they came along, waiting for a chance to grab something and run. The next day on the way to school we'd brag to each other about what we had managed to get.

When I got to be fifteen or so, my parents started letting me go into the resistance zone during school vacations. Practically my whole family was fighting in one way or another, my brother, my brother-in-law, all six of my uncles. I became a messenger boy during the summers. During the school year I was a student. My family belonged to society in Binh Duong and my parents made sure I finished school instead of giving myself entirely to the resistance.

When the war ended, in July 1954, all of the fighters in my family got ready to go North, including my brother, whom I idolized. By the end of 1954 or early 1955 the Vietminh army began to gather, moving down the country to the embarkation points in Vung Tau and Binh Tuy. I was going to go with them as far as Xuyen Moc, the port they were leaving from. I remember my father telling my brother that it was his duty to go, then putting his hand on my brother's shoulder and telling him to take care of himself and to write. My mother just stood there, though I knew she felt exactly the same way my father did. Finally, my brother bowed to them, his arms folded in front, the way children did to their parents at that time. Then I followed him out of the house.

The oxcart train we joined stretched for miles and miles, taking all the resistance troops from Zone D. It started in Tay Ninh, then wound down through Binh Duong and into Bien Hoa—two thousand oxcarts they said, and over twenty thousand *bo dois*. It was immense, a national outpouring. Students walked alongside the carts with families that were going with the convoy to see their sons or fathers off.

At each village, the people would stand along the roadside, cheering and waving and offering food. At night the villages would be ready with food and water. They would put on performances to entertain the fighters. We students would sing and put on our own shows every night. During the days we walked along, listening to the soldiers telling their stories about the battles they'd been in and the heroic actions they'd seen.

We were on the road twenty-eight days from Binh Duong to Xuyen Moc. It was the most exciting time of my life. I wanted to go North with them so badly I could taste it. All of the students did. But we were told to stay and study or work. We had already won a great victory over the French, and in two years we'd all be united again.

In Xuyen Moc we set up a tent city, waiting for the Polish ships that would come to take the *bo dois*. We cooked around the fires, telling stories and visiting—everyone was full of excitement and expectancy.

When the day finally came I walked with my brother to the dock, holding his hand. He told me, "You stay home and take care of father and mother; you're the only one left."

HUONG VAN BA

COLONEL, PEOPLE'S ARMY OF NORTH VIETNAM

A ranking artillery officer in the North Vietnamese Army. Small but wiry, with that Vietnamese quickness you often see in men who were good fighters. I located him through the friend of a friend of a friend, and it was only after careful probing by mutual acquaintances that he agreed to an interview.

When we finally got together he was friendly and direct. He spoke only in Vietnamese, so the entire interview was done through an interpreter. Later I discovered that he understood English well. He wanted to be sure there would be no misunderstandings.

HUONG VAN BA: *Going North*

WHEN I WAS TWELVE YEARS OLD I QUIT SCHOOL TO FIGHT THE French. Like everybody else I hated them and the village officials who worked for them. At first I joined the Vanguard Youth. Our job was to make propaganda, talking to people in the villages and giving musical performances.

About a year after I joined I was sent to a three-month course in Marxism. I was taught about dialectical materialism and the tasks of Vietnam's revolution. The classes were conducted by former political prisoners who had been released from Con Dao prison. I liked it tremendously, maybe because I was so young. I especially liked the breaks. The teachers would tell us about Russia, and about the happy lives people led there and the social justice. Everybody admired the USSR and the sort of society they had made. Some of my friends and I would try to draw pictures of Karl Marx and Engels. Everyone wanted to become a Communist.

When my studies were finished I joined the Ve Quoc Doan, the National Guards League. I was thirteen. We were organized as local forces and I was assigned to liaison duty. During the day I hung around the French posts (I knew how to speak a little French). I talked to the soldiers and made friends with them. I'd get as much information as I could and draw maps of their positions. At night I'd guide the resistance forces in to attack.

One day a Vietminh medical team came into my village to offer medical services to the people and to set up medical training courses for soldiers. The head of the team was a German-trained doctor who had returned to Vietnam to join the resistance forces. He liked me—I was more educated than the other boys, and more active—and he asked my commander to let me join the team. So I was transferred to serve under the administrative committee. But eventually I decided I didn't like medicine, that I really wanted to be a soldier. So I switched back.

And I did like being a soldier. My spirits were always high. I had boundless enthusiasm for it, regardless of the hardships and dangers we had to face. I was fighting all over the South, in many battles. Some of the ones I remember best were the fights against Ba Cut's Hoa Hao in Ca Mau and Can Tho. [Hoa Hao is a religious sect that was centered in the Mekong Delta and kept its own private army. Anti-French at the beginning of the war, the Hoa Hao later fought the Vietminh for control of the central Delta provinces.] I was in the 307th battalion when we captured the district chief in Can Tho, then ambushed the relief column.

Along the way I was admitted to the Communist Party—in 1949. Ho Chi Minh had supposedly dissolved the Party in order to unite everyone behind the resistance. But in fact the Party only became secret instead of open. In the South, two other political parties were organized under covert Communist leadership: the Socialist Party, to attract intellectuals; and the Democratic Party, to draw property owners, business people, and other prominent figures. Superficially, these groups were independent. But in reality their core leaders were Communist Party members.

When the Geneva Conference was convened [May 8, 1954] we were stirred with both hope and worries. But we were told that it was our job to fight, that the Party would take care of diplomacy. It wasn't any of our business to worry about that. We'd win at the negotiating table when we won on the battlefield. So I kept fighting. When the cease-fire order came on July 20th, 1954, I was a deputy artillery platoon leader in Battalion 307, the most renowned unit in the Southern resistance. I was twenty-one years old and I had been a soldier for nine of those years.

Afterward we were told that since we hadn't won a complete victory, we were going to have to accept a temporary partition of the country. In two years there would be a general election to reunify the nation. With this news, people in the South, like myself, agreed to regroup North. We believed that in two years the country would be reunited and that we'd be able to go home. Had we known there wasn't going to be any election, we never would have left our homeland.

While we were preparing to leave, the Party cadres mobilized everyone from Saigon to Ca Mau to visit and say goodbye to those who were going. It was an emotional scene. We were told that those who were going North and those who were staying behind had the same glorious and important task.

We left from Vung Tau aboard a Russian ship. Immediately after I arrived in the North I was sent to Thanh Hoa Province, where I was assigned to do fieldwork with the peasants and to continue my political studies. I wasn't happy about this. But I was a Party member, and we were taught that Party members must always be in the forefront—the first to bear the hardships and the last to enjoy the fruits.

There were certainly hardships. I missed my parents terribly. Sometimes I'd find myself crying at night. I hadn't been at home much, since I had joined the revolution at such an early age. But my parents had raised me and given me a precious education during my childhood. My friends were equally unhappy. They all wanted to go back as soon as possible.

But you know, time cured my homesickness. After a couple of years I got used to it. And besides, I was busy with daily work. There wasn't time to dwell on my family. After I was twenty-five or so, there was nothing left to cry about. I had no more tears.

In fact I had no personal life at all. Party members were not supposed to think about their personal lives. Their job was to carry out the Party's orders. Inside I didn't agree with this at all. But it didn't make any difference who agreed and who didn't. You still had to follow the Party's decisions. You follow the rules of the game where you live. In any society people want to have a happy life. In a Communist society, if you want to have a happy life, you have to have a good position in the Party. To move up to a good position, you have to comply with Party discipline and effectively carry out the Party's orders. Do the opposite and you get purged—punished and kept down. So it didn't matter what I thought. Sometimes you have to act in certain ways, whether you think you should or not. Besides, at that time, young Vietnamese had a political ideal. I had that, and I also had a personal ambition—to become a military leader. That was what I wanted.

It was a terrible disappointment in 1956 when we realized there wouldn't be any elections. Of course we had had hints. Once Vo Nguyen Giap [the victor of Dienbienphu and minister of defense in Ho Chi Minh's government] was asked when we would go South and if he thought the country would be united in two years. His answer was that the job of carrying out the revolution had no time limit on it. I remember a speech given in Hanoi by a visiting Russian dignitary. His message was that the North should build a strong and wealthy socialist society, and eventually the South would follow. Listening to him, it was clear to me that the Russians were not in favor of liberating the South by force. Even in 1957, when Le Duan [secretary-general of the Communist Party] was questioned by representatives of the regrouped Southerners, he said that the situation "was not yet favorable."

Meanwhile, the Americans had arrived in the South to replace the French. I didn't know much about the Americans. I believed what the Party said about the French—they were colonialists who had come to Vietnam to rob our resources. We had defeated them. But now the Americans had come. If the French were colonialists, the Americans were neo-colonialists, financial exploiters who were out to force our people into their own kind of enslavement.

That's what we were told, and I believed it. I was still young. I knew nothing at all about the Americans myself. When they brought Mr. Diem to Vietnam, the Vietnamese people had never heard of him. What they did know was that Diem must be a creature of the Americans. The United States made a big mistake when it put some unpopular overseas Vietnamese in power. Why didn't they choose some respected and virtuous figure in the South as leader?

Anyway, we didn't accept Diem's regime. We belonged to the resistance forces. We had a well-trained army, the strongest in Southeast Asia, second only to China's. We could win any battle. I certainly didn't expect the war to last very long. And if the Americans hadn't intervened, we would have beaten the ARVN quickly. [ARVN—Army of the Republic of Vietnam (South Vietnam).]

In 1959–1960 units began to move South. I remember in 1959 a delegation from the South visited the artillery officers' school where I was an instructor. I entertained them with a demonstration of antiaircraft machine guns. Some of my friends left for the South in 1960. I received my own orders in the middle of 1962 while I was still an instructor at the artillery school. But prior to my own departure, I was assigned as a trainer for others who were going.

The camp we used for this training was located at Xuan Mai, Ha Dong Province. It had previously been the base of the regrouped Southern Division 338, but the entire division had already left for the South. Instruction for those who were being sent included military and political subjects as well as classes on the current situation in South Vietnam. Of course, the exact nature of the training varied, depending on the kind of unit involved. But the physical part of it was tough and exhausting for everyone. Infantry units were conditioned mainly to walking, running—building endurance. They were trained to carry seventy to eighty-five pounds on their backs, and the training went on night as well as day. It included marches of seven or eight hours with backpacks loaded down with stones. It was tough. They had to be prepared to deal with anything.

A lot of the field training was conducted at night, to reduce the chances that local people would get suspicious about what the training was for. For the same reason the soldiers would not wear their military uniforms, just regular clothes.

Food rations for the trainees were tremendous—3.2 dong worth of food per day. This was compared with the standard civilian food ration in North Vietnam at that time of .60 dong and the regular army ration of .90 dong; 3.2 dong was higher than Ho Chi Minh's own ration.

Most of the trainees were anxious to return South, so they were patient and worked hard. The instructors weren't harsh with them—there was no shouting or punishment. The main thing was to educate them, to motivate them to like the training. Ho Chi Minh said that when trainees weren't enthusiastic and didn't get good results, it wasn't their fault. It was because the instructors had failed to make them understand the purposes and the necessity of the training. Or because they had failed to make it challenging.

Among those who were being prepared to go were Northerners as well as Southerners. Even though some of the Northerners had fought in the South before [prior to 1954], they were not as enthusiastic as the Southerners. The Southerners were really anxious to get back to their homes and families.

At that time the tactical theory was that artillery couldn't be successful in breaking through the kind of defensive systems they were using in the

South. But I was able to demonstrate to a visiting team of generals the effective use of artillery, H-12 rockets, DKZ-75s, and mortars. I set up blockhouses and barbed wire fences as targets in the demonstration and showed how they could be destroyed.

I served as a trainer for almost two years. It wasn't until May 24th, 1964, that I myself was able to leave.

TRUONG NHU TANG

MINISTER OF JUSTICE, PROVISIONAL REVOLUTIONARY GOVERNMENT

A covert urban organizer since the mid-1950s, Tang was one of the founders of the National Liberation Front. (His autobiography, A Vietcong Memoir, *was published in 1985.) Although he was one of the losers in the purge of non-Communist officials that took place after liberation, he recalled with great warmth his first meeting with Ho Chi Minh.*

TRUONG NHU TANG: *Meeting Uncle Ho*

IN AUGUST [1946] WE FINALLY ARRIVED IN PARIS TO BEGIN OUR studies. A student reception committee welcomed us at the Gare du Nord and took us out to the university, where we were given rooms in the Maison de l'Indochine, the Indochinese student residence. Two days later we all received invitations from the Maison president to a get-together where we would be introduced to several Vietnamese delegates who were attending the negotiations on independence being held at Fontainebleau.

At the stipulated time, several individuals in business suits were on hand to tell us that they had been sent by President Ho Chi Minh "to convey his warmest regards and welcome you to France"—also to invite us to meet with the president the following morning at eleven. This unexpected announcement caused a murmuring in the group. Somebody sitting behind me whispered, "Who is Ho Chi Minh?" Another voice answered, "I don't know, I've never heard of him." Someone else, more politically aware, said, "Look, he's the president. He's negotiating with the French for equality. We've got to see him."

The next morning, promptly at ten, a number of cars arrived at the

Maison to drive us to Montmorency, where a country house had been provided for Ho. The house belonged to Raymond Aubrac, the World War II resistance chief in Marseilles who was close to the French Communist Party. His wife, with whom Ho was on cordial terms, was a member of the National Assembly. As our caravan pulled to a stop in front of the house, we could see a group of people gathered on the steps to greet us. Standing in the middle was a frail-looking older man who was introduced to us as President Ho. With him were Pham Van Dong and other leading figures of the revolution, not a single one of whom was familiar to any of us.

Looking on with a kind of confused interest, I was immediately struck by Ho Chi Minh's appearance. Unlike the others, who were dressed in Western-style clothes, Ho wore a frayed, high-collared Chinese jacket. On his feet he had rubber sandals. In contrast to the tense-looking younger men around him, he gave off an air of fragility, almost sickliness. But these impressions only contributed to the imperturbable dignity that enveloped him as though it were something tangible. I had never thought of myself as a person especially sensitive to physical appearances, but Ho exuded a combination of inner strength and personal generosity that struck me with something like a physical impact. He looked directly at me, and at the others, with an expression of intensity and warmth that was magnetic.

Almost reflexively I found myself thinking of my grandfather. There was that same effortless communication of wisdom and caring with which my grandfather had personified for us the values of Confucian life. I was momentarily startled when Ho reached his arm out in a sweeping gesture, as if he were gathering us in. "Come my children," he said, and sat down on the steps. We settled around him, as if it was the most natural thing in the world. I sat next to him, already infusing this remarkable person, who seemed so like Grandfather, with the schoolboy reverence I had felt towards the personal heroes adopted from my reading of history: Gandhi, Sun Yat-sen, and especially Abraham Lincoln. Lost in thoughts like these, I was not observing my comrades closely, but my impression was that their attention too was rivetted on Ho, as he told us to call him "Bac" Ho—Uncle Ho—instead of Mr. President. Then he was asking each of us in turn about our families, our names, our studies, where we were from, how old we were. He wanted to know too about our feelings towards Vietnam's independence, a subject on which most of us had only the vaguest thoughts. We certainly hoped our country would be free. But beyond that we had little to contribute.

When Ho realized that among our group there were students from the

North, South, and Center of the country, he said gently, but with great intensity, "*Voilà,* the youth of our great family of Vietnam. Our Vietnam is one, our nation is one. You must remember, though the rivers may run dry and the mountains erode, the nation will always be one." To Western ears such phrases may have sounded artificial. To ours the simple sentimentality was evocative. It was the concrete language of slogan and poetry that Vietnamese leaders had always used to rally the people to a political cause. Ho went on to say that when he was born Vietnam was a nation of slaves. Since his own adolescence he had been struggling for liberty, and now we had the fortune to be free and independent citizens, a fortune that our parents and grandparents had not enjoyed. Eighty years of slavery had diminished the nation, but now it was time to reestablish the heritage given to us by our ancestors and recover from our backwardness. If our people were to gain an honorable place among the peoples of the world, it would depend largely on us, on our efforts to study and learn and to contribute to the national family.

It was a message that combined ardent and idealistic nationalism with a moving personal simplicity. Ho had created for us an atmosphere of family and country and had pointed to our own role in the great patriotic endeavor. Before an hour had passed he had gained the heart of each one of us sitting around him on those steps in front of Aubrac's house.

TRAN VAN TRA

COLONEL GENERAL, PEOPLE'S LIBERATION ARMED FORCES (VIETCONG)

The general who commanded VC forces in most of South Vietnam, the so-called Bulwark Theater. This is from his war memoirs, published in Ho Chi Minh City in 1982. Several weeks later the book was withdrawn from circulation, most likely for its candor and ardent Southern orientation. Tra himself was purged and isolated, though recent reports (summer 1985) say that he has been partially rehabilitated.

TRAN VAN TRA: *Uncle Ho's Parting Words*

I REMEMBER THE FIRST TIME I MET UNCLE HO, IN 1948, AT VIET Bac [in the North]. Since the outbreak of the Southern resistance on

September 23, 1945, that was the first time a Southern delegation . . . had gone to Viet Bac to report to Uncle Ho and the Party Central Committee. Our route passed mostly through areas temporarily occupied by the enemy. We had to organize ourselves as a well-armed combat unit so that we could be ready to defend ourselves and fight our way through when we had to, even though all along the villagers gave us whatever help they could.

We walked all the way along the eastern side of the Truong Son range, climbing mountains and fording rivers and streams. At some places we had to go by sea, at Cam Ranh and Nha Trang. We traveled six months without rest.

The French were following our movements closely and tried to ambush us in the mountains of Pham Rang, at Doc Mo, and in Khanh Hoa. Finally, they parachuted troops into Van Dinh, west of Hanoi, hoping to take us by surprise and capture our entire delegation. But each time they failed. . . .

When we reached Viet Bac we were eager to meet Uncle Ho, to fulfill a long-term desire. When we did meet him, we were all moved. Here was our teacher, our father, the incarnation of our homeland, the image of our people. He had a high forehead, a thin beard, a pair of bright eyes, a kind face, and a calm, fragile air. I didn't yet know about his great ideas and his noble virtue. Just looking at him, I suddenly felt I had endless confidence in him. I respected him and felt intimate with him. His skill could conquer everything. He was the quintessence of talent. It was so fortunate that our nation gave birth to such a person, whom millions of people followed and loved.

On the day our delegation was to return South, Uncle Ho, the Central Committee, and the government gave us a going-away dinner. In front of everyone, Uncle Ho called me over and presented me with a beautiful sword. In a warm voice that reached the bottom of my heart, he said, "I'm giving you this valuable sword so that you can take it back to the people of the South and use it to kill the enemy. Tell the people that the Party and I will always be with them. If we are united in serving the country, we are bound to win!"

His words have never faded from my mind, or from the hearts of the Southern people.

HOANG HUU QUYNH

ENGINEER

Trained in Moscow, head of the Ho Chi Minh City Technical Institute before his defection. The interview was in France.

HOANG HUU QUYNH: *Ten Years to Grow a Tree*

I WAS BORN IN QUANG TRI. MY GRANDFATHER WAS A HIGH-LEVEL mandarin and all of my family were literate, educated people. In 1946, when the French occupied my village, the family split up and scattered. My uncles joined the resistance. My father was a teacher, but he also left the family for the resistance.

In 1947 or 1948 there was conflict in the resistance between the intellectual and proletariat factions. In Quang Ngai, south of Hue, they even murdered each other, and it was during that period that my father was assassinated.

After he died, my mother was hardly able to support the family. One of my younger brothers was given to an uncle who was going to Saigon to try to find work. There just wasn't enough food on the table at home. The next year, 1954, the year of Geneva, I was given to another uncle who was going North. It meant one less mouth to feed. I was ten years old.

I remember everyone talking about two years, two years to reunification. I was well treated in the North. Ho Chi Minh had said, "It takes ten years to grow a tree, but a hundred years to grow a man." So I was sent to school, and I liked it.

THE VENERABLE GIAC DUC

BUDDHIST OPPOSITION LEADER

Booming voice and a large smile. He heads a small community outside Boston housed in one of those Boston six-family triple deckers, now painted the bright yellow that Vietnamese Buddhist monks favor. It's in an old Jewish neighborhood, presently changing. The old folks sitting in the corner park speak

Yiddish as they watch young Vietnamese and Cambodian mothers do their shopping, trailed by small black-haired children.

Giac Duc has a doctorate in Oriental philosophy from the University of California. Sitting in the third-floor chapel, he can expound equally well on Mahayana sutras or the techniques of political mobilization. Remembering the struggle against Diem he said, "I felt I had two burdens on me, a spiritual burden and a political burden. It was one thing to have compassion. But you also have to realize your compassion. You have to teach spirituality, but you also have to motivate the people to struggle. . . ."

THE VENERABLE GIAC DUC:
Buddhists and Catholics, the Beginning

WHEN I WAS EIGHT YEARS OLD, I ENTERED THE THANH SAM MONastery in Ha Dong Province, North Vietnam. That was in 1943. After the Geneva Conference in 1954, I left for the South. It is often said that almost all those who went from North to South Vietnam at that time were Catholics. But that isn't true. Almost three hundred thousand Buddhists were among the million refugees. Some went because they had been wealthy and some went because they were intellectuals. An entire Buddhist intellectual movement relocated from North to South at that time. Buddhist professors and learned monks. Eventually they changed the intellectual face of Saigon.

I went for two reasons—one personal, one religious. My family had a long tradition of anti-French politics. My father, one of Ho Chi Minh's nationalist opponents, had been killed by the Vietminh. So I was afraid of the Communists because of my family background. Secondly, we thought that the Communists would make life difficult for Buddhists in the North—there were already indications of that in areas that had been Communist strongholds for a long time.

At the same time, Buddhism in the South needed to be strengthened and developed. In the real South—in the Saigon area and the Delta—Buddhism had fallen into decay. Many of the intellectuals had been westernized by their association with French culture. Also, strong sect movements had gotten established—the Cao Dai and Hoa Hao. So Buddhism had to be more strongly built up among the people. It was for that reason too that I went.

When I first arrived in the South I was living at the Bac Viet Pagoda outside Saigon. At that time there was no feeling against Diem among the Buddhists. Even Thich [Venerable] To Lien, who was the spiritual leader of all Vietnamese Buddhists, had accepted him. Of course Diem was Catholic. But To Lien had said that he had nothing against Diem's appointment.

Nevertheless, in 1955 I became aware of Diem's anti-Buddhist attitude, and it angered me. That year the government did not allow Buddha's birthday to be celebrated as a national holiday. I got very angry about that, perhaps because I was so young, or perhaps because my family's political background made me more sensitive to this kind of thing. But when I consulted with the elder monks about what to do, they weren't excited about it at all. They said that from the religious point of view, such things are transitory and unimportant. They said that whether there was a national holiday or not, Buddha was still Buddha and Buddha's birthday was still his birthday. But I was angry and wanted to do something. Eventually they said, "Okay, you do whatever you feel you need to do."

That was the first demonstration I organized. Near the Bac Viet Nghia Trang Pagoda was a refugee camp where many Buddhists from the North were living. I knew a lot of the younger ones who had been students in Hanoi and I was able to get together a march of about two thousand people to protest the government's action. We marched two miles down the road, with lots of Buddhist flags waving from the crowd and about a hundred monks walking in front. I had been picked up by an ardent Buddhist cyclo [pedicab] driver and was riding at the head of the march.

Two miles down the road the police were waiting for us. There was no violence. They just cut out the front hundred or so marchers, surrounded us, and arrested us. The rest of the crowd dispersed and went home. Those of us who had been arrested were taken to Giadinh prison. The police asked me if I was a Communist, and I told them, "Not at all. All of us are anti-Communists." Whatever they thought about my answer, they kept us in Giadinh for three months.

Except for the terrible overcrowding and the heat, the treatment wasn't too bad. The other prisoners seemed very surprised when a hundred monks joined them. They made room for the old monks to sit down, and they demonstrated their respect for us in various ways, exempting us from the cleaning chores, for example.

I don't think my experience in jail politicized me. Perhaps it gave a spur to my activism that came out later on. But I always seemed to be active and politically aware—that was part of my nature. At any rate, after I got out of jail I became part of a group that was setting up private Buddhist high schools. We opened three high schools where the faculties were made up of monks and nuns; it was the beginning of a Buddhist parochial school movement in the South.

The movement had two reciprocal objectives. On the one hand, we wanted to make Buddhist spirituality more a part of the everyday lives of the people. And education was one of the best ways to do that, especially since so many Saigonese were curious about the Buddhist intellectuals who had come down from the North and were now available to teach their children. On the other hand, we were anxious to introduce Western learning to the monks and nuns. We wanted to orient them to the modern world. Two of the high schools were near monasteries, so they stirred up an interest in Western thought and Western education that had never been allowed before.

Up until then, the monks had been so secluded they weren't even allowed to read newspapers or write in the Vietnamese script [*quoc ngu*, the modern Vietnamese phonetic alphabet]. They were only permitted to use Chinese characters. But the idea of making the monks more fit for the modern world had been started in the North by Thich To Lien at the beginning of the 1950s. Before that he had been the strictest of conservatives. But on a trip to Japan in 1952 he found that the Japanese monks had a broad understanding of the modern world, but were able to combine that with a close adherence to tradition.

Thich To Lien had brought the idea back from the World Buddhist Fellowship Meeting that Vietnamese monks could do the same. Perhaps he believed that the monks would have to be much more aware than they had been of the times they were living in. Whether he had a political purpose or not, I don't know. But there was no doubt about his commitment to educate the religious to their secular world.

At about the time we were setting up parochial schools in Saigon, monks in the center of Vietnam were establishing high schools right in the pagodas themselves. These were called Bo De high schools. The first one was in Hue, then they spread to every province in the South. In 1955 and '56 I worked in the parochial schools as a teacher and administrator. Then I moved to Hue, where I studied for a while, then taught history, social studies, and mathematics in the Bo De school.

All the while I was developing organizational and administrative skills, and participating in the movement to increase the interpenetration of Buddhism and the national life. At the same time I had not lost my anger at Diem. Initially I had not regarded the government's decision about Buddha's birthday to be part of a concerted policy of discrimination. But soon afterward I saw I had been mistaken. Buddhist refugees from the North were not receiving the kind of good resettlement lands that Catholic refugees were getting. They were being discriminated against right down the line in all the government's assistance programs. So you could say that while I was learning to put together and run organizations, I was also nurturing a dislike for the Diem government.

In 1958 I worked with several Buddhist monk leaders—Thich Tri Quang, Thich Don Hau and others—to set up an institute for Buddhist studies in Nha Trang. We established a large monastery along with it, and I was named secretary-general. It was in 1959, too, that the Diem government began to push the doctrine of *Nhan Vi* [humanism], a kind of national policy against materialistic thinking.

Unfortunately, *Nhan Vi* was Catholic in conception and in spirit. It emphasized the doctrines of the Trinity and of creationism, and was critical of Buddhist teachings. What was worse, everybody who wanted a good job in either the government or the army had to study *Nhan Vi*. *Nhan Vi* courses were set up in Vinh Long under the jurisdiction of Bishop Ngo Dinh Thuc, Diem's older brother, and army officers and district and provincial-level administrators began to go through the curriculum.

The complaints started coming to us immediately. At first we did nothing. But before long it was clear we would have to take some kind of countermeasures.

VOLUNTEERS AND CONSCRIPTS

In the North and the Southern resistance areas, some volunteered for the army, some were drafted. These accounts are from military interrogations of Liberation Army soldiers who were captured or who rallied. After reading box after box of reports like these and comparing them with live accounts, you learn to discern fact from fiction. These have the ring of truth.

NGUYEN TAN THANH, *Senior Captain, Deputy Commander, South Long An, VC Main Force, from Long An*

I JOINED THE VC WHEN I WAS THIRTY-FIVE YEARS OLD. I WAS MARried and had four children. I was leasing farmland—one hectare [about 2.5 acres]—that was very poor in quality, almost sterile. That was why the owner rented it out to us. Despite working hard all year round, we got only about 100 *gia* of rice out of it. Of this amount, 40 *gia* went to the landlord. We borrowed money to buy ducks and geese. We lived a very hard life. But I cultivated the land carefully, and in time it became fertile. When it did, the owner took it back; my livelihood was gone. I had to go back to my parents, to raise ducks for my father.

I was poor. I had lost my land and I didn't have enough money to take care of my children. In 1961 propaganda cadres of the Front [National Liberation Front] contacted me. These guys had joined the resistance against the French, and after Geneva they had stayed underground in the South. They came to all the poor farmers and made an analysis of the poor and rich classes. They said that the rich people had always served the French and had used the authority of the French to oppress the poor. The majority of the people were poor, not because they wasted their money but because they had been exploited by the landlords who had worked with the French. In the past, the ancestors of the poor had broken ground for tillage. Then powerful people had seized their land. Without any other means to live, the poor had become slaves of the landlords. The cadres told us that if the poor people don't stand up to the rich people, we would be dominated by them forever. The only way to ensure freedom and a sufficient life was to overthrow them.

When I heard the cadres, I thought that what they said was correct. In my village there were about forty-three hundred people. Of these, maybe ten were landlords. The richest owned five hundred hectares [1,236 acres], and the others had at least twenty hectares [49 acres] apiece. The rest of the people were tenants or honest poor farmers. I knew that the rich oppressed the poor. The poor had nothing to eat, and they also had no freedom. We had to get rid of the regime that allowed a few people to use their money and authority to oppress the others.

So I joined the Liberation Front. I followed the VC to fight for freedom and prosperity for the country. I felt that this was right.

PHAN THANH LONG, *Sergeant, NVA*

BEFORE I JOINED THE ARMY, I THOUGHT THAT IF I HAD TO GO IN, I wouldn't mind being assigned to some unit in the city. Of course it was very naive of me. When the draft notice did reach my hands, I wasn't happy, but I wasn't upset either. I didn't feel anything at all. Of course a lot of guys enlisted. There was a big propaganda drive that year to get guys to join up. [The first American ground forces arrived in South Vietnam in March 1965.] They were calling on everyone to enlist in order to save the country. They said the country was being threatened by American aggression. That was the time when the Americans had started bombing the North. Everyone's patriotic feelings were really stirred up. When you saw the airplanes dropping their bombs you really got aroused. Everyone felt a deep anger against the Americans.

But I had a girlfriend . . . she's a teacher now. Then she was only eighteen. When I got my notice she told me, "If you can think of a way to stay behind the lines it would be much better. If you go South you never know when you might return. In the middle of the fighting down there, there's only a little chance you'll come out of it alive." My oldest sister also got very upset when she heard that I had been drafted. She didn't want to see me leave the family. She told me that she wished I could stay home, even though she knew there was nothing we could do about it. When I picked up my knapsack and was about to leave the house, she broke into tears. We were hugging each other and crying. Both of us were crying.

At that point a recruitment cadre showed up and ordered me to hurry up. Then he told my sister that she should be encouraging me to go instead of making things so painful. My sister let him have it. "We love each other in this family," she told him. "Don't be so rude to me." She really put this guy in his place. Of course I had to leave anyway.

But not everyone had to go. I used to be friends with the two sons of Nguyen Duy Trinh—Nguyen Truong To and Nguyen Truong Thanh [Trinh was a member of North Vietnam's foreign ministry and a politburo member]. They were both sent overseas to study instead of having to do their military service. It was the same for Tran Duy Hung's son [Hung was mayor of Hanoi] . . . also exempt from the draft. Almost every district or province Party committee member had a son studying abroad. The chairmen of every one of Hanoi's precincts also got their sons out of the country to study.

For me, after my induction and three months' training I was headed into the South along with the other recruits who were being sent to the front lines. I wasn't happy about it, but there wasn't any way to discuss it either. Hundreds of thousands of others were in exactly the same position.

Up until the time we left none of us had ever seen any of the wounded who had come back from the South. The government thought that the sight of disabled veterans would deter guys from going themselves. All the disabled who came back North were sent to highland areas like Lang Son or Vinh Phuc, or to areas along the coast around Haiphong. In Military Region 4 the wounded were sent to eastern Quang Binh Province. Once they got to these areas, the wounded vets were allowed to write home. But they weren't allowed to tell their folks about their handicaps. They had to say they were in good shape. The government never disclosed information on either the dead or the wounded.

It wasn't until I reached the banks of the Ben Hai River at the 17th parallel on my way South that I first saw wounded soldiers. A group of them were marching back, down from the Truong Son range. Behind them came the transportation teams (carrying those who couldn't march). The teams were busy all day long with the wounded and the dead. I was thinking about my chances of escaping the same fate.

NGUYEN VAN HOANG, *Second Lieutenant, NVA, from Hanoi*

MY GRANDFATHER WAS A CONFUCIAN SCHOLAR, A MANDARIN AT THE Imperial Court in Hue. Because he was anti-French, he decided to quit his government position and retire to a little farm in Ha Dong. With his few acres of paddy land, he kept himself busy farming and disassociated himself entirely from politics and from the French authorities. My father joined the Workers' Party and became deputy secretary of the Ha Dong Party branch. Later he was assigned to the Ministry of Cultural Affairs and transferred to Hanoi, where I grew up.

When I was in school my mother wanted me to do my advanced studies in electromechanics. She was sure that hydroelectricity would be developed in the North and that I could have a good career in that field. My father had different ideas about it. Painting was a tradition in our family, and he wanted me to continue it. He's got a strong will, and in the end I enrolled at the Institute of Arts and Trades. When I graduated I became a teacher.

Generally speaking, not all of the artists in North Vietnam follow the regime wholeheartedly. For an artist like myself, nothing is more beautiful than the ability to live your life freely. And there's not much appealing about the Communist regime in that regard. But I volunteered for the army anyway because of a personal tragedy. During one of the air strikes in Haiphong my fiancée was killed by an American bomb. Immediately afterwards I decided that I had to go South to fight. At the time—this was in the summer of 1967—I thought that the Liberation Army was riding the crest of a wave. If I didn't join up right away I'd miss my chance to take revenge. I reasoned that the Americans must be bombing the North in retaliation for their defeat in the South. I thought the NLF [National Liberation Front] was on the verge of winning the decisive battle and that they would take Saigon in the very near future. I desperately wanted to go and kill a couple of Americans to relieve the bitterness I felt.

When my family learned that I had volunteered they were very unhappy about it. My mother cried for several days and nights straight. My father didn't cry, but he was obviously in distress. The day I left, my mother told me that both of them had been up the entire night, and that my father had been weeping along with her. When I said goodbye, my father told me, "You have to look after yourself, son, and try to return safely. For myself, I'm just trying to think of this as a study trip abroad for you. But be careful. Try to follow discipline and not get punished. And don't be too daring in the fighting. Don't make yourself a useless sacrifice. You are an educated man. It's not your vocation to be a soldier. That's a career that anyone can follow who knows how to pull a trigger. I'm unhappy that you're going. I want to see you back again."

Personally, I didn't think it was going to be that dangerous. In general, most of the people in the North were very confident at that period. Many people were volunteering, without any idea of what kind of hardship and violence they were letting themselves in for. As far as I was concerned, I trusted the government and believed what they were saying. I really thought the revolution was near victory.

My father and my uncles saw it differently. One of my uncles was Hoang Tan Linh, the deputy chief of the Central Cadres Organizing Office in Hanoi. When he heard that I had volunteered he said, "Why are you joining? Don't you know the war in the South is a colossal sacrifice of troops? They're sending soldiers to the South to be killed at a merciless rate. They've taken most of the young men from Hanoi and from all over already, and they'll keep taking them. In war there has to be death. But this war isn't like when I fought against the French. Now the losses are in the thousands and tens of thousands. If you go now there's only one fate—unbearable hardship and possibly death—a meaningless death."

This uncle was a ranking cadre and he always said that in the end we would win. But he stressed to me that this was a period when the sacrifice of troops was necessary. The government was intent on fighting hard and violently, and they needed massive manpower. He said the destruction that was going on was savage and frightening beyond what I could imagine. [For a period of time before 1967, Nguyen Chi Thanh, the overall military commander in the South, followed a strategy of direct confrontation with American and ARVN forces. Liberation Army casualties were enormous.] That was what he meant by a "colossal sacrifice."

But even if I had understood that, I still would have gone. In my family I was considered a very strong-willed person, like my father. Once my mind was made up, there was no budging me. I wasn't happy about joining the army. In fact, during my basic training I used to slip home every two or three days because I was so homesick. But I was absolutely determined to go South—that was irreversible.

But I'll tell you, had I realized that everything we were hearing about victory was nothing more than a big bluff, I never would have left.

BUI VAN BINH, *Sergeant, NVA, from Hanoi*

I WORKED AS A LABORER IN THE VANGUARD YOUTH IN HANOI. VAN-guard Youth members are between sixteen and thirty, but I joined when I was fifteen. I added a year to my age so that I could volunteer—all the members were volunteers. The government had made promises: exemption from military service; elimination of bad social classification, like if you were from a landlord, capitalist, bourgeois, or petit bourgeois class. Also the privilege to go abroad to study, and to get a good job. Almost 90 percent were volunteers from landlord and bourgeois families. They hoped that after three years of voluntary work their political status would be rehabilitated and that they could train themselves and reform their class consciousness.

The Vanguard Youth was organized like the army into battalions, companies, and platoons. The main job was to clean up each time the city was bombed. In each city there was one corps of about five hundred people—the equivalent of a battalion—except in Hanoi, which had two, the 51st and 49th. The 51st was a girls corps, the 49th boys. The 51st's job was to repair and patch up the roads in the city after they were hit. The 49th was supposed to build a pontoon bridge across the river to take the place of the Long Bien Bridge after it was damaged in an air strike. Each of the 49th's companies was stationed at a ferry quay—Phu Vien, Thuong Cat, Chem, or Kim Lien. I worked on this bridge for two years. Then the Americans stopped bombing, and immediately after the government dissolved the youth corps. [Lyndon Johnson ordered a bombing halt in March 1968. Hanoi didn't become a target again until Richard Nixon resumed the attacks in retaliation for the Spring Offensive of 1972.] I had to join the army and go South. The government didn't keep its word about exemption from service. None of the promises were respected. Most of the others shared my fate . . . except for a small number who were transferred into other work battalions because of their ill health. Two years of hard labor, just wasted.

NGUYEN VAN HUNG, *Private, NVA, from Hai Duong Province*

I WAS TWENTY-EIGHT YEARS OLD WHEN I RECEIVED MY DRAFT NOTICE. My father had been a deputy village chief under the French regime, so I was classified as what was called a "middle farmer element." This was an undesirable classification, and of course my father had worked with the French. So even though he died when I was four I still had this bad classification. In addition I was an only son, and the head of my own family as well. By law I should have been exempt from service, but by 1967 there was such an emergency in the South that the authorities were taking everyone they could between eighteen and thirty-five. It didn't matter if you were a good element or a bad. So in April 1968 I found myself in the army. [The Tet Offensive at the end of January resulted in approximately 40 percent losses for the Vietcong, North Vietnam's partner and ally in the South. As a result, infiltration of Northern troops into South Vietnam was stepped up dramatically.]

When I got the draft notice I knew I was destined to go South. And I knew the chances of coming back were very slim. About a hundred guys from my village had gone, starting in 1962, and none had returned. Their parents and wives were waiting for them up to their eyes in fear. But nobody had gotten any news. The government was very explicit about it. They said, "The trip has no deadline for return. When your mission is accomplished you'll come back." Uncle Ho had declared, "Your duty is to fight for five years or even ten or twenty years." So it was clear to me that the whole business was going to be long and dangerous. I was really agitated when I left for the army.

I especially resented the government's callousness about my family situation. After I received my draft notice, my wife began crying at night. She wanted me to petition against being called up. I knew that wasn't possible. So I had to swallow my bitterness and convince her that sooner or later my fate would be set, so I'd better go. It hurt to see my baby and wife left alone. But I didn't dare say anything openly.

But once I was at the training camp, I began to understand that the fight for the South had to be done. Actually I must say that I already believed the Americans were a hundred times crueler than the French. And the French—everybody remembered it—had created the starvation of 1945. [In fact, the great famine of 1945 was caused primarily by the Japanese, who had requisitioned much of the country's rice reserve for their own use and had forced Vietnam's peasants to plant such crops as peanuts and jute instead of rice. In the North, two million out of a population of fifteen million died.] I was sent to basic training from April to

August. They called it military training, but in fact it was two-thirds political. On the military side, the main drill was to learn how to carry heavy loads while climbing hills and walking through jungles. Next was how to use weapons like the AK-47 rifle . . . then combat tactics: shelling, sapper training, camouflage techniques.

But right from the start, we had to learn the basic political drill: Fight the Americans and save the country. The political cadres stressed that soldiers are part of the proletariat, that our job was even more important and more honorable than what the people were doing. It was our duty to liberate the Southern population that was in misery under the domination of the American imperialists. After a continuous week of this my morale was a lot higher than it was when I left my village.

The second part of the political indoctrination was even more important. That was the part about class struggle. Here the emphasis was on going through the whole story of the wretchedness and suffering that you, your grandparents, parents, wife, and children had gone through. One soldier told about how his grandfather was tied up and beaten to death by landlords because he couldn't pay the rent on his land. His mother was raped and he had to work as a servant. But thanks to the revolution he was now a soldier who had the opportunity to liberate the South from the domination of the American imperialists and from feudalism so that all class discrimination could be eliminated. Another guy cut his finger and used the blood to write an application to volunteer for the South. Even with my strong family feelings, I was still affected by the boiling sentiment of the meeting. I felt really encouraged. Most of the people in my unit were tremendously enthusiastic during the entire training period.

HOANG THIEN LOC

SINGER

The interview was in a Thai refugee camp. He had not left because of any disillusionment with the system, but because the purge of ethnic Chinese in 1978 had left him without a family and desperate.

HOANG THIEN LOC: *A Chinese in the North*

MY PARENTS' PARENTS CAME FROM CHINA TO VIETNAM. MY PARENTS were born in Vietnam. So although ethnically they were Chinese, they spoke Vietnamese without any accent.

I grew up and went to school in Thai Binh. My father was a traditional doctor. His skill was to cure people with herbs, leaves, and natural methods instead of with modern drugs and injections. I grew up like every other Vietnamese kid. There were never any feelings of prejudice between ethnic Chinese and pure Vietnamese. And there were no government policies of discrimination.

The Americans first bombed North Vietnam in August of 1964 when I was in seventh grade. But the first raid in Thai Binh came a couple of years later. The Bo Bridge was hit, right in the middle of the city—after that they changed the name to Doc Lap [Independence] Bridge.

When the raids started in Thai Binh, people began moving outside the city, including the schoolchildren. My family had to move to the east of the city. But my school moved to the western outskirts, so I had to stay in the cottage of one of the villagers there. Many of the students had to do that. We brought all our own rice and other food with us, and we had to pay something to the houseowner in addition.

Three other students lived with me in the house. We slept two to a bed in the single room. The peasant who owned the house worked very hard on the collective farm he was part of. His was one of about fifty families who lived in the hamlet and made up the commune. But even though they worked so hard, they still loved the students who were staying with them. It's the tradition among Vietnamese to give respect to literate and educated people.

During the week we stayed in the hamlet, but on the weekends all the students would go back home to visit their families. At that time my parents were living about twenty kilometers [twelve miles] away. Every weekend I went there by bicycle, with my friend sitting on the back. At home there was time to relax and enjoy the family atmosphere together with my brothers and sisters. Then on Sunday evening I'd ride back again with my supplies for the week.

We built the school ourselves. All the teachers and students built it. It was really nothing more than a big cottage made out of bamboo, with walls that you could see through easily. But it was fine for hot weather. At least there was plenty of fresh air.

We had six classes going to the school—four ninth-grade classes and two tenth-grade. We followed the same program of studies that we had followed in the city. Since there were about fifty students in each class, the school had to be divided into two shifts. One shift went from seven to eleven in the morning; the other from twelve to four in the afternoon. I was on the morning shift. I'd get up at five or five-thirty, look over my lessons for the day, then go to school with my friends. Almost always we'd leave without having breakfast. Then, when we got back we'd all help prepare lunch, usually rice with *nuoc mam* [fermented fish sauce] and vegetables. Among the four of us, we ordinarily had enough money to cook meat maybe two times a week. None of us considered the diet a hardship. Everyone lived pretty much the same way, so there wasn't anything better to compare it to.

Our daily routine was almost always the same. After lunch we would take a nap, then we'd get up and do homework for a couple of hours. There was a lot of studying to do. But everyone knew that was the only way to a good future, so we did it. That was about the only thing we did do. After dinner we'd take a walk around the hamlet, talk with friends, or read, usually the Party newspaper or propaganda books published by the government. There wasn't much else available.

I can't say that we had much joy in our lives. We had boys and girls in the school, but no one had any special relationships—no boyfriends and girlfriends. In general things always seemed the same. There was no variation. Even the clothing was plain—the boys wore dark shirts and pants, the girls black pajamas. At night we'd use the oil lamps if we wanted to read. But the oil was expensive and the lamps had to be covered very carefully to keep the Americans from seeing lights from the air. Many of the houses never used lamps at all. It saved money, and they really didn't have anything to do at night anyway. In my house, we were in the habit of going to sleep by nine o'clock.

Life in the countryside was more boring than life in the city. It was also a lot harder. We had meat because we brought it from our homes. But some of the peasant families couldn't afford meat for months at a time. There was almost nothing to buy in the store except rice. Very little in the way of other foods or merchandise. Even private pig or chicken raising was closely controlled. The peasants would have to sell any animals they raised to the government at the official price, so there wasn't much incentive. They even had to gather the pigshit and submit it to the commune for use on the ricefields. There was an official equivalent of pigshit to rice—the peasants would be given a certain amount of rice in return for the shit they had gathered. But the control system didn't work all the time. Families that raised chickens almost always would kill one for dinner when they had any big celebration, like a death anniversary or a marriage, or any other important event.

The only thing that broke the routine of life were the air raids. There were never any on the hamlet itself, but there were a lot in the vicinity. Every time the American planes came, the P.A. system would alert the people. It would announce, "Now the planes are a hundred kilometers [sixty-two miles] from us. . . . Now the planes are fifty kilometers [thirty-one miles] from us." When the alarm went off we'd run to the bunker next to the school. We'd wait there for the all-clear signal: "The alert is ended. All activities resume as usual."

One raid hit Dai Lai village, which was only a few kilometers away. We could see the explosions and the fires. It was a terrifying sight. Right after the raid the whole school was ordered to go to Dai Lai to help. When we got there it was so awful that we were in a state of shock. The village had been hit by napalm. More than half of it was burned. Hundreds of people were dead and many others were burned terribly but still alive. Some children were burned over half of their bodies and were screaming and crying for their mothers. I saw one small child's body in a bunker that was still glowing. The body looked like a blackened pig. I was so scared I couldn't move.

The tragedy in Dai Lai was the worst thing I had ever seen. I knew that sometimes soldiers used to stay in Dai Lai. But there were none there the day the Americans came. Many of the village children became orphans—a large group of them had been taken on a trip to another village that day. While they were gone their parents and relatives died in the raid. There was no protection. Antiaircraft in the Thai Binh area was almost nothing. The antiaircraft guns were concentrated around the big cities like Hanoi and Haiphong, not in small places like Thai Binh. The Tan De ferry was even too small to carry heavy weapons into the city.

Not long after the Dai Lai attack my school burned down. Nobody knew how it happened; it wasn't an air raid or anything. Some people said it was burned by the Biet Kich [ARVN special forces], but others said that angry people in the area had done it. There were Catholics in the Thai Binh region who everybody said were anti-Communist. So the rumor went around that they had burned the school. I didn't know who did it, but when it happened we had to build another school. We had to buy the bamboo in another village and bring it to the school by bike. Then we built it again, the same as we had the first time.

When Dai Lai was bombed I was in my last year of school. In earlier years there had been a lot of enthusiasm about the war. You could feel the pride and self-confidence people had about helping the South. But by 1968 many people were depressed and tired. Very few of my friends wanted to go into the army. That was especially true after Tet Mau Thanh [the 1968 Tet Offensive]. At the beginning of the offensive we heard all about victory after victory. But after a couple of weeks we didn't hear any more news. The Saigon regime was still there and the U.S. planes were still bombing. It was obvious the radio wasn't telling the truth. That was the time when suspicions about the government began to rise.

We also got news through Saigon radio, which reported how many *bo dois* were being killed. Hanoi radio never talked about that, only about how many enemies were wiped out. But word about our casualties spread from people who listened to the enemy radio, so people didn't completely believe the statements that we were always winning.

But it was dangerous to listen to Saigon Radio or other foreign radio stations like the BBC or VOA. It was a crime to listen to "enemy radio." If you were caught it meant jail. We still listened to it, but very carefully. For the students, if you got in trouble with the police you'd have to leave school. And that would mean going into the army. Almost everyone I knew was studying as hard as they could so they could keep their grades up and stay out of the war.

For myself, I wasn't concerned about the army. Ethnic Chinese were not forced to serve, so the only ones who went were volunteers. Even the ones who volunteered had to have their parents sign a paper giving their approval. So I wasn't worried about the army.

My own dream was to be a singer. From the time I was five or six years old I loved to sing. I sang in all my class performances and I sang whenever my teachers or my friends' parents asked me to. I also entered into all the school and province competitions and I always won some kind of prize or award. Singing was the only thing I really wanted to do with my life.

When I graduated from high school I passed the examination and was accepted into the college of pedagogy to be trained as a teacher. But at the same time I received notification to report for a military physical. After the physical I was classified "A," which meant that I would be drafted. I didn't believe it, because my nationality was Han—Chinese— so I was supposed to be exempt from the army.

My mother got so angry about this that she went to the Thai Binh military committee to complain. They told her that there must have been some mistake. But they still didn't give her the papers that would have allowed me to go to college. My family was sure they were trying to purposely keep me out of higher education. But personally I didn't care much about that. I wasn't interested in going to college and becoming a teacher anyway. I knew that the people in Thai Binh's cultural organizations knew who I was because I had won so many singing prizes. And people from the Thai Binh Orchestra, the Nam Dinh Orchestra, and the Third Military Zone Orchestra had already talked to me about joining them.

But no one was able to get permission from the military committee to let me join. They said that since I was draft age, by law I wasn't allowed to join any of the performance groups. But at the same time, they didn't force me to go into the army. I am sure their objective was to keep up the impression that ethnic Chinese were exempt, but to force me to volunteer for the army by cutting off all my other future possibilities. The propaganda would have been that the government never forced ethnic Chinese to join the army, but they volunteered anyway.

I was completely depressed about losing what I thought was my golden opportunity to become a professional singer. But I was definitely not going to go into the army. None of my family wanted me to go either. I didn't have any idea what to do with myself. My future seemed dead. Finally a friend of mine taught me how to repair watches. After I learned how to do that, I opened a small watch repair shop on wheels and fixed watches on the street. At least I could earn enough money to live on that way. Watches cost a fortune, and most people either had very old ones that were made in France or very bad ones that were made in China. So there was plenty of business for a watch repairman.

I did that from 1970 to 1972. In 1972 I got a job as a turner in a lathe factory. My life during that whole period was ordinary and depressing. I lived with my parents and brothers and sisters. I was twenty-one and I didn't see any future for myself at all.

All that changed in 1974. That year the head of the Thai Binh Orchestra and Dance Band (*Doan Ca Mua Thai Binh*) asked me if I was still interested in being a singer. He said that if I was he thought he could arrange it with the military committee. I couldn't believe it. In my heart I had long ago given up the hopes I had. But Mr. Thai, the orchestra head, was able to intervene with them. He said that he told them a singer's job is to keep up the spirit of the people and even of the army, and that is even more important than a soldier's job. Maybe that convinced them, or maybe they just didn't need soldiers so much anymore by that time.

Whatever the reason, at the end of 1974 I was sent to Hanoi to study solo performance. I was still there in April 1975 when the South was liberated. Afterwards all the performers wanted to go South. Everybody was anxious to see what it was really like. All of our political performances and songs were about how the Southerners had suffered under the yoke of *My-Nguy* [American-Puppets]. We were singing songs for the peasants about how "each kilo of rice goes from North to South." There was another one for factory workers about "Each meter of textile for our Southern brothers."

The image of the Southerner that was engraved on my own mind while I was singing was of an anguished but determined woman in black pajamas with a black-and-white checkered towel on her shoulder. It was an image from a picture posted everywhere during the war that emphasized how poor and unhappy the Southerners were. On the other hand, after liberation a lot of rumors began to spread about the capitalist life and the kind of luxury goods they had in the South. Some of it sounded unbelievable—air-conditioning machines, hot water from pipes inside houses, very tall buildings. When the Thai Binh Orchestra was told to prepare a program of performances for the South, I was very happy. I couldn't wait to go.

LE THANH

MECHANICAL ENGINEER

I saw him twice, the second time a year after the first. The change was dramatic. The first time he, his wife, and young son were sharing a two-bedroom apartment with his wife's sister and her family. He spoke very little English. Times were hard.

A year later he could converse easily. His in-laws had moved to their own place and his work was going well: more money and more responsibility at the factory where he maintains heavy machinery. A skilled mechanic, he also takes care of the small apartment complex where he lives. He seems to embody the positive picture of Vietnamese immigration depicted by various State Department studies: hardworking, energetic people supporting themselves while adjusting to new lives in the United States.

He had planned his escape meticulously, telling no one except the few friends who were essential to getting the boat and supplies. Not even his father knew; he was afraid an emotional reaction might suggest to the block committee or work committee that something was wrong in the family. For the same reason, he didn't tell his wife until everything was set.

In a remote stretch of Haiphong harbor, the thirty-foot sailing junk with twenty-two refugees aboard was becalmed for several hours shortly after its midnight departure. Just before the wind came up again the boat was spotted by a sentry on a little island outpost. Bullets crashed into the boat and broke the main mast. Crouching behind the gunnels shielding their children, some of the women were screaming curses at Thanh for getting them killed.

As we talked in the apartment, friends of his dropped by to visit. They had been on the boat, and the wife had done more than her share of the cursing. Recalling the scene, they all had a good laugh. After their escape from the harbor, it had taken two months to get to Hong Kong.

LE THANH: *Coming of Age in the North*

MY FATHER WAS A FACTORY WORKER, AN ORDINARY PERSON. HE hadn't the slightest interest in politics. During the French war he didn't take anyone's side. It was all he could do to support us, even with my mother's salary from the warehouse where she worked.

I was one of six children. The house we grew up in was one large room, maybe sixteen or seventeen yards square—kitchen, living room, dining room, bedroom all in one. For light we had oil lamps, for water there was the tap at the end of the street, the same tap everyone else on the street used.

In my house we all woke up around five-thirty. My mother would cook breakfast and lunch—breakfast for everyone, lunch for her and Father to take along to work. In fact, breakfast and lunch were both the same: rice with *nuoc mam* [fermented fish sauce]. For dinner we ate steamed vegetables, either from the little garden we planted around the house or from the market. To go with the vegetables we had cooking oil that we got from the government storehouse. The oil came from our Chinese and Russian brothers.

We could afford to buy real fish once or twice a month. Meat or chicken cost more, so we didn't have them so often. I remember the smell of meat from my childhood, but not the taste of it. There would be so little to go around that we didn't get much more than the smell. The exceptions would come at Tet [the New Year] and at the yearly mourning celebrations for our grandparents. You know, in Vietnam we celebrate death anniversaries instead of birthdays. At my house the celebrations would center on a whole cooked chicken.

People who lived in the countryside could add to their diets by fishing or raising chickens and ducks at home. But for the city people there was only the government food ration. When I was six we moved from the province of Thai Binh to Haiphong, the port city about fifty miles from

Hanoi. We lived on the ration. It was the same for everybody. Our family was neither better nor worse off than other worker families. At the level we lived on, food was a preoccupation. At dinner there was time to sit around and chat, a relaxed time when we could share our feelings of being a family. We could also share our dreams, and these were mainly of food—meat, chicken, fish. Our talk was about these things and other things we would like to have, so that life could be more comfortable, easier. Thoughts about individual freedom, rights, that kind of thing never entered into it. How could they?

In the mornings I went to school. My shift was in the morning; in the afternoons another shift of students would use the school. At noon I'd go home to take care of my younger brothers and sisters and have lunch with them. In the evenings my father came home before my mother—he had a bicycle and it took him only about twenty minutes to get back from the factory. As soon as he got home he'd leave to do the shopping. Rice, vegetables, and wood for the stove were the most important things, also the most expensive. The shopping would take forever because of the lines. Lots of people queuing up and only a few clerks in the stores.

After dinner I'd help my parents do the housework, cleaning, washing dishes, laundry. It was also my job to fetch the water from the tap in the street. I'd wait in line trying to be patient, waiting for my turn. When I finally got to the head of the line I'd fill up four ten-gallon containers, then I'd carry them home on my shoulder pole. This water was for everything from drinking to taking baths. Hot water was a luxury since we didn't want to waste precious wood to heat it up. But if someone was sick, we would heat up the water for them. Also my mother and sisters liked to take baths at home, standing in a tub and ladling bowls of warm water over themselves. The boys and men usually went down to the river to wash.

Sunday was the day off. But it was a day off without private time, filled with meeting after meeting. National holidays that fell on Sunday were called Socialist Sundays. These holidays—Ho Chi Minh's birthday, for example (we did celebrate *his* birthday)—were days of hard work. Young children would have to go out to pick up trash and clean the streets. Older children would be put to work digging canals or doing other manual labor. Workers would compete against workers, factory would compete against factory, city against city—everyone would try to surpass last year's production record.

Over the next days the newspaper would report the highest achievements. The workers, factories, and cities that won would be awarded a flower or a flag from Chairman Ho and a certificate that they were national heroes. There were different kinds of heroes: hero of the army, hero of the people, hero of work, hero of production. But there were never any material incentives, no rewards of money or food. It was explained that material rewards were the mark of a spiritually inferior society—capitalist society, where the aim is to exploit the workers and appeal to people's lowest instincts.

People would ordinarily work double time and more on Socialist Sundays. Everyone volunteered for these competitions. There wasn't really any choice. You didn't get paid, but if you didn't volunteer you would have problems—problems with your job and problems with your food rations, things that nobody was going to take any chances with. In public nobody said anything negative, but at home my parents would complain about it once in a while. They resented not being able to spend their holiday peacefully with the family. But even at home there wasn't any real anger. Mostly people were resigned to it.

My parents' one dream was to see their children graduate from the university. They weren't Communist Party members and neither of them had been revolutionary fighters, so education was the one way the family could raise itself up. From the time I got to high school I was fixed on the idea. I studied as hard as I could, always with that goal in front of me. Natural sciences were my favorite subjects. But like everybody, I spent more of my time in school on national history than on anything else.

Our curriculum revolved around the story of Vietnam's two thousand years of struggle against all kinds of foreigners. We studied case by case and story by story the lives of all of Vietnam's national heroes—Tran Quoc Tuan; Tran Hung Dao, who chased out the Mongols in the thirteenth century; and especially Emperor Quang Trung, who surprised and defeated the Chinese at Tet in 1789, unifying the country after a hundred years of division.

Other subjects may have been interesting or they may not have, but everybody learned these stories with tremendous pride and enthusiasm. As we grew up they built in us a great patriotic feeling. Our national heroes had loved freedom and were ready to sacrifice everything for it. That feeling got instilled into us, into our bones, that we had to be worthy of our history. We were the sons and daughters of a heroic people, and we should live lives as heroic as those of our ancestors.

We learned more recent history too, mainly about the struggle against the French colonialists. We were taught how brutal the French had been, how they had enslaved Vietnam. We looked at pictures of what the French had done—rows of Vietnamese shackled in stocks, heads of murdered Vietnamese patriots displayed by French soldiers. We read biographies and memoirs of militants who had died under French torture or had spent years in jail. We also learned that our great victory over the French had put an end to French colonialism in the entire world, and that people all over the world paid respect to us because of that.

These lessons were linked to others about the Communist Party that had led Vietnam to victory. The stories of Party leaders who had given their lives or had been imprisoned for so long impressed all of us. Of course we were most impressed by the life story of Ho Chi Minh, the great father of Vietnam who had been fighting for independence since his youth. Looking back, I can tell you that the whole thing was effectively done. Vietnam's national history and the history of the Vietnamese Communist Party were portrayed together, in parallel. While we were drinking in the history of the nation and learning to love our country, we were also learning to identify the nation and the Party. A high school graduate might not know much about mathematics or science, but he certainly knew about the country and he knew about the Party. There wasn't a single schoolboy who didn't have total confidence in the Party's leadership and credibility. We all dreamed about one day becoming a Communist.

At the same time we were also taught about Ngo Dinh Diem, who had taken over in the South. Unlike the Communist leaders he hadn't done anything at all for the country. He hadn't been in jail; he hadn't sacrificed a thing. Instead he had lived a long time in France and had been trained by the Americans. He worked for the Americans, who didn't want Vietnam to be unified. It was their orders he was obeying when he had refused to hold elections in 1956. Worse than that, he oppressed the people of the South who wanted to unify the country as the Geneva Agreement had said.

We understood that the Americans were behind Diem and that they were exactly like the French. And we knew how cruel the French had been. In my mind I associated the Americans with the French. Both of them were imperialists. The United States was the leader of the capitalist countries. They were the enemies of all poor people. They were rich because they stole labor from the people they had enslaved. And even in their own country only a few people at the top were rich while the majority went hungry.

We saw from films the great gap between the people in the North and the South. We saw the students who were beaten in the streets of Saigon and dragged off to jail by the police. We saw the poor people of Saigon begging for food and the peasants living wretched lives. The same films showed the Americans and Southern military officers with their luxurious cars and houses.

The most powerful of all these films was shown in about 1960, a film about the Phu Loi prison where the Saigon police kept suspected Communists. This was an inhuman place where prisoners were brutally tortured. Many of them looked like walking skeletons. This film was shown all over North Vietnam, in schools, factories, and offices. Along with it they showed a documentary about Hitler's concentration camps. The people in Phu Loi looked the same as the ones in the Hitler camps. The difference was that in Phu Loi Vietnamese were torturing and killing their own brothers.

Like everybody I knew, I was enraged about the Southern regime and the Americans. I hated them. Many of us felt ashamed that our brothers were suffering in the South while we weren't doing anything but going to school. Some people even started complaining that the Party was too weak, because it wasn't taking any revenge for what was happening. I was at a pitch of anger. I wanted to do anything I could to save the people in the South. We had to destroy the Americans now just as our ancestors had to destroy other foreigners.

We saw other films, too, about Russia and China. These films showed the comparison between presocialist life in those countries and life now. We could see with our own eyes the huge progress that had been made. We also knew that the Russian and Chinese people had given us great amounts of aid in the war against the French, for free, without any conditions, as part of the "international obligation" of the socialist camp. We took pride in the accomplishments of the Russians and the Chinese, which far surpassed those of the French and the Americans.

When I was twelve I took my first step toward becoming a Communist. I joined the Youth Red Scarf League [*Khan Quang Do*]. It was an honor to be accepted as a member. For every school assembly or festival I would proudly put my red scarf on. Our main activity was learning and performing traditional dances, popular songs, songs about the great national heroes, songs about the atrocities of the different foreign invaders and about our own devotion to the country and the Party. I remember one of the favorites went "No one loves the red scarf as much as the youth / The red scarf reminds us of our Uncle Ho's teachings!" When we weren't practicing or performing we were playing soccer or volleyball. After I joined the Youth League I had almost no free time. My whole day outside school was taken up by the league.

As I got older I moved up from the Youth League to the Vanguard

Youth, and from there to the Young Communists League. So by the time I was sixteen I was well along on the three preliminary steps to becoming a full-fledged Communist. I was following the path that would take me to the university and that would give me a good future. I was enthusiastic about it too. I volunteered for everything. All these activities appealed to the idealistic nature of a young man. They gave me a chance to do something for the country and the people.

I think that almost all of us in the youth organizations felt pretty much the same way. We had no private lives to speak of. Although we were teenagers, we didn't have any girlfriends. I told myself that I should live as a real Communist lives, the pure life of a revolutionary. We tried not to even think about girls. We would feel guilty if we caught ourselves singing some romantic song. At that time the Party had a slogan called "Ba Khoan"—"The Three Delays": "If you don't have a child, delay having one. If you aren't married, delay getting married. If you aren't in love, delay love." So we delayed love. Instead we built up our feelings about the mountains and the rivers and the flowers in the places we lived. We loved these things and we felt strongly that we were ready to die for them.

When I was finally accepted into the university, it was a great honor for my parents and my family. For my parents, their dream was being realized. I basked in that feeling. For myself, I didn't have any great ambitions at that point either for a career or a family. But I had grown up poor. All my life I saw my parents struggling to make a living. Their lives and everybody else's lives I saw were a constant round of drudgery. Everything was done by hand, drudge work. After I started in the university I got the idea that I could become a mechanical engineer. I began to formulate the idea for myself that I could become a national hero too. Not a hero of fighting, but a hero of invention. I could develop new ways of doing things that would help take the burden of work off people.

At the university I also got more involved than ever in Communist youth work. I began to study Marxism-Leninism intensively. I distributed leaflets and talked passionately in meetings and assemblies about Party policies and about the brutality of our enemies in the South. Since I was a good speaker I was chosen to give speeches to high school students about the war. Before the speech they'd give me material about atrocities the Saigon regime had perpetrated. I had documents about Diem's life and about how the Americans had set him up as president against the aspirations of the people. I'd talk about the infamous 10/59 law that put former Vietminh outside any legal protection. While I talked about Diem's campaign to kill Communists, I'd show pictures of families that had been murdered by his police.

I don't know how articulate I was, but my sincerity influenced people. I believed completely the things that I was saying. If I was speaking about the victims of America-Diem, I was as angry as if I myself were one of those victims. My talks drew loud applause from the audiences. They'd assemble all the students in a high school outside in the school courtyard and I'd talk to them there. I'd really get them motivated. Party and Youth League leaders praised me for being so active. I thought that now I'm becoming a real Communist, I'm becoming worthy. I followed the slogan *"Dau Can Thanh Nien Co Dau Kho Co Thanh Nien"*—"Where the need is, there the youth are. Where the difficulties are, there are the youth."

In 1965 when the Americans came, life began to get much harder. At the clinics and hospitals the supply of medicines dried up. Before then treatment was available if you got sick. Afterwards, especially in the village and district clinics, they relied on leaves, herbs, roots, garlic—all the traditional medicines. It was pretty much a case of recovering naturally or dying of whatever you had. During the bombings everyone suffered. Hatred for the Saigon side and the Americans grew even stronger than it had been before. A lot of young people volunteered for the army at that time.

But there was also a lot of anxiety. Everybody was excited by news about our great victories in the South and about the opposition movements that were fighting against the inhuman regime in Saigon. But there was no news from my friends who had gone South—nobody was hearing anything. A lot of my high school friends had gone into the army after they graduated—all of them who didn't have good enough grades to get into college. After they were sent South nobody could communicate with them—you couldn't write or receive letters. Not even their parents could. So there was a lot of confusion about what was really going on and a lot of tension. When people would complain or ask questions they were criticized or arrested by the security police. It was easy to be accused of harboring "reactionary" or "defeatist" thoughts.

Not long after the bombing began all the schools had to move to the countryside. Everybody went, teachers, students—they even dismantled the laboratories and set them up in the villages. We were able to keep studying, but we also had to work. We helped build bunkers and repair bomb damage. We helped organize air raid procedures. We also worked in the ricefields, taking the place of young peasants who had gone into the army. All the students had deferments the whole time I was at the university, up until 1967—I graduated in 1966. But we were part of the war effort anyway.

Nobody could get away from the war. It didn't matter if you were in the countryside or the city. While I was living in the country I saw terrible things. After a bombing raid the students would be sent out to help take care of the people and start cleaning up and rebuilding. I saw children who had been killed, pagodas and churches that had been destroyed, monks and priests dead in the ruins, schoolboys who were killed when schools were bombed. When I saw these horrors my only feeling was that I wanted to kill Americans.

Many of my friends joined the army after the university. But by that time I had begun to see things a little bit differently. One thing was that I had begun to think about why antiaircraft guns had been set up near many of the places that were bombed, right next to the schools and the pagodas. The official explanation was that they had to protect these places. But it didn't take too long to realize that the U.S. planes were dropping bombs where they saw the guns firing.

I began to ask questions about that at the Party meetings and to talk with my friends about it. I also asked questions about why nobody was coming back from the South. It began to seem like an open pit. The more young people who were lost there, the more they sent. There was even a kind of motto that the whole generation of army-age North Vietnamese adopted—they tattooed it on themselves and they sang songs about it— "Born in the North to die in the South."

When new soldiers were taken into the army, their families would be oriented about it. They'd be told that the soldiers were sacrificing themselves for the country and that they should be proud of it. They were also told that the battlefield was uncontrollable. Nobody could say how long the war would take or how long it would be before the soldiers came home.

When soldiers died, most often word would get back to their families through friends who had returned because they had been wounded. Usually there was no official notification. Sometimes families would go to the government to ask for information. But it was a terrible situation for them, because anyone who spread word about soldiers dying would get into trouble with the police.

But even so, when messages got back that relatives had been killed families would often gather for quiet, private funerals. Usually the police would just close their eyes to such things. If the deaths were officially reported, then there would be a large collective ceremony.

But the deaths weren't the most demoralizing part of the war. The wounded were, the ones who came back without arms or legs. If people saw how many of them there were and what they looked like it would have been terrible for morale. People would begin to hate the war. So when the badly wounded veterans came back they were kept in isolated camps for a long time before they were allowed back to their families. But information would always get out—messages would be smuggled one way or another. Often parents would do anything they could to try to find their children. It was as if the nation were in mourning, searching for its children.

One story about the wounded was told all over Hanoi—everybody knew it and everybody was sure it was true. I think there's no doubt it was at least based on truth. But the important thing of it was that it expressed the people's sorrow over the tragedy of the war. It was about a soldier who had gotten married and then was wounded in the South. When they brought him back, they put him in an isolated area. But his wife got word he was back and she finally found out where he was. It turned out to be a hospital for the severely wounded where relatives were absolutely not allowed, but the wife found a way to smuggle herself in. When she found her husband he had no arms or legs. She was so shocked, she couldn't look at him and ran off.

The husband felt utterly abandoned and desperate. Somehow he managed to drag himself to a ditch next to the hospital that was full of rainwater, and he drowned himself in it. According to the story, the wife was brought before the court and sentenced to seven years in prison for killing her husband. That story epitomized the horror that the soldiers and their families were experiencing. It was the kind of feeling they could never express openly. But that didn't mean it wasn't there. It came out in stories like this that circulated all over. People believed them because they accorded with the kinds of things they knew were true.

As far as I was concerned, I wasn't in favor of fighting to the last man. A lot of others weren't either. Why didn't we stop the fighting so that we could concentrate on building the country? I knew that something was wrong and that we weren't being told the truth about the war. But the more questions I asked, the fewer answers I got.

Because I was questioning things, eventually I was classified as a "halfway element." That meant I was better than a reactionary or rightist but I was no longer considered a good citizen. Because of this classification, I wasn't taken into the army after I graduated. Instead I was assigned a job at one of the largest factories in Haiphong. I was twenty-one. Most of my friends from high school were already dead.

For the young men who were still alive there wasn't any future. Many parents tried to keep their sons out of the army. They would hide them when they were called up by the recruiting center. Anyone who didn't show up automatically had his rice ration cut off. But families would buy food on the black market or just get along by sharing whatever they had. They would survive that way while they tried to scrape up enough to bribe a recruiting official to fix up the files. Other draftees mutilated themselves or managed to find other ways to fail the physical. People with money were able to pay doctors to disqualify their children.

These kinds of things were easier to do in the three big cities—Hanoi, Haiphong, and Nam Dinh, especially in Hanoi and Haiphong, where the government officials and Party leaders lived. Many of them were looking for ways to keep their children out too, so the recruiting wasn't done so strictly. And people had more money in these places, so corruption was more a normal thing. Also, it was simply easier to hide in the cities and there was more information about how to stay out. The result was that the big majority of the Northern army was made up of young people from the countryside. They were just more naive. They believed the propaganda more easily. They didn't have the same chances to get out of it.

In my family none of the four brothers went. My youngest brother dropped iodine in his eyes before he went to take the army physical. We bribed the examining doctor to fail another. The third one tried to hide from the draft, but he was caught and put in jail. My parents did everything they could to help us stay out. My older sister had married a disabled veteran when he got out of camp. After hearing what he had to say, my mother told us, "Stay at home. We'll share the food with each other. God will decide. Whatever happens you can stay alive at home. Going South means going to die."

NGUYEN NGOC OANH (LE THANH'S WIFE): *Seamstress*

I GREW UP IN HAIPHONG, IN THE CITY. MY FATHER MANAGED A tailor shop. Before the revolution he had been a famous tailor. When the revolution came they took his shop away. He was still a tailor, but afterwards he managed the shop he used to own. He started teaching me how to sew when I was eight.

My father didn't like the Communists. Under the French he had been allowed to practice his trade freely, but under the Communists there were controls that he didn't like. But he really wasn't a political man in any way. We weren't a political family.

I started school in 1956 when I was seven years old. I don't remember there being much political indoctrination in the early sixties. But in 1964 and 1965 they began teaching more politics. That was especially true in 1965, when all the schools had to move out of the city because of the bombing.

It wasn't just the schools. A lot of the factories and shops moved too. My whole family went to live in Thuy Nguyen, on the outskirts of Haiphong—my parents, my four brothers, and I. The family we moved in with had three children of their own. We all slept in one big room. The adults put curtains around their beds for privacy. It was very much like one family.

Of course there were problems—little conflicts people had with each other, petty insults, that kind of thing. The biggest problem was that as city people we were used to a more generous, open style of living. The people in the country were very poor. You could feel that they were a lot more careful about things, more narrow and restricted. But all in all the problems were minor, not nearly what you might expect given how crowded we were. Our family had been ordered to move to the outskirts and the people in Thuy Nguyen were under an obligation to provide for us. So everyone made the best of it.

I went to school during the day. After I came home I'd work with my father in the shop. Regardless of what my father thought, I looked forward to becoming a Party member. I was accepted by the Youth Union, which was very competitive—a real challenge. That was the only road to a bright future. But I was enthusiastic for only a couple of years in school. As I grew up I became less interested. I began to get tired of the meetings and singalongs. After a while they didn't seem interesting or productive.

Like most schoolchildren I wanted to go to the university so that I could have a good profession. But I belonged to a petit bourgeois family, so I knew I didn't have a chance. Instead I stayed home to help my father and learn to become a seamstress. I didn't think about marriage until rather late. The first thing was to have a job, some kind of profession. Then you could think about a family.

In those years we didn't talk about boys. It just wasn't a subject you talked about, or even thought about. No parents taught their daughters anything about boys or anything about sex. My mother was like everyone else's mother. She just said, "Take care of yourself!" In her view all boys were bad. There was no way to learn about sex either from your mother or from school. The closest we got to it was in the biology lessons when we read about animal reproduction. After that we could draw some conclusions for ourselves. But not many of them.

As far as the war went, I didn't have any strong feelings about it one way or the other. When I met Thanh I had no concern whatsoever about his political views. My parents were always reminding me to look for a good boy. That meant one who came from a good family and had a bright future. My parents liked Thanh and so did I.

When we left Vietnam it was completely his idea. He didn't even tell me until three days before we left. When I heard the news I was really scared. I had a little baby. And I was unhappy about leaving my parents. But my husband said, "I'm going. You'd better come with me—or else we'll have to break apart from each other." So I had no choice.

Le Thanh didn't go South. Others did. Even for the most enthusiastic, the Ho Chi Minh Trail was a dreadful experience. For many, the worst part was meeting the wounded who were going the other way. Some were so frightened they deserted. These poor souls led a limbo existence in the Laotian jungles, hovering around the way stations and medical posts, hunting and stealing to keep themselves alive. But most continued on, toward the South.

TRAN XUAN NIEM, *Second Lieutenant, NVA, from Hanoi: Try to Keep Your Faces Intact*

I GREW UP LONESOME. IN MY FAMILY THERE WAS ONLY MY MOTHER, my sister, and me. My father had been killed by the French before I was born. My mother never remarried, but she devoted herself to caring for my sister and me. Despite the loneliness we loved each other very much.

Because of my father I grew up with a burning resentment against foreign invaders. These feelings were reinforced by the school instruction and political teaching we got. I had complete faith in the Party and in Uncle Ho. I devoted myself to my studies so that when I became an adult I could join the revolution and answer the call of the nation. I wanted to help bring peace and happiness to the people. (My mother's favorite saying was, "Study hard and be polite.")

After I joined the army and went through basic training I was sent South down the Ho Chi Minh Trail. At places along the sides of the trail were the hulks of military vehicles and graves, graves of NVA soldiers. They were arranged neatly and had the names and dates of death inscribed on them. There were graves all over in some areas. Inside, I was sure that everyone was frightened. But nobody said a word about it.

On the section of the trail going toward Kontum every day we saw groups of wounded soldiers coming home. When we exchanged a few words they told us, "You'll see all kinds of pleasures in the South." The ones who were marching had mutilated arms. Those who had lost their legs were carried [by trucks] under camouflage. Some of them had been burned by napalm. Others were deformed or blind. We used to say to each other, "On arrival in the South try to keep your faces intact."

NGUYEN TRONG NGHI, *Platoon Political Cadre, NVA: Our Future Selves*

ON OUR WAY TO THE SOUTH WE OFTEN MET GROUPS OF WOUNDED who were going North. Some had lost their arms or legs, some had been burned by napalm. Some had malaria. They all looked like skeletons. Every day we would meet them walking or riding in the opposite direction, groups of two or six or ten of them. We told each other that some day we would be like that. We began to feel the war.

Sometimes the men asked the lower-ranking cadres questions. The answer was that war always brings death and that we shouldn't bother ourselves with morbid thoughts. No one argued with the cadres. But everyone was frightened, especially when we met those men for the first time. It was horrifying. It was like looking at our future selves.

PART TWO
STRUGGLE

THOUGH THE WAR FOR THE SOUTH WAS DORMANT FOR SEVERAL years after 1954, it never really slept. Violence accompanied Ngo Dinh Diem's assumption of power. At the beginning, he could barely call downtown Saigon his own. To exercise leadership, he first had to assert his right to it.

He did so with striking speed. First Diem crushed the forces of Saigon's Binh Xuyen crime syndicate, then he took on the sect armies of the Cao Dai and Hoa Hao. Emerging from these confrontations with enhanced credibility and strength, he turned his attention to the Vietminh infrastructure that had stayed behind, launching "Denounce Communists" and "Kill Communists" campaigns that struck innocent non-Party veterans along with underground Communist operatives.

Born into a Catholic family (his older brother was bishop of Vinh Long, later archbishop of Hue), Diem found his chief support in the Catholic community, particularly among the recent Catholic refugees from Ho Chi Minh's North Vietnam. Wooing them, he alienated others, most dangerously the majority Buddhists, who began to organize themselves politically in response to government threats and discrimination.

Although Diem paid lip service to the democratic urgings of his American advisers, his real instincts were for Vietnamese-style power politics—familial and feudalistic. As a result, even as he consolidated power, he was becoming increasingly unpopular and isolated. An organizer for the National Liberation Front in its early years reported that contacts among the religious sects, the legal political parties, and the Buddhists were all fruitful. "In each group we made overtures, and everywhere we discovered sympathy and backing."

In 1960, Diem was very nearly unseated by a paratrooper rebellion with ties to opposition political figures. By 1963 he had alienated everyone but his closest supporters. Army officers, peasants, politicians, students, newspapermen, and Buddhists were all giving voice to sharp and persistent grievances. So frustrated were American leaders by Diem's refusal to accommodate his various constituencies that they were ready to desert him for any successor who gave promise of stability.

The incident that triggered Diem's slide into oblivion was the self-immolation of an elderly Buddhist monk from Saigon's Xa Loi Pagoda. The summer of protests that followed prepared the way for the military coup that finally toppled the president and his family on November 1, 1963, bringing to a close the first phase of South Vietnam's existence as an independent country.

IN the wake of Geneva, North Vietnam had its own problems. As Diem had labored to consolidate power in the South, so Ho Chi Minh went about building a strong Communist regime in the North. But if Diem's challenge had been to assert his personal ascendancy, Ho's was to create an unshakable base of support for the Party. And to do this, he had to reform the society he now ruled.

Toward this end, in 1955 and 1956 the politburo carried through land and social reform campaigns, redistributing farm holdings and indoctrinating the population in the principles of class struggle. Executions of those classified as "rich landlords" may have amounted to forty thousand. The terror occasioned a peasant revolt in Nghe An Province (Ho's birthplace) and brought public apologies from Ho and Minister of Defense Vo Nguyen Giap, who told the Tenth Party Congress, "We have executed too many honest people."

The Southern Vietminh soldiers who had regrouped North were another problem for Hanoi. Most of these had left their homes expecting to be repatriated after two years. With their strong regional loyalties, many Southerners were uncomfortable living in the North, and when the unification election never materialized, frustrations ran deep.

It wasn't until 1959 that the Party felt strong enough to resume open warfare in the South. An infiltration route for troops and supplies was hacked out of the jungles covering the Truong Son mountain range and extended down through eastern Cambodia into the old resistance strongholds of South Vietnam's Tay Ninh Province. In the first years, 50 percent of those who attempted the journey died en route. Those who made it were often on the trail for five or six months.

But with reinforcement from the North, the guerrilla war in South

Vietnam intensified rapidly. In a vain attempt to pressure Ho's government into withdrawing its assistance, in 1964 the United States began bombing Northern targets. But the war only widened and grew more vicious. By 1965 Lyndon Johnson had decided that it could be won only with the help of American combat troops.

On March 9, 1965, the first marines waded ashore at Danang. Within three years, more than half a million American troops were "in country." At the beginning U.S. generals were optimistic. In several conventional battles North Vietnamese and main force Vietcong units were seriously bloodied. Then the war of attrition set in. Moving over to tactics that emphasized ambush and infiltration, revolutionary forces were able to inflict a growing number of casualties on their opponents. The sapper and mining specialists, the "special operations men," came into their own.

On January 31, 1968, the careful tactics of attrition dissolved before the fury of the Tet Offensive. Assaults on Saigon and every provincial capital in the South were coordinated with popular uprisings inside the cities, meant to topple local authority and meet the assault groups halfway. The long-planned-for "General Offensive and General Uprising" was at hand.

For the revolutionary forces it was a disaster. The popular uprisings never took place. After the initial shock, ARVN and American forces brought their firepower to bear on an enemy that finally was out in the open. Vietcong casualties ran to 50 percent, ushering in two years of running, hiding, and slowly rebuilding strength.

In the aftermath of Tet, North Vietnamese troops flooded South to fill out the decimated Liberation Army. From 1970 on the revolution was largely a Northern show. Northern troops manned the front lines and the Democratic Republic became a "giant rear area," providing manpower and resources. Its people suffered accordingly.

By that time, the United States was winding down its presence, "Vietnamizing" the war in response to growing domestic opposition. When American ground support was finally gone, the two Vietnamese sides squared off against each other. The 1972 Northern "Spring Offensive" was stopped by desperate ARVN resistance and massive American air power. But the Paris Peace Agreement that followed only set the stage for a last showdown, this time without any intervention from the United States.

The final campaign of a 10,000-day war kicked off in the winter of 1974–75. By March South Vietnam's army was crumbling. By April the war was essentially over. On April 30, tanks from the North's 203rd Armored Brigade rumbled onto the grounds of Saigon's Presidential Palace. The fighting was over, but for many the struggle to survive continued.

XUAN VU

THE WAR CORRESPONDENT AND PROPAGANDA CHIEF GOES NORTH

XUAN VU'S STORY: *In the North*

SO I WENT NORTH. MY REPUTATION AS A WAR WRITER HAD PRECEDED me, and the people in charge of transplanting Southerners wanted me to continue documenting the revolution. How could I best do this? That was the question. What subject would offer the scope and grandeur I was looking for? At this point, 1954, there was no more war, so martial glory was out. Building socialism was in. The great themes of personal sacrifice and reconstructing the nation could be displayed in peace as well as in war. And maybe best on the kolkhoz, the collective farm.

If Balzac was my guiding star, on this project Mikhail Sholokhov could be my patron saint. Sholokhov had written *the* great epic of rural Soviet life, *Virgin Soil Upturned*. Now socialist Vietnam was starting its own historic experiment in collectivization. How would people respond to the new values, to brotherhood and the common good? The drama of making barren land productive and the simultaneous drama of personal transformation among the farmers beckoned. Vietnam would have its own Sholokhov—and who better than me?

To pursue this vision I got myself sent to one of the new collective farms, around Vinh, south of Hanoi. My first impression of the place was depressing; it was poverty stricken, no different than the countryside around it. At first I was overwhelmed by how severe everything was, such a contrast to the lush farmland in the South. I lived in a crowded barracks, a thin plywood plank for my bed with a flimsy plywood writing table squeezed in next to it. The food was sparse, mainly rice. Just about enough of it to live on. Occasionally there'd be something to go with it, a little dried fish or meat, nothing else.

What was worse, I couldn't for the life of me see that any noble human motives were transcending all this grimness. I worked as the kolkhoz secretary and watched everything carefully, trying to gather material for my Sholokhovian opus. But instead of a heroic struggle, what I saw were mostly dispirited people doing careless work. They didn't seem to give a damn about what they were doing. The land itself was new, it hadn't been cultivated before and it took an unbelievable amount of work to clear it and get it ready. And nobody really wanted to do it. There were no tractors as there were in the *Virgin Soil Upturned* kolkhoz, but there were water buffalo—ten of them when I got there. By the time I left, they had all sickened and died. Nobody took proper care of them. If some peasant had owned them he would have treated them like the family jewels. There were petty squabbles going on constantly, and sometimes more serious fights. People didn't have any tolerance for each other. They always seemed edgy and defensive. There was a bad atmosphere in the place.

As I got to know the people, I found out that a lot of them felt they had gotten stuck. Many of the collective farmers were Southerners who had come North after Geneva, like me. Ho had invited everyone North with these great gestures of welcome. The Southern resistance fighters who went expected to be treated like heroes. Whatever they expected, a bunch of them had been shipped to this collective, and these guys were burning with resentment. They had fought for years against the French—now this was their reward? They couldn't believe it. They took out their bitterness on everyone around them—the kolkhoz officials, the other farmers, anyone who happened to be there.

Another group who thought and acted the same way were the former prisoners, people who had been held in French prisons during the war. They came from Con Son Island and other horrible dungeons, and some of them had spent many years in jail. Now they were mad as hell. They thought they had sacrificed enough. We had won, we had a new country. What they had gone through ought to be recognized. Instead, they had ended up here. Between them and the regrouped Southerners there were enough foul tempers to make every day miserable.

The third big group of people at the kolkhoz were the local peasants who had been exemplary workers on their own land. But in the kolkhoz they got lazy. They were pissed off the same as the others were, but they were lazy on top of it. They seemed to think that all the drudgery they had put in before had earned them a rest and that here was the place for them to take it.

What made matters even more depressing was that the nearest village was an empty ghost town. All of the people had left for the South, just as most of us in the kolkhoz had come North. We knew very well why we had come North—we had either been in the army or in jail. We were all revolutionaries. But why would a whole village just have picked itself up to go South?

As time went by I got more and more anxious about all this. There was nothing to write about, at least nothing I wanted to write about. Aside from the virgin soil part, I couldn't see any parallels at all with what Sholokhov had described. And I was stuck myself. My wanderlust hadn't exactly prepared me to get bogged down in a place like this. But there was no way to leave. In the end I stayed for a year—a year of wasted time.

I might have been there longer except for one of my friends who had come North with me. He was also a writer, but he had gotten a job with Radio Hanoi. I had written to him that I was having a hard time and that I didn't see any novels being written about the kolkhoz, at least not by me. He managed to persuade his bosses to give me a job at the radio station, too. So I finally got out. My friends on the kolkhoz were practically in tears, at least the ones from the South. All of them missed their families terribly and hated where they were and what they were doing. But they couldn't find any way out of it.

Anyway, in 1955 I went to Hanoi to work in the literature department at the Radio. Every night we would broadcast stories. I collected material for them, wrote quite a few myself, organized whatever background was necessary—I wrote and produced the show.

But I was becoming more and more homesick—for my country and for my family. And I didn't see myself developing the talent I thought I had either. I certainly wasn't putting down any roots in the North. The people in Hanoi seemed cold. They were agreeable enough at work, but they would never invite you to their homes or to whatever was going on. It was hard to develop relationships that were more than skin deep. There just wasn't the open friendliness that was part of the Southern style of life. As a result, the Southerners tended to stick together—Party members as well as non-Party people. We felt like foreigners, and the feeling didn't disappear with time.

Altogether, I wasn't happy with my decision to go North. It had been a mistake, not on political grounds, but on personal grounds. So I decided to leave. Marvelous innocence! I just got on my bicycle—it actually belonged to the radio station—and rode down to the International Control Commission headquarters [the three-nation group established to monitor the implementation of the Geneva Accords] so that I could get myself sent back. I was a little hazy on exactly what the procedure was, but I was pretty sure that all you had to do was ask.

Outside the ICC office a Vietnamese guard took down the license plate number of my bike and asked me what I wanted. I told him. He said, "Fine, I'll give them the message. You can come back this afternoon."

Needless to say, as soon as I got back to the radio station, my boss called me in and asked me where I had been. He accused me of wanting to go back to the South. I told him, "Yes, that's right, I do."

Later, a big meeting was called, a "struggle" meeting. I was the object of the struggle. All the bosses at the radio station sat around. They "analyzed" my mistake. They told me, "Brother Vu, this isn't the way," pointing out why it wasn't right to want to go back. The meeting lasted for hours. They weren't rough, they hardly ever raised their voices. But they persistently accused me, explaining, insulting, badgering, until I had "recognized my mistake" in a satisfactory way. Afterwards I was forced to read an article over the radio, to prove that I hadn't escaped.

It was a bad period. By now everyone realized that there wouldn't be any unification election, that there was no way to get back. Many of the Southerners began to get desperate. One of our friends even managed to escape, somehow getting from Hanoi into Laos where he presented himself at the South Vietnamese Embassy. They flew him back to Saigon, where we later heard he became something of a celebrity.

As far as I was concerned, the ICC affair had taught me a lot. I just kept my mouth shut and worked. After a time I was switched from the radio station job to a job with the Writers' Association—better because it meant more straight writing: short stories, fictionalized accounts of the French war, sketches of battles and incidents that I had covered. All of it was published in the literary magazine *Van* (*Literature*).

Just as I was getting used to this new situation, I got a notice to present myself for "land reform." What was called "land reform" was actually a kind of socialist reconstruction movement that affected everybody, not just peasants. The intention was to reform the entire country, to make everybody conscious of the class struggle and to make sure that everyone adopted a correct attitude—that meant a proletarian attitude.

The idea was that there were Three Gates you had to go through to prove you could be a member of the new society. First was the Gate of Blood. That meant fighting in the resistance. If you had been a fighter against the French, you had been trained by bloodshed. You had demonstrated your loyalty that way. Second was the Gate of Imprisonment. If you had been jailed and tortured by the French, and had resisted in prison, then you had proven yourself that way.

But neither one of these gates—or even both of them—was enough. You not only had to have proven yourself by fighting the outside enemy, you also had to overcome the inside enemy. You had to be able to struggle against yourself and against your background. You had to prove that you were loyal to the revolution with your whole heart, and that you could renounce all your other loyalties—to your family especially. You had to cut your roots to your parents and grandparents and to any property you might have—renounce anything that separated you from the poor peasants and workers. This was the last gate, the Gate of Social Reform. Without going through this gate, the first two weren't worth anything.

Even though I worked for the literary magazine, technically I was attached to the propaganda and training section of the army. That had been my section in the South. So they sent me for social reform to a unit of soldiers who had been brought up from the South in 1954 and were now quartered in a village about a hundred kilometers north of Hanoi.

Altogether there were about a hundred of us. We met in an old temple that had been converted into a school. All of the soldiers, myself among them, had to sit crosslegged on the ground. The trainer spoke to us from the stage at the front of the temple, where the altar used to be. No talking was allowed and no movement. Every day we would sit there for hours. When you got stiff or cramped from sitting crosslegged, you were allowed to change your sitting position, but only in a certain way. First by folding your left leg back, then when that got excruciating, by folding your right leg back. No sitting with your knees hunched up or stretched out, or anything that looked different or showed a lack of discipline.

The trainer was always someone with a "good" class background, most often a poor peasant, or at least his father and grandfather had been poor peasants. Most often these people were political cadres who had been chosen for the correctness of their views. They taught the lessons of proletarian class consciousness. "Who Feeds Whom" was one of the topics—a kind of elementary Marxist analysis showing that the poor feed the rich. We had books that outlined the lessons we were listening to. And the speakers would use real examples, not just abstractions. For example, they would talk about situations in the village where we were living, about landlords who had exploited the poor and had gotten their wealth through the labor of others. Then they would bring in peasants from the village who would tell their own stories.

While we were meeting in the temple, the villagers were going through their own land reform. Poor peasants denouncing richer peasants in front of the entire village, children denouncing their parents, people's trials that might end up with the isolation or execution of someone who had been an exploiter. It was a charged atmosphere. Inside the temple we felt it. It made what we were going through more dramatic. You had a tendency to think of the whole thing as a game that everyone was being forced to play. But it was deadly serious. What was going on outside reminded you just how serious.

The lectures on "Who Feeds Whom" and another fifteen or so topics would drone on all morning. After lunch we would break into small discussion groups to go over the morning's lesson. The group leader would begin by saying, "Okay, who feeds whom? You, Comrade Lam, you tell us." And Lam would start off, repeating what he had heard and read and adding some examples of his own. We'd go around the whole group like that.

The small groups were also used for self-criticism. Each person had to write a detailed autobiography which highlighted everything he had ever done that was against the revolution. If you were educated in a French school you had to describe how your thoughts had been formed by the colonialists. If your parents were business people or owned land you had to tell about how they had acted against the interests of the people—and how you yourself had profited from it. If you had made any mistakes of your own, you had to include those in your confession. For example, if at some point you had put your own self-interest before the interests of the revolution. Maybe you had fought alongside the French for a while, or maybe you had chosen to continue your studies instead of joining the Vietminh. Or maybe you had stayed behind because of your girlfriend. Whatever you had done that showed you lacked the right class consciousness had to be confessed, and then denounced. And the whole time you had to look sad as hell.

Everyone understood what was expected. Even if you couldn't really think of anything, you had to exaggerate some inconsequential incident or make something up. What they wanted was for you to deny yourself and to accept the consciousness of the Party. You had to root out everything that was part of you that didn't conform to the correct way of thinking. Maybe it sounds impossible, but there was a lot of good psychological insight in what they were doing. After you had written or said something terrible about your parents or grandparents or about something very personal, you really felt as if you had betrayed them. Even though you might be saying to yourself the whole time that you didn't believe it and were only saying it because you were being forced. Still you had created a distance between yourself and whoever or whatever you had denounced. You had broken a bond that tied you to something outside the revolution.

My class background wasn't good. My father owned land. I denounced him and I denounced my education. All the while I was saying to myself, This isn't me. Other soldiers with bad class backgrounds said the same kinds of things I did. What they were saying to themselves I don't know. The ones from poor peasant families, the good root people, didn't say much. They weren't expected to. People who had really juicy self-criticisms had to speak in front of the entire unit. Exemplary poor peasants would also speak, for contrast. Nobody objected to any of this. It wasn't possible. You just accepted it passively. Individuals with truly bad parts to their personal histories knew they owed what was called a "blood debt" to the people. They felt lucky they were being allowed to reform themselves.

After it was all over, the unit's political officer signed the self-criticisms. That was proof that you had "passed" the land reform course. You had gone through the third gate. Then the whole thing was filed with your personal dossier, for future reference.

I don't know whether land reform accomplished what they wanted it to. It was traumatic enough for me. But there was a lot of quiet talk about the murders that happened in the countryside. People whispered about a peasant rebellion in Nghe An that the 325th Division had to put down. Of course there was no official information on any of this. None of it was ever reported in the newspapers. But the troubles were confirmed indirectly by Vo Nguyen Giap [North Vietnamese minister of defense] in a big speech he gave in Hanoi's central square. I remember he was wearing civilian clothes instead of his uniform, a sign that he was speaking for the Party. He said that the land reform had had some successes but that there were also some mistakes. The Party's policy was right, but in certain localities it had been carried out incorrectly. He didn't seem terribly repentant about it. There was a rumor, though, that Uncle Ho had cried in a Central Committee meeting when he heard about the executions. But I don't know. He was an awfully foxy guy.

Back at the literary magazine I began revising my reporter's notes for a book on the war in the South. It was published in 1960, to some acclaim. I was even talking with the film people about making a movie of it, though nothing came of it in the end. At the time I was living across from the National Theater, in the center of Hanoi. From my window I looked out on a huge billboard above the corner of Pho Hue and Trang Tien streets, the city's biggest intersection. SEE FULL COMMUNISM IN THIS GENERATION it said. Underneath the words were the happy faces of a worker, a peasant, and an intellectual. Around them were smiling chil-

dren. The funny thing was that the faces were all Caucasian, not Vietnamese. I always assumed they were Russian faces.

Then, in 1960, the Russians got involved in an affair that provided
entertainment for the whole city for almost a year. Through the loud
street corner radio speakers we began to learn about the split between the
Russians and the Chinese. From eight to eight-thirty each night, the
loudspeakers would broadcast Radio Peking on a direct hookup. They had
done it for years. Then from eight-thirty to nine would come the direct
hookup with Radio Moscow. That had also been going on for years. But
now the two stations began abusing each other. The Chinese would insult
Khrushchev. Then the Russians would come on and insult Mao. Some
nights the tone would be intellectual and civilized, with the commenta-
tors presenting these abstract political analyses about who was a revision-
ist and who wasn't. Other times they would get vitriolic, denouncing
each other in the crudest terms.

The whole thing was a tremendous diversion. People would gather
around the street corners and listen avidly to the night's programs. It
went on for a year before they finally cut it off. Afterwards the billboard
came down too. Maybe the Caucasian faces were too symbolic. Someone
might think we were taking sides.

About the same time, the situation in the South started getting a lot
more attention. Radio programs, newspaper articles, all sorts of meetings
talking about liberating the South and unifying the country. The street
corner loudspeakers kept up a steady stream of information and commen-
tary—morning, lunchtime, and evening—any time that people were on
the streets. You heard it constantly. Southerners would come in from the
Front [the National Liberation Front] to talk about what was happening
and to drum up enthusiasm. There was an endless flood of talk about
getting rid of the Americans and *My-Diem*—America-Diem.

Even foreign speakers began showing up. Anna Louise Strong, an
American writer, gave speeches about how awful the United States government was. She was an ancient, white-haired lady who was helped on
to the stage by two girls who looked Chinese. "The United States," she
said, "is like an octopus, trying to take all the land in the world. American mothers will never let their sons go to Vietnam." Bertrand Russell
sent a tape that was played over and over. "I can't come myself, but I am
sending this message. . . ." Letters from Jean-Paul Sartre and other
French intellectuals were printed and broadcast. It seemed as if the whole
world was supporting us and the Front.

I believed all of this. I thought, Yes, the United States is the aggressor.

Their advisers and money are keeping Diem in power. I was optimistic that we'd be able to win, that the country could be unified. Everyone felt the same. There was great enthusiasm, or at least that was how it seemed. Maybe some people had reservations about whether we could really beat the Americans. But if they did, they certainly didn't say it out loud. Even me. I knew how these things worked. I knew how the newspapers and radio did propaganda. But they were your only sources of information. So even after you discounted the fakery and distortion, you were still left with a picture of how things were going that was basically the one you were hearing.

No question. In the first years there was a lot of excitement and commitment, the same as there had been in the French war. But before I finally went South myself, an uneasy feeling began to creep into the atmosphere. By that time the villages were emptying out. The young people were all going to fight in the South, and they weren't coming back. Here and there I would hear snatches of information or gossip that many of the youngsters were unhappy about having to go. A friend at work would say something about his son, or more likely his son's friends. More often it would be some general remark about how somebody had heard that they were having problems with some of the young men. People were just worried. Especially the ones with children. But this wasn't the kind of thing anybody spoke about openly. There wasn't any public discussion. It was like my boss while I was still at the radio station. Up on the wall we had a beautiful picture of Ho Chi Minh, with a fatherly smile on his face. One day my boss looked up at the picture and said very softly to me, "Vu, you see that old guy up there. He killed my dad." (His father had been executed in the land reform.) Then he shook his head and whispered, "Shhh." Nobody was going to say anything out loud about Uncle Ho. And nobody was going to say anything about the war either. But underneath there was a lot of unhappiness, at least after the first enthusiasm wore off.

All this time while I was working for the magazine I hadn't given up my own hope that someday I could go home. Even though I had "passed" the land reform, I hadn't exactly gotten rid of all my subjective feelings. Actually, I hadn't gotten rid of any of them. Personally, everything looked dark. I felt stymied as a writer. I didn't have a fundamental understanding of the Northern psychology or of their way of using language. I had re-done all my old stuff. But where were my wonderful new experiences? I didn't see any new horizons anymore. What made me even more pessimistic was getting to know the great North Vietnamese writers. One of the reasons I had gone North was to meet these people, who were really the giants of Vietnamese literature. Some of my friends and I had achieved a certain amount of fame in the South. But none of us were in the same class as the older Northern writers like Nguyen Huy Tuong, Nguyen Tuan, Kim Lan, Nguyen Hong, or To Hai (To was Vietnam's Hans Christian Andersen). These people were our uncles, our teachers.

Eventually I got to know all of them. Almost every day we would meet to drink tea or beer and talk—the whole circle of writers. The older writers had all been in the resistance and they were happy to be back in Hanoi after living in the jungle. They were wonderfully open. They would talk to us about how to plan out a novel, how to build a plot, how to use irony. Nothing could have been better for someone like me.

But as time passed, I could see each of them becoming more and more depressed. They just couldn't produce like they had before. The problem was that we were all being given such terrible projects to write about. The culture and propaganda people wanted works of art about all the good things, about factory life or collective labor in the countryside. But only the good things. What you wrote about had to be round like a ball, perfect. But a good writer has to pick something complicated, something he can analyze from the inside and from the outside. On these projects we were doing, if you wanted to criticize something, you were only allowed to scratch a little here or a little there. You could never get to the inside, to the ulcer that might be at the heart of it.

One of the older writers was the great humorist Nguyen Cong Hoan. He suffered more than any of them. During one of our talks he told me, "I have strange eyesight. When I look at a person, I ask myself, Why is he walking around on two legs? Three legs would be more normal. Nowadays they say that everybody has to have two legs, but that's just not the way I see it."

One writer who did manage to say what he wanted was Nguyen Huy Tuong. Tuong was one of the most famous of that generation. He was a Party member who had joined the resistance in 1945 and was now one of the leaders of the Writers' Association. Tuong wrote a short story entitled "The Sunday Story" about a village after land reform—about the suspicions, the fear, and the breakdown in friendships and family relationships. Somehow Tuong arranged to get this story published in an anthology of short stories. He had colluded with the editor to sneak it into this book that was chock-full of stories that were "round like a ball." "The Sunday Story" got past the censor, probably because it was stuck in the middle of a large collection. Afterwards Tuong was forced to make a thorough self-criticism and to renounce the story.

Tuong and the others had all become famous under the French. And the contrast between what they were allowed to write then and what they could write now was depressing. Most of them were French-educated, too (although some, like the storyteller To Hai, were self-taught)—and some even liked to speak French rather than Vietnamese. All of these guys could see the handwriting on the wall. They knew they were on their way out. What I saw in them reinforced the troubles I was having myself. I was dying to get back home. Finally, I got my chance.

Xuan Vu's story continues on page 178.

NGUYEN CONG HOAN

Released from Nha Trang prison, the future Assembly deputy returned to his studies in Saigon in a more militant frame of mind.

NGUYEN CONG HOAN'S STORY: *In Opposition*

I WENT BACK TO THE UNIVERSITY IN A DIFFERENT FRAME OF MIND. my experience in Nha Trang prison had helped give me a political understanding of life. Maybe it wasn't very sophisticated, but it was strong. Nha Trang had been a real blow to my self-respect. After all, I was a university student, the only one from Phuoc Giang. I studied hard, and I was doing well. I was on my way to becoming a scientist who could help the nation, while before I was a peasant boy who had never even thought about the future. But with as much prestige as I had—at least among my family and the villagers—they had arrested me. Even though I was completely innocent of anything. If they could arrest and beat me, they could arrest anybody. In fact it was obvious they were. I started thinking that with this kind of government nobody in the country was safe. I didn't have the vaguest idea what to do about it. But I did have a good understanding at this point that the government was against the people.

Of course, that made my feelings about the poor in Saigon even stronger. I didn't know how to do anything about the government politically, but I knew I could at least try to help these people the government was treating so callously. So in a way you could say that prison had turned me from an observer into an activist—a social activist even if I wasn't a political activist.

At first I started going with some friends of mine to visit orphanages.

We would make friends with the children, play with them, take them out on little trips. Then we began organizing classes for them. We formed a small group of socially minded students from Phu Yen Province, and I became the informal leader. I really enjoyed it. The time we spent with the orphans was always rewarding. You could show them there were people who cared for them and loved them like an older brother. And of course they responded.

Before long I got involved with the Buddhist student organization. I didn't have a strong religious feeling at that point, but I naturally gravitated toward them because it was only the Buddhist youth that had a program of social help. By now I was spending all my weekends working with the orphans and teaching them. Then we began a program to give free instruction to poor students in Saigon to help them prepare for the baccalaureate exam. And I got heavily involved in that too.

This was happening in the winter of 1963 and through 1964. [Editors' Note: Vietnam has no seasons in the Western sense, only a dry season (approximately December through May) and a wet season. However, throughout the book we have translated seasonal references into terms familiar to American readers.] I was now a committed social activist. But after 1963 the political situation in Saigon got worse, and I started getting drawn into political action too.

Ngo Dinh Diem was overthrown in November 1963 partly because the mass opposition had undermined him, especially the Buddhists. The group of generals who took his place only lasted a couple of months before they were kicked out by another general named Nguyen Khanh. Khanh was a real disaster. While he was in power protests and mass demonstrations became a way of life. Then in February 1965, Khanh was dumped and two more generals took over—Nguyen Van Thieu and Nguyen Cao Ky.

All these changes were connected to the people's unhappiness with the different military dictators who were running the country. Different groups like the students, Buddhists, Catholics, and the labor organizations found out that they could organize and demonstrate. They saw their actions could put a lot of pressure on the government, and that the pressure could undermine the government and lead to a new one. So the mass opposition movements were gaining real strength. All the different groups were hoping that the more they struggled, the more responsive the regime in power would have to be to their demands, which were mainly for more democracy, peace, and social welfare.

Inevitably I got involved in these political demonstrations, since I was a student and a member of the Buddhist youth organization. In 1965 and 1966, I became a political activist as well as a social activist. Not that I ever took a leading role in the street demonstrations, but I participated in them more and more.

The Buddhist demonstrations would usually start in the big An Quang Pagoda. Mass meetings and lectures on political topics were going on all the time there, almost all of them on the subject of more democracy. In particular we wanted elections. The Buddhist organizations were always agitating for elections.

Monks and student militants would address the meetings at the pagoda, talking about the need for constitutional reform and for elections instead of military dictatorships. The monks Tri Quang and Thien Minh were the leaders and the most effective speakers. The meetings hung on every word. When they'd say, "The people must choose the government!" ten thousand people would be listening to them so intently you could hear a fly buzz. They would say, "Under these circumstances, what can we do? We must express our need for democracy! We must go out to the street!" And the whole meeting would stand up like one person and the demonstration would be on.

Almost always the police would be out there waiting for us. You could never tell what might happen. Sometimes there would be confrontations, fights. The police would charge with their batons and tear gas grenades and we would fight back, throwing rocks. It all depended on whether the monk in charge wanted a fight, because all the Buddhist demonstrators would follow the monks' directions precisely. We could just as easily sit down and allow ourselves to be beaten, or turn back to the pagoda and avoid a clash. But the idea was to pressure the government, and often that meant a street battle.

From 1965 on I also became more aware of the war, and more worried about it. That was the year the Americans arrived in force. As more of them came to Vietnam, I could see what kind of effect they were having. Each time I went home to Phu Yen I'd take a bus. One of the stops was in Cam Ranh, which had been such a beautiful place. But now it was choked up with night clubs. Prostitutes and pornography stores were all over the place. It had turned into a pornography city. The same kind of thing was happening in Saigon, where there were more and more prostitutes and beggars. The Americans I saw looked strange and different. I didn't hate them, but I was certainly disturbed by what their presence was doing to the country.

But the war itself was much more disturbing. By this time it wasn't a guerrilla war anymore. People were being killed by the thousands, on the government side and on the other side. But on both sides it was the poor people who were suffering, who were being killed off and who were killing each other off. The wealthier people found ways to protect themselves and keep their children away from the fighting.

In the center, in Phu Yen, it was especially bad. Korean troops were operating there and they didn't have any scruples at all about killing all the men in a village if they thought the village was being used by the Vietcong. So the peasants were scared to death and there were crowds of refugees. My parents became refugees too, along with most of the others from my village. It just wasn't safe to live there anymore.

As far as I was concerned, I didn't think much about the Front—the Vietcong. But some of my friends from the Buddhist movement joined them, people who were sincere and warmhearted, people I liked. But I never considered joining myself. I knew they didn't have the mass of the people with them, and I especially didn't like the violence of their methods. So I was quite opposed to fighting for them. It wasn't so much that I was exactly a pacifist. I had been involved in a lot of street demonstrations that turned into fights. But I believed that we could change things in a relatively peaceful way, through political methods. And the way to do that was to struggle, to demonstrate, to keep the pressure on. That's what appealed to me, to face the government directly as proponents of peace and democracy. The Vietcong couldn't pretend to do that, and that's why they didn't have the people with them.

In 1967 I graduated from the university with a degree in physics and chemistry, and in September 1967 I began my graduate studies. At the end of January 1968, I was with my family in Tuy Hoa for the celebration of the Lunar New Year when the Tet Offensive started. It began around midnight with what everyone first thought were firecrackers. When we realized a battle was going on we rushed out of the house and ran toward the beach. Thousands of people were on the beach watching the explosions and the planes swooping down and the great balls of orange fire. We stayed on the beach for two days, until it was all over. Then we walked back and looked at the bodies that were lying all over the streets, mainly civilians and Vietcong guerrillas.

The horror of this experience strengthened my feelings of pacificism, and also my religious feelings. I prayed for peace. I took a vow that if peace came I would become a monk and retire to a pagoda. Then I wrote my prayers and my vow in the form of two poems so I could make my feelings as clear as it was possible for me to make them.

Actually, my personal religious beliefs had been getting deeper over the past year or two, and Tet gave it even more of a push. Before, I had simply thought of myself as Vietnamese. I hadn't really considered my attachment to traditions and customs as religious. But the more I thought about the poverty and political oppression and the killing, the more I came to see that Vietnamese Buddhism embodied the most noble traditions of the country. The longing for peace and the struggle for social welfare and justice were the essence of Buddhist ethics. In Vietnam, Buddhists had historically led the fight on behalf of the oppressed; the Church had always allied itself with the poor.

Most recently, Buddhists had fought against the Diem dictatorship. But before that, the Buddhist pagodas had protected the Vietminh during the French war. By contrast, Catholicism had come to Vietnam with the French and was allied with the government. Catholicism was Western, like the French were Western. But Buddhist ethics and the values of the people were the same thing. The main object of the Buddhist is to do good in his present life in order to build merit for his soul, for his future life. Buddhism is above all a social religion. It was this social emphasis that attracted me more and more.

As I became personally more involved with the Buddhist Church, I continued studying. In 1969 I finished my master's degree in chemistry and started working on my doctorate. I also kept up my social and political activities, which now had taken on more of a religious coloring. But by 1971 we had been going to the streets for years. The feeling began to set in that we couldn't go on doing that forever, at least not with any effect. Now, finally, there were elections coming up—this was the October elections of 1971. A lot of my friends in the Buddhist youth movement thought I should run for an Assembly seat from Phu Yen.

After giving this idea a lot of thought, I decided to do it. The mass opposition movement seemed to have peaked a year or so earlier, and I didn't have great faith anymore that we could actually change things by that route. But running for office would give me a chance to appear everywhere and talk freely against the regime. Then, if I won, I would have parliamentary immunity. I could speak out in any way I wanted, and nobody could stop me. I would be able to join the opposition group in the Assembly and we could coordinate strategy with the Buddhists and the students who were still going down to the street.

So I ran. There were twenty candidates for two seats, and the other nineteen were professional politicians, people with money who had parties behind them. But even though I was only a student and I didn't have any money or experience, I had certain advantages.

The main advantage was that most of the other candidates were afraid to speak out against the government—and there was a lot of antigovernment sentiment among the voters. I ran on three issues: (1) Peace, (2) For the Poor, (3) Against the Government. By "against the government" I meant that I was against social injustice and economic inequities, I was against illegal arrests and imprisonment, and I was against the suppression of free speech. I called my campaign "The New Wind."

When it came time for me to give my first big speech, all my friends were worried. The only public speaking I had done was in front of small student groups, or when I was teaching. So they were afraid of what might happen when I got out in front of a crowd. So was I. But when I actually stood there, I found that all I had to do was speak from the heart about the things I knew and felt strongly about. We were all surprised by the effect.

Everywhere I went people seemed to know me. Maybe they didn't know me personally, but they knew my background. They knew that my family was poor and that I had grown up as a peasant. So many of the poor people felt a bond with me. I also had the support of the Buddhist Church, and that meant a lot in the countryside. When the results came in, I had won by a huge landslide. There were a hundred thousand voters in Phu Yen. Even with twenty candidates and the usual government corruption and fraud, I got fifty-four thousand votes. So in October 1971 I went up to the National Assembly.

After that I began to think in bigger terms. Specifically, I thought maybe I could become province chief of Phu Yen, something like a state governor in the United States. According to the Constitution, the province chiefs were supposed to be elected. But in fact they were always appointed. What would happen was that each year the Assembly kept giving the president the right to appoint chiefs. In the Assembly, the regime would bribe or intimidate everyone they could, and it was always enough to put across the bills they were proposing.

They never tried to approach me directly, but from time to time they'd make an attempt through my wife. That was a typical way these things were done. If a bribe came through your wife, everyone could always say it was just a present to her. Of course there was nothing political about it at all, just a birthday present or a Tet gift. Then at night the wife would whisper to her husband that she had gotten something from someone. The husband would never have to touch it. Ostensibly he might not even know about it.

They also tried to use my wife to threaten me. She would hear "rumors" that someone had made a threat on my life, usually from the Tuy Hoa police chief. The police chief was the regime's agent there. So if he told my wife that his men had heard something about a plot, what it meant was a direct threat from the regime—and not just to me, but to my family as well.

There was nothing to do about this kind of thing. If I showed I was afraid, or that I was vulnerable to this kind of pressure, I would lose whatever effectiveness I had. They'd have a key to control me with. So I couldn't react in any way. But I did become more careful about things like traveling. I never disclosed my plans in advance—what villages I'd be visiting or what my schedule was. In actual fact, I wasn't too worried by the threats, maybe because they were spread out. They came now and then, but I got used to them. They were a fact of political life. Besides, I was sure that if anything happened to me, there would be a big reaction from the people in Phu Yen. That was my main protection.

Only twenty or so opposition Assembly people were able to stand up to this kind of thing—individuals like Tran Van Tuyen and Kieu Mong Thu. Sometimes others would vote with the opposition bloc, but it was never enough to make a real difference. Still I kept hoping that if we could intensify our opposition inside the Assembly and combine our movement with the mass opposition on the streets, we could force the government to move. But my hopes were never fulfilled.

Nothing showed the position of the democratic opposition to Thieu better than the freedom of the press campaign that went on in 1973. The Saigon newspapers were up in arms about a new round of censorship, and of course there was a lot of violence from the police. One night during this conflict, the journalists were holding an all-night vigil at the Press Club, which was across the street from the National Assembly building. It was a very tense atmosphere. Everybody expected the police to attack. So a group of five or six opposition assemblymen decided to try and stop it by staying up with the journalists. We thought that since we had parliamentary immunity we would be able to protect the newspaper people from being physically assaulted if there was a confrontation.

At midnight the police arrived and moved in on the Press Club. We all locked arms with the journalists and identified ourselves out loud as assemblymen, although of course the police recognized all of us quite well. As they came toward us we started shouting "Immunity, immunity!" It was like whistling in the wind. They just waded in and beat the hell out of everybody who was there. Dinh Xuan Dung [one of the assemblymen] was knocked to the ground. Then the police hauled off most of the journalists—some conscious, some unconscious—and they took Dung along with them. They threw all of them into the paddy wagons and roared off, leaving us to lick our wounds with the rest of the journalists.

We were all absolutely enraged that these bastards would just ignore our parliamentary immunity and that they had the gall to attack elected members of the Assembly. After we had gotten ourselves together, we walked back across the street to the Assembly building. We were just smoldering with anger.

One of our group was Ho Ngoc Nhuan, a leader of the opposition bloc. When we got across the street I saw Nhuan poking around in corners and kicking through the street gutters muttering to himself. I said, "Nhuan, what are you doing?" He hissed out, "I'm looking for something that will burn, I'm going to burn this place down, this filthy place!" He was talking about the Assembly building.

A little while later we were still in front of the Assembly talking about what to do, still gritting our teeth in anger. While we were standing there a paddy wagon pulled up in front of us and four guys got out carrying a body, one each arm, one on each leg. They threw the body down on the Assembly steps, then they got back in the wagon and took off.

We had been frozen during the few moments this took. But as soon as the police drove off we ran to look at the body. When I bent over I saw it was Dinh Xuan Dung, the assemblyman who had been beaten unconscious and taken off with the journalists. He lay there with his eyes closed, without moving or breathing. I thought he was dead. I put my face down next to his and started to cry, first quietly. But then I couldn't control myself and I began sobbing.

While I was sobbing away, I thought I heard the corpse say something. I looked down and Dung's eyes were open. He was whispering, "Hoan, shut up you idiot, I'm not dead!"

But though he wasn't dead, he had been very badly beaten. We carried him inside the building, then we began to make plans. By the next morning we had contacted all our friends, the students, unions, Buddhists, press—everybody in the opposition—telling them to be in front of the Assembly building by ten o'clock.

When ten o'clock came the streets around the Assembly were full of angry, chanting people. In front of the crowd I carried Dung's "body" slowly down the stairs and into the street where we had a stretcher ready for him. Then, with Dung as a visible symbol of the regime's complete contempt for the people and for the country's democratic institutions, we marched off to the Presidential Palace yelling, "Down with Thieu! Democracy! Liberty!" We made as much noise as we could parading past the Palace. Then we went back to the Assembly and gave a few last speeches before we broke up the demonstration. Afterwards, we carried Dung to the hospital; they kept him for a couple of days before they let him go home.

But even though our opposition bloc wasn't an effective force for real change, the 1973 Paris Agreement gave all of us tremendous hope. We weren't afraid at that point that the NLF would take over. But Thieu had openly said he was against the agreement and it was clear to everybody that he had only signed it because the United States had forced him to. So we felt that what we had to do was protect the agreement and try to make sure it was carried out. All the opposition factions in Saigon shared this feeling that they had to join in a formal "Third Force"—that is, people who weren't part of the government and weren't part of the Front, but who would have a role in the Council of National Reconciliation and Concord that the agreement set up.

We saw the agreement as giving us a way out of the war. It stipulated that the political future of the South would be decided by the people through "free and democratic elections" under international supervision. The government and the Front were supposed to set up the Council of National Reconciliation and Concord to make sure the elections took place. We knew that if the government and the Front were facing each other in an election, they'd both be looking for support from the middle. And we were the middle, the Third Force.

So we began to organize support for the middle way. We sat down with the people around Big Minh, the Southern general and political leader who was most conciliatory toward the Front, to try to draw him into our plans. We set up a National Concord and Reconciliation Force and went all over the country organizing local branches. We got together our backing from the Buddhists in all provinces and from the other opposition factions. We wanted elections, and we wanted a clearly defined and substantial Third Force. We worked like dogs to make it happen.

At first we were optimistic. But by the middle of 1974 we had lost hope. Thieu wasn't budging an inch. He refused to set up the National Council. He refused to move into negotiations with the Front. Elections were obviously never going to happen. On the contrary, he was arresting the leaders of our local Reconciliation Force branches, arresting journalists friendly toward us and bribing assemblymen to allow him to run for a third term.

While this was going on, the Communists were stepping up their military attacks. By 1974 there really wasn't anything left of the Paris Agreement. There was just no hope. There was no way to move the regime and no way to stop the Front.

By the beginning of 1975 the government's military situation was deteriorating fast. Then at the beginning of March the Communists took Ban Me Thuot. That was the beginning of the end. After Ban Me Thuot the government forces just crumbled.

I knew we were in the middle of a disaster. Nobody in the opposition had any leverage left. There was no way to influence events. There was simply nothing to do. I was in a totally passive position—as if I was back in the Nha Trang jail, letting them beat me because I couldn't do anything about it.

NGUYEN THI TY
(NGUYEN CONG HOAN'S WIFE):
Assemblyman's Wife

WHEN HOAN RAN FOR OFFICE I WAS TREMENDOUSLY HAPPY. HE WAS warmly supported by the people in Phu Yen. I was proud for him. But I was also afraid. Because he was in the opposition, he had enemies. Sometimes I would hear that someone had planned to bomb our house and kill all of us. I was worried sick, but what could I do? I'd think, It's up to God what happens to us.

When my husband was in the Assembly he had a lot of trouble with the Tuy Hoa police chief. My husband had denounced the chief in the National Assembly for corruption and for illegally arresting people. His attack got into the newspapers in Saigon, so the chief was very angry. I was afraid he'd try to get to my husband through me and the children.

On Tet there's a tradition of gift-giving. It's a wonderful opportunity for corruption—bribing under the cover of giving gifts. On Tet of 1973 a close aide of the chief's came to the house at midnight [a traditional time for Tet visits]. I could see through the window that the chief himself was sitting in the car in front of the house. The aide gave me a big box— he said it was a gift from his boss to me and the children.

I opened it immediately. Inside there were pastries, cakes, different kinds of teas—and together with them were three gold luong. When I saw these I told him, "Oh no, you have to wait until my husband gets back from Saigon." He kept insisting that I take it. He said it was a free gift from his boss, absolutely free, that no one was asking any favors of anyone. When I still refused he began to tell me that if I didn't take it— this free gift—that his boss would punish him severely. But I wouldn't take it. When Hoan came back he told me I had done exactly the right thing. Of course I knew I had.

Nguyen Cong Hoan and Nguyen Thi Ty's stories continue on page 187.

TRINH DUC

While most of the Vietminh army regrouped North, the Party left behind a network of underground operatives: secretaries to oversee major war zones and small staffs composed of the most skilled agents. Delighted by the opportunity to live in the Democratic Republic, Trinh Duc was at first dismayed by the news he would be staying in Saigon.

TRINH DUC'S STORY: *Village Chief*

AFTER GENEVA, THE SAIGON INTELLECTUAL ASSOCIATION WENT UNDER-ground. There were fewer of us and all communication was very guarded. We still continued our proselytizing work, but much more cautiously than before.

One of the most likely prospects at Hoa Hoa High School was the school's woman principal. You could tell from the way she taught us that she was a sympathizer. I began to cultivate her, at first just to be friendly. Then, when she turned out to be receptive, I started giving her litera-ture. Even after I was transferred out to Nghe An High School in the middle of the year, I kept up my contacts with her.

But others besides myself had noticed how impressed she was with the revolution. Student informers for the police denounced her and she was arrested. I found out later that the police found in her house a copy of the Chinese Communist Party constitution, a Chinese political magazine, and a booklet on student organizing, all of which I had given her. It didn't take much for them to get my name out of her.

At about ten in the morning, the police came to the restaurant and forced the manager to tell them the address of my brother's house, where I was still living. I was sitting in the living room writing a leaflet when they came up to the house. In my bedroom were six big trash bags full of documents on the Geneva Agreement. They had just arrived the previous day and I hadn't had time to get them distributed. When I sensed some-body was in the room, I looked up. Cops were all around. I jumped up and tried to run, but they grabbed me before I could take a step and began to slap me. They lugged a jeepful of material along with them to the Hoa Hoa police station in Giadinh.

I wasn't especially surprised by what had happened. Diem had launched what he called the *To Cong* (Denounce Communists) Campaign and many people were being arrested. I also knew that Hoa Hoa was supposed to be the toughest police station in the city, the place they brought the worst elements, so I didn't have any illusions about what was going to happen to me there. I had also talked to people who had been in jail and had been tortured. As we drove to the police station I was going over in my mind what I had heard. So I was resigned to it; I was prepared for it mentally.

When they first brought me in they didn't even ask any questions. They just threw me into a room and beat me until I was unconscious. When I woke up I was in a cell with a lot of other prisoners. They told me that when I was first carried in everyone thought I was dead, and that later an official had come into the cell to give me a shot with a syringe.

That night the prisoners took care of me. The next morning the police dragged me to the torture room again. They threw me down on the floor and tied my hands and legs. Then they pressed a cloth hard over my nose so I had to breathe through my mouth. When I opened my mouth they poured water down my throat—gallons of it. I had to swallow, swallow, until my stomach began to swell up. I felt like I was gagging to death. Then one of them stood on my stomach, forcing the water to come up out of my mouth. After that they began to ask questions about my network. Of course they knew that the principal wasn't the only one and they wanted me to reveal all the names.

In fact, I did have all the names in my head, and all the code names—at that time I had more than sixty people working for me. But how could I tell them? I knew they would do exactly the same thing to them that they were doing to me. So I refused. Every time I refused, they'd start beating me again. But that just made me more determined not to tell them anything.

After they brought me back to my cell I began to swell all over. My clothes had to be cut off my body. I couldn't walk. When my cellmates carried me to the hole in the floor to piss, I pissed blood. I was sure I would die. Then the next day it started all over again.

They interrogated me for twenty-two days. During the whole time I wasn't able to stand up or walk. Every day they carried me to the interrogation room. Back in the cell I could only crawl. But I kept to my story that I was only a messenger, that I didn't know anything. I didn't tell them a thing.

I think there were several things that helped me survive spiritually—I never thought I would survive physically. The first was that I knew they would torture and kill my entire network. So if I talked, I myself would be killing my comrades. The second was hatred. Maybe that was the main thing, because there wasn't anything reasonable about that feeling. Whatever they were doing to my body, my mind was in a hot fury the whole time. And it just got hotter. I always challenged them, constantly. I'd scream at them, "Kill me, kill me, you bastards!" I got angrier and angrier until there wasn't anything left but hatred.

Another thing that helped me survive was pride. I was very proud that I hadn't broken, and I knew my cellmates respected me tremendously for what I was enduring. They gave me medicines and food they had gotten from their families. They took care of me. I got great spiritual support from them. I knew that I was living as a real Communist, sacrificing myself for others. That sustained me.

On the twenty-third day, General Nguyen Ngoc Le came to see me. At that time Le was chief of police for South Vietnam. He introduced himself and said that he respected me for not revealing the names of people. Then he said that he would give his word as a general that I would be released if I only told them how the network was set up and kept going—I wouldn't have to give him any names at all.

I told Le that I didn't know anything I hadn't already told the police. My job was only to deliver messages and distribute literature. Often I didn't even deliver the literature but shoved it into the toilets at school. The reason they had found so much of it at my house was that I hadn't been delivering it.

After Le left, the torture began again, though not so regularly. Every few days they would take me out for interrogation. Sometimes they used electric shocks and sometimes the water treatment. They also stuck needles under my fingernails. But mostly they just beat me. After each session they would give me a couple of days to think. Then just as I'd start recovering, they'd take me in for another. The whole period lasted five months.

When the interrogation was finally over, they sent me to the Cho Quan prison hospital. I think they finally got tired of beating me. At Cho Quan I was allowed to have visitors. Even after I was as recovered as I was going to be, my brother arranged for me to stay there longer by bribing one of the hospital officials. Years later, after I finally got out, I found that my case had become famous in the revolution along with the case of Mrs. No, who is now [1985] Party boss of Dong Nai Province. She too had undergone intense torture without divulging anything. Our two experiences were written up as models for cadres to study.

From the hospital I was sent to one prison after another, first to Phu Lam, then to Catinat. I was transferred to Catinat because another one of the people in my network had been picked up and had named me. He was a labor organizer in the Con O battery factory, a factory that had originally been located in North Vietnam but had moved entirely to the South after Geneva. The whole factory moved—owners, workers, equipment, everything.

From the moment Con O set itself up in Saigon there were strikes. In fact, we were behind the trouble. Our organizers, including the guy who had been arrested, were constantly arousing the workers. Of course our strategy was to let them strike over labor issues while we remained as far behind the scene as possible. But by the same token, the owner was forever trying to implicate the strikers in politics.

So when they arrested one of our organizers, it was a real breakthrough for them. They moved me to Catinat because that was where the case was being investigated. They even put me in the same collective cell with this guy, probably they hoped an informer would be able to pick up some information. But I managed to get him by himself by using two other cellmates to shield us. I put my face right up next to his and told him, "Look, you don't know anything about me, but I know everything about you, your whole background. Tomorrow when you talk to the interrogator, you deny everything. If you don't, I'll have you killed. This is the only way you're going to survive."

The next day he retracted his denunciation. Aside from that he kept his mouth shut.

Finally I ended up in Giadinh prison [now called Le Van Duyet] in the outskirts of Saigon. The collective cells there were so hot and airless that we split the group into two so we could take turns—one group sleeping, the other fanning with the mats they gave us to sleep on.

In Giadinh I was able to make contact with other Party members through prisoners whose jobs brought them into different cells—the food servers and janitors. Morale among the prisoners was very high; there was a high level of anger against the jailors. I took advantage of every opportunity I could to raise it even higher, to keep the prisoners impressed by the need to struggle without letting up. I knew that everything I could do to warm up the atmosphere would sharpen their sense of purpose and help keep their spirits alive.

The easiest way to do that was to organize the struggle against the prison regime. The more we antagonized the guards and the more conflict we had, the angrier the prisoners felt toward them. So we made demands for more showers, more water, better food, more time outside the cells—all things we knew they would refuse. When they did refuse, the other Party members and I organized hunger strikes. We wouldn't eat anything for days. The prison was full of constant chanting and jeering from the inmates.

At first the guards would arrest the leaders and throw them in isolation, but we always had new leaders ready to take their places. Of course none of the real organizers were ever identifiable as leaders. When that didn't work they brought in water cannons. They finally gained control of the cells after they attacked us with vomit gas grenades. That finally shut everybody up.

After a number of these episodes, they transferred the most stubborn prisoners out of Giadinh to Bien Hoa prison. At Bien Hoa I was shoved into an isolation cell for a month and a half, a tiny dark room with a weak light bulb that shone night and day. With Hoa Hoa, Phu Lam, Catinat, and Giadinh, I was in various prisons for almost five years. Then they moved me to Phu Loi.

Phu Loi was the worst place I had ever seen. It was even more crowded and filthier. The food ration kept everybody on the edge of starvation. They also had what they called the *Hoc Tap Va Cai Tao* program—"re-education and reform"—phrases they had taken from the Party. Every day former Communists who had rallied to the government would come into the cells to teach, to talk about how bad communism was and then give out literature, which had to be read and discussed.

I refused to listen to it. I told them I couldn't read Vietnamese and that I just wasn't going to have any part of it. I told the others not to participate either. So they chained me up, my arms squeezed together behind me, and they threw me into isolation. After a while the pain was excruciating. My body hurt all over anyway. It always did when the weather was wet—that was a leftover from the beatings they gave me in Hoa Hoa.

I was in isolation that time for two weeks. When they let me out they told me I didn't have to participate in the studies, but that I had better not disturb the group anymore. I said okay to that.

There was a group of sixty-eight Chinese cadres in Phu Loi whom they considered especially hard-core. Eventually they moved us all into cells at the National Police Headquarters. Then they announced they were going to send us to Taiwan. When we heard that, we told them that we would kill ourselves immediately rather than be sent there—a mass suicide. We were completely ready to do it too. We knew that none of us would stay alive for a day on Taiwan.

When I was in the National Police Headquarters it was 1961. I was thirty years old and I had been in jail since I was twenty-three. The whole springtime of my life was spent in jail. Sometimes when I was alone I thought about my personal life, that I would have liked to get married and have a family. But I never dwelled on it or thought, That's enough. I was a very ardent revolutionary.

Sometime in 1961 I was transferred with the other Chinese hardcores to Con Son Island. This was the place everybody feared most, like the Devil's Island of the Vietnamese prison system. They loaded the sixty-eight of us onto the ship in chains, along with about a hundred and fifty others. The whole group sat in two long lines facing each other, all of us chained by the feet to the long iron bar that ran the length of the deck.

It took the better part of a day for the trip to the island. But when we got there, the boat didn't pull all the way into a dock. Instead it stopped offshore in chest-deep water. Then the guards unlocked our chains and kicked us out of the boat. In the condition most of us were in it was all we could do to struggle through the water and up onto a kind of rocky landing area. There we saw there were two paths that led off this landing area up to the prison. One had a sign that said Ngo Dinh Diem Road. The other sign said Ho Chi Minh Road. A guard with a bullhorn was bellowing that those who chose the Ngo Dinh Diem Road could look forward to returning home to their families one day and enjoying a bright future. But the Communist road was the road to hell. Those who took that would never return. I took the road to hell, along with eleven others.

As we came up the path from the rocky area, a gauntlet of guards with sticks was waiting for us. The blows came down, knocking people to the ground, then smashing down onto their backs and heads as they tried to crawl through the rows of guards. By the time I stumbled past the last one, I was barely conscious. I could only make out a blurry impression of the prison in front of me.

It was just as well I couldn't. There was no way to be prepared for life in that place. The "Ho Chi Minh" prisoners were separated from the others. We were kept alive on two small bowls of rice a day, with no meat, vegetables, or anything else. Everybody developed beriberi, some more seriously than others. When we were sick the officials would come along with vitamin capsules—only one vitamin C capsule would make the red spots on your legs disappear. Then they would ask if you still chose the Ho Chi Minh Road. They would wait until someone looked like he was on the verge of death—then they'd come by with the capsules and syringes full of vitamin solutions, and they'd say, "If you want a shot, then separate yourself from the Communists." I was swimming in hatred. I broke their goddamn needles.

Con Son changed me. At least it changed me finally. When I was young I witnessed a great deal of injustice, and I hated the people who I saw doing such terrible things. But that hatred wasn't ingrained in me. Later I saw how people I loved were brutally tortured, and I had more hatred. Since I had been in prison that kind of thing had been happening to me personally for many, many years. Con Son was the culmination of it. I felt as if I had become like hardened steel. My human feelings were leaving me, I knew that. I was more than capable of doing the same things to my enemies that they were doing to me—no question. Without a moment's hesitation. The same and worse.

IN 1964 I was released. Ngo Dinh Diem was dead, and the generals who overthrew him had also been overthrown. The new president was another general named Nguyen Khanh. To celebrate the success of his coup, Khanh declared an amnesty under which about five hundred prisoners were freed. I was shipped back to Saigon on the exact same boat, chained up to the same iron bar. At Chi Hoa, the central prison, the guards told us that we were to be released—that's when we first heard it. I said, "Don't joke!" But then after a while my name was called. Even then I didn't believe them. I had been in jail for ten years—through three generations of South Vietnamese presidents and three generations of American presidents.

After they gave me my release papers, I took a bus back to Cholon, to my brother's house. My brother was still there, still running his restaurant. He had been picked up right after I was, but had only been in jail six months. When he saw me, he was overcome with happiness. We both were. We spent the next three months celebrating. We had parties every night, one feast after the other. My nephews, nieces, my sister-in-law's family, the restaurant workers and their families, each night somebody would be there to help us celebrate. I was back from Con Son, and that called for a hero's welcome.

The second day I was back, the Party contacted me through a messenger. I was to take a rest and recover my strength. Then they would give me my orders. In the meantime, I was supposed to keep in contact with the other ethnic Chinese who had been freed with me. My rest period lasted three months.

At the end of that time I got a message telling me to be ready to leave.

Since my identity was known, I would have to go into the jungle and take up my new job there. The other eighteen were to come out at approximately the same time, but by other routes. I made my last contacts with them, then reported myself to the local police station for the last time. Since my release, I had had to report myself to them—first every three days, then every month. Now I told them that I was going into the hospital for treatment of problems I had developed while I was in prison. Then I was ready to leave.

On the day of departure I met my liaison in the Cholon marketplace. I asked her if she had eaten soup yet. She answered, "Not yet." Then I said, "Let's go and have some." That was the arranged code. Then we took a bus to Cu Chi, where I was led into an ordinary village house and found myself being conducted through a maze of tunnels that started from the covered hole in the house's bunker.

The main tunnel in this system was called Tong Nhut Road. It connected village to village and in some places had entrances from almost every house. In those places if there was an enemy attack, an entire hamlet might disappear.

I was amazed at my first sight of this underground network, but later I got to know it very well. The Cu Chi tunnels served as a defense, a trap for Americans or ARVN troops, a supply area, and a stop for new recruits coming out from Saigon into the jungle. I was delighted to find that the chief of personnel in Cu Chi was an old colleague of mine from the Intellectuals' Association. But when he asked me to stay on as his assistant, I told him I was anxious to get as far from Saigon as possible.

The trip from Cu Chi to Cuc R [Cuc R (COSVN) was the headquarters area that controlled the war through most of the South and served as liaison between the war front and the command center in Hanoi] took a month of travel by foot, bicycle, and sampan. When I got there they treated me at first like a beginner at revolution. I had come in with a group of other former prisoners, and we all had to rewrite our autobiographies, as if we had just been recruited. The cadres explained to us that this was because we had been out of the system so long and hadn't been able to follow the political developments or the course the revolution had taken. Consequently, our point of view was not up to the times. I wasn't happy about this, but after it was explained to me, I accepted it as being reasonable.

The main thing in the autobiographies was to write about the mistakes you had made in prison. You had to examine yourself thoroughly. You weren't expected to write only about the actual errors you had made, but also about your weaknesses, the way your thoughts had changed, or if you had questioned your commitment to the Party—things of that nature. I wrote about something that had happened in Con Son in the period not too long before I had been released. At that time they had put the Ho Chi Minh Road prisoners together with the others. Every morning the whole prison had to stand before the puppet flag and sing the puppet national anthem. So every morning I had stood there in front of the enemy flag. I lent my presence to it. I participated in it.

The way it worked was that you wrote your self-criticism, and then it had to be approved by the others in your group. So you read it in front of everybody and listened while they criticized you for what you had done, your justification for it, everything that had happened. I acknowledged my mistake and my weakness in doing what I had done. The others criticized me, but they also said they understood. They accepted my self-criticism. Afterwards, the whole report was submitted to the Party cadre. After he approved it, they gave me back my status.

After that, my training began—military and political at the same time. The courses taught about the National Liberation Front, which had been organized a few years before. [Formally established in December 1960, the NLF was the political umbrella organization for the Southern revolutionaries.] We learned the entire program by heart, and we were instructed in how to carry it out. I also took a course in labor organization, which was especially important because of the number of workers in the rubber plantations that were under our control.

While the political courses were going on, I was also trained in guerrilla warfare. I learned how to use a carbine, AK-47, grenades, the different kinds of mines—how to make them and how to disarm them. I also learned field tactics and studied the strengths and weaknesses of the enemy.

When I was finished with the training, they assigned me to the Hoa Van Committee [the Chinese department]. All the headquarters areas including Hoa Van were stretched out away from COSVN along the Cambodian border. It was a very rugged jungle area that provided good protection and easy movement across the border. But it didn't provide much food. Rice had to be brought in, and there were very few vegetables to go along with it. The soldiers did a lot of hunting, but that wasn't in any way a stable source of extra nutrition. There was just never enough food.

I had been thinking about this situation while I was at COSVN, and when I got to the Hoa Van Committee area I proposed that they put me in charge of improving the life of the department. For a while on Con Son I had been chief of the prisoners who worked raising vegetables and I knew I could do it well. So I planted vegetables. Before long I was raising enough for the Hoa Van Committee, for Radio Liberation, which was next to us, and even enough to send up to COSVN.

While I was in charge of farming, it was also my job to lecture the new ethnic Chinese recruits who had been sent to the Hoa Van Committee for training. After the farming got established, I became more and more involved in this training. Eventually, I began to make trips to Cu Chi to bring the Chinese recruits up through the jungle. Cu Chi was the main safe area near Saigon that we could use for initial orientation and for gathering these people. The Saigon government knew what was going on, but if they tried to come into Cu Chi it always cost them dearly, so usually they left us alone.

As time went by I took more of a direct role in the actual recruiting process, directing the liaisons who were bringing recruits out from Cholon and occasionally making trips into the city myself. During 1965 there were a great number of volunteers. The Americans had finally brought their own forces into Vietnam, and one of the results was a huge outpouring of young people who wanted to fight against them. During one period I was able to bring five hundred recruits out just from Cholon.

All of them knew they would never have an easy life in the jungle, and that nobody could tell them how long the fighting would last. They came only because of their ideals and because they were willing to sacrifice themselves to save the country. Once we got them to Tay Ninh [the head-quarters areas] we gave them three months of military and political training, then sent them into the field. Often they didn't live long. In the battle of Dong Xoai—the first large, conventional battle we fought—forty ethnic Chinese cadres were killed. Just cadres; that doesn't include the number of Chinese *bo dois*. A good many of them had been my recruits.

IN 1967 I was sent to Long Khanh Province [approximately fifty miles northeast of Saigon] as part of a special mission to reinforce the local political cadres. Long Khan is a highland area that produces tea, coffee, fruit, and rubber. A high percentage of the peasants are ethnic Chinese, but the cadres in the area were mostly Vietnamese who didn't even speak their language. That was one reason they had failed to mobilize the people behind the revolution.

My first appointment was as deputy secretary of the Party branch in Bao Binh village; then after a few months I was moved up to secretary. My job was simply to guarantee control of the village and the region around it. It was a matter of constantly demonstrating the presence and the invincible strength of the revolution so that the peasants would have no doubt about which side was going to be there longest and which would have the most effect on their lives. In Bao Binh I was in charge of political, security, and social welfare operations—all of them coordinated to win the villagers to our side and keep them there. I spread propaganda, collected taxes, attacked local military posts, and made sure that the officials appointed by Saigon were no real threat—either by making arrangements with them, intimidating them, or if necessary, executing them.

Within a year I was named to the Xuan Loc district Party branch secretariat and put in charge of three villages, Nam Lo and Bac Lo in addition to Bao Binh. My area included a number of hamlets that we called *xoi dau*—contested areas. *Xoi* means "sweet rice," and *dau*, "beans." So a *xoi dau* area was a mixed area, one subject to both our control and Saigon's. Vinh was this kind of hamlet. During the day the people followed the government. But at night the government officials would go back to the district or province capital to sleep, and then our cadres would come out to do their work.

The Saigon-appointed hamlet chief in Vinh was a man named Thuan. We had an agreement together that if he did nothing to hurt us we would let him alone. There would have been no problem killing Thuan, but there was no real reason for it either. If we had, the government just would have sent someone else to take the job, and maybe the new one would be tougher and more effective than Thuan. So in a situation like this it was much better to compromise. Besides, I knew everything about Thuan and his habits while he knew nothing about me. So he understood that he was the vulnerable one.

In addition to keeping a truce of sorts with Thuan, I also did business with him. It was the business that eventually led to his death. At that time the Saigon government was making an attempt to keep rice and medicine out of the hands of the Vietcong by restricting the supplies available to hamlets in disputed areas. Local people were put on a strict ration that was calculated according to how many individuals they had in their household. The idea was that if they didn't have anything extra, they wouldn't be able to smuggle anything to the guerrillas.

In this kind of hamlet the people always suffered terribly. They weren't able to keep more than a week's worth of any kind of supplies on hand. Their food intake was severely limited, and they were under constant government pressure. Under those circumstances, it was natural that they sympathized with us and hated the government.

Thuan wasn't much different from a lot of the Saigon hamlet chiefs— he saw his job mainly as a way of making money for himself. The rationing program was ideal for him. It gave him a chance to steal large amounts of supplies by making up false lists of the number of people in Vinh. The government made food available for the number on the list, and he bought it at the official price. He then took the rice, sugar, and so on and sold it on the black market at many times what he paid for it.

Working like this gave him six hundred extra kilos [about 1320 pounds] of rice every month. I knew all about what he was doing, and I made an arrangement with him to sell me three hundred kilos, the basic supply I needed for the cadres of my three villages. But I refused to pay him the black market price. I figured that if I left him with half his profits instead of all of them, he should still be happy. I was allowing him to stay in business and I wasn't making life difficult for him. He could make do with the official price. Thuan agreed, but he wasn't happy about it. He wanted me to pay him the black market price.

But our arrangement must have preyed on his mind. It was just un-bearable to him that he was losing thousands and thousands of piasters. One day he left a message in our "letter box" that he wouldn't sell me rice at the official rate anymore, that if I wanted it, I'd have to pay the black market price. That night he stopped sleeping in the hamlet.

As far as I was concerned, this was a frontal challenge. The price wasn't even that important. But if I let him do this, that would have proved he was stronger than I was. The revolution would have lost face in the ham-let. So I convened a Party branch meeting in the Bao Binh and we decided to execute him.

In Thuan's case this was an easy decision to make. He was a greedy, self-serving individual who wasn't popular with the villagers. Had he been well-liked, it would have been harder for us. Before killing someone who was popular, we'd have to try to do something to discredit him. Executing someone would always instill fear in people. But if they liked the individual, if he was a good man, it would also turn their hearts against the revolution.

Anyway, that wasn't a problem with Thuan. I ordered one of our people in the hamlet to start tracking Thuan's movements and schedule. At the same time I chose a team for the actual execution. When the tracker told us that Thuan left the hamlet by jeep every day between four and five, I set up an ambush for him on the national route. I dressed the execution team in Saigon army uniforms and trained them to act like Saigon sol-diers. When they were ready, I sent them out to do the job. They could have just shot him, but I wanted him alive so I could explain his crimes to him. I wanted him to understand the justice of his sentence.

The plan worked perfectly. One of the guerrillas pretended to be a half-drunken puppet soldier trying to hitch a ride. His act managed to get

Thuan to stop; then the other two came out from their hiding places and they arrested him. If the ruse hadn't worked, they would have just shot him as he drove by.

After I talked to him and explained everything I ordered my men to shoot him and carry his corpse to the hamlet that night. We attached a declaration to his shirt, informing people of his crimes and of his sentence. I'm sure that even if the villagers weren't happy about his death, they weren't unhappy either. We had gotten rid of a corrupt oppressor, and we had demonstrated to everybody our strength and effectiveness.

There were other situations that turned out differently. Another one I remember was a hamlet chief who had given us misleading information about the strength of a military post we were going to attack. Acting on his information our plan of attack was incorrect and I lost fifty men. Afterwards I ordered the hamlet chief to be killed, but the execution team only succeeded in wounding him in the legs. Before we could make another attempt we found out that the post had been reinforced just a few days before our attack and that the hamlet chief probably hadn't known about it. So I called off the execution.

In my position I had to play the role of a political cadre and also be a guerrilla chief. It was a very hard life. I needed to encourage my men and set an example every day.

The hardest mission I set for myself was preparing the battlefield for an attack on the Bao Binh army post. Before any attack on a post, we tried to get a detailed plan of the defenses and the inside layout—where the bunkers were, the heavy weapons positions, the barracks, how many soldiers there were, and so on. Sometimes we could get this information from an agent or informer inside the post, but sometimes we had to get it ourselves. Usually it was a sapper's job to penetrate into the post, make a mental map of it, then come back and build a sand table model for us to study. For the attack on Bao Binh post I decided to do it myself, to set an example, and also so I would know what the job was like.

When I went in, I had three gunners supporting me outside. I had to camouflage my body and crawl through the cleared area inch by inch, constantly checking for mines. When I got to the barbed wire fences, I had to lift up the bottom line without breaking it, so the next day there would be no trace of anyone going through. I had to watch everything and remember everything so I could crawl back exactly the way I came in. And I had to do everything while I was more frightened than I had ever been in my life. No one could do this kind of mission without wetting his pants.

The one part of my life that wasn't difficult in 1967 was getting married. My wife was a nurse who was part of the village social welfare network. She had also been in prison for many years—in fact she had been one of the Con O strikers in the mid-fifties, when she was very young. So she had been part of my network then too. Of course I hadn't known her at that time.

When we got married I was already thirty-six. My superiors were worried about my situation—with a cadre my age who was still single, there was too much risk of an illegal relationship that could ruin my career. So they encouraged me, and at the same time they encouraged my wife. With all the encouragement, finally, we decided to do it.

THE Tet Offensive brought on the worst time of the war. Long Khanh was not a key area, and my villages certainly weren't, so the offensive didn't have as much immediate effect on us as it had elsewhere. But we still were prepared for it. The slogan was "Each One Ready to Die to Save the Country!" We knew about the "General Uprising," and I firmly believed we'd win. But afterwards the effects were terrible.

First of all, casualties everywhere were very, very high, and the spirit of the soldiers dropped to a low point. Secondly, afterwards the enemy changed over to what we called the "two-pincer strategy." They began to reoccupy posts they had abandoned before—they mostly let the ARVN do that. Then they began to send out guerrilla forces to ambush us in the jungle. That was the second pincer. After a while there was nowhere to turn. I would send units out on supply missions and they would disappear. People would be killed while they were cooking or going for water. Sometimes I could find out what happened to them, sometimes I couldn't.

During the period 1968–70, I was ambushed eleven times and wounded twice. It seemed the enemy had learned a lot about how to fight in the jungle. The Australians were especially good, but the Americans came as close to getting me as anybody.

Early in 1970 I was ambushed along with eight others in a jungle clearing. The nine of us were walking single file across a vegetable field that the villagers had carved out of the jungle, on our way from one hamlet to another. It was a cloudy night. The moon was partially covered over and no one could see much. I knew I should have taken the line around the clearing, keeping to the jungle, but I was in too much of a hurry. Toward the middle of the clearing there was a clump of banana trees. Just as I pulled even with them, I realized there were some shapes in the trees. They saw me at exactly the same instant, and instinctively I flattened to the ground.

Just at that moment claymore mines fired off on the path behind me, huge explosions. The instant they stopped I crawled back along the path right over where they had gone off. As I crawled I felt some of the bodies, then squirmed off at a right angle toward the jungle. Firing was going on all around. At least two bullets hit my backpack before I got to the tree line. I had to leave the bodies there in the field. I kept thinking how demoralizing it would be for the peasants when they came out in the morning.

So many were killed in 1969 and 1970. There was no way we could stand up to the Americans. Every time they came in force we ran from them. Then when they turned back, we'd follow them. We practically lived on top of them, so they couldn't hit us with artillery and air strikes. During those years I had to reorganize my unit three times. Twice, the entire unit was killed. Each time I reorganized, the numbers were smaller. It was almost impossible to get new recruits.

Worse than the Americans were the Australians. The Americans' style was to hit us, then call for planes and artillery. Our response was to break contact and disappear if we could, but if we couldn't we'd move up right next to them so the planes couldn't get at us. The Australians were more patient than the Americans, better guerrilla fighters, better at ambushes. They liked to stay with us instead of calling in the planes. We were more afraid of their style.

Finally I had only a dozen men left in my third unit. By that time the situation was so bad in all the local units that the decision was made to consolidate our forces in Long Khanh district T-4 with the forces in T-7. The T-4 forces gathered to make the move, six hundred men. We were about three or four kilometers [two to two and a half miles] from Binh Phu when we were hit. They opened up on both ends of the column, then hit us with air strike after air strike. It was a slaughter. There was no place to run, except to try and disappear in the jungle. I was wounded in the side, but I ripped my shirt off and pressed it into the wound to stop the bleeding. Somehow I kept crawling. Four others came out with me. All of them were wounded, though not as badly as I was.

When we finally got clear of the battle area we collapsed from exhaustion. We didn't have any food or water with us. We were sure the Australians were all around. For the next few days we lived on bananas while we tried to figure out how to hook up with T-7.

The trek through the jungle could have been a trek through hell. We drank groundwater and ate leaves and green bananas. And when we got there, conditions in T-7 were no different from conditions in T-4. Food was still an insoluble problem. Long Khanh didn't grow rice, only fruit, so basic rice supplies had to be brought in from a distance, mainly from the storage areas in Cuc R or along the Mekong River in Cambodia. At one point we were eating a bowl of rice every two days. The rest of the diet was manioc and jungle fruit. It was no wonder that a lot of guerrillas began to go over to the other side, into the *Chieu Hoi*. [The *Chieu Hoi* (Open Arms) program was an amnesty plan for Vietcong who gave themselves up to the government. Over the term of its existence, it took in more than 250,000 enemy soldiers.]

There's no doubt that 1969 was the worst year we faced, at least the worst year I faced. There was no food, no future—nothing bright. But 1969 was also the time I was happiest. I destroyed several American tanks from the "Flying Horses" tank battalion that was stationed in Suoi Ram. I did it with pressure mines that our bombmakers made from unexploded American bombs. Each mine had seven kilos [fifteen pounds] of TNT. I was given an award as a champion tank killer.

The year 1969 was also the period when the true heroism of the peasants showed itself. Although we were isolated from the villagers, many of them risked their lives to get food to us. They devised all sorts of ingenious ways to get rice through the government checkpoints. Their feeling for us was one of the things that gave me courage to go on.

Another thing was the conviction the Americans couldn't last. In 1969 they began to pull out some of their troops. We believed that eventually they would have to withdraw altogether. We knew that even though we faced tremendous difficulties, so did they. They had terrible problems, especially at home. We didn't think their government could stand it in the long run. That gave me heart.

One of the things that demoralized a lot of guerrillas were the B-52 attacks. The fear these attacks caused was terrible. People pissed and shat in their pants. You would see them come out of their bunkers shaking so badly it looked as if they had gone crazy. The B-52s always came in groups of three. They dropped two different kinds of bombs. We called one *bomb dia*, "lake bomb," and the other *bomb bi*, "gravel bomb." Lake bombs were so powerful they blew gigantic ten-meter-deep craters in the ground, like a small lake. The other kind, *bomb bi*, was filled with steel ball bearings. *Bomb bi* hits would mow down the jungle. They'd leave a swath clear enough to drive a jeep through.

After a bomb raid you'd think that all the guerrillas would be dead, but that wasn't so. I was hit by four B-52 attacks, in Tay Ninh and Long Khanh. Each time COSVN alerted us about an hour beforehand. We were never caught aboveground. No one was hurt in any of the attacks I experienced. But other times there were a lot of casualties. Even when there weren't direct hits, the pressure from the explosions would kill people in their bunkers. For some reason, men were killed more easily by concussions than women. Female guerrillas would often survive attacks that killed men who were in the same bunkers. We didn't know why, but we theorized that men's testicles were especially vulnerable to pressure. Whatever the reason, we learned to make bunkers with two openings instead of one, so that the pressure inside would be dissipated—T-shaped, with the two entrances on either side of the top of the T.

Toward the end of 1970 things began to get better. We started gaining more control. I could feel the optimism starting to return. One of the ways you could tell this was that the peasants felt more comfortable about contacting us and giving us support. They didn't have to be heroes to do that anymore, especially after 1971. ARVN was taking over from the Americans at that time. There was a test of "Vietnamization" in southern Laos on Route 9 and ARVN lost a lot of men. [The South Vietnamese army launched an attack on the Ho Chi Minh Trail in southern Laos on February 8, 1971. They were stopped short of their objectives by Vietcong and North Vietnamese troops and pushed back into Vietnam with heavy losses. It was the first time the ARVN had operated without American advisers.] After that we felt easier.

The supply situation also got a lot better. I was able to make an arrangement with lumbering people who were coming into Long Khanh to harvest timber. I allowed them to do whatever they wanted in exchange for rice. They bribed everyone in sight. They even made direct arrangements with the ARVN commissariat. There were never any searches, and I was able to supply the North Vietnamese main forces in my area as well as my own people.

Other supplies were more available, too, partly because the money situation was better. Several times I was ordered to escort cash shipments from Cuc R to Long Khanh. Big 100 kilo rice bags stuffed with dollars. From there my messengers took it into Saigon where the dollars were exchanged for piasters and distributed to our agents to buy food and medical supplies, and to pay bribes.

One result of our better conditions was that in 1972 I brought my wife out to visit me. We had been married in 1967 and in 1968 we had our first child, born in Bao Binh village. But by 1969 our situation was so bad that I had sent her and the baby back to Saigon to live with my brother. I had arranged to get all the right identity papers for her and she was living a normal life in Saigon. She worked as a nurse in Quang Dong hospital. She worked there right up to 1975. But from 1972 on she came out on regular visits to Bao Binh. So by the end of the war I had three children, a boy and two girls.

The only major trouble I had in Bao Binh after 1971 was during the *Gianh Dan Gianh Dat* [land and people campaign] when we struggled with the Saigon troops over the village while the Paris Peace Conference was going on. Everyone knew there was going to be a cease-fire, so both sides were trying to get control of as much territory as they could. At one point we were holding about half the village, and the fight was going back and forth. [A "village" in Vietnam is usually spread out over a large area and may consist of several different hamlets.] Then we were hit by planes. The air attacks were so severe that we were forced to withdraw. All the villagers on our side either had to run away or accept ARVN control.

But that was a temporary setback. Afterwards Long Khanh wasn't especially active, in 1973 and '74. It wasn't one of the main battle areas. Then during the spring of 1975 I was ordered to Vung Tau to organize the ethnic Chinese there and to help prepare the city for liberation. [Vung Tau is a coastal fishing area south of Long Khanh.] From the liberated area of Long Khanh I went by foot to the Saigon River. There I joined a flood of refugees from the center of the country who were trying to get to the ocean. Flotillas of sampans were heading down the river. It was the easiest thing in the world to merge into the crowds. There were no controls or checks, nothing to stop anyone who wanted to infiltrate along with the refugees.

Early in the morning I arrived on the beach at Vung Tau and met my contact right on schedule. The recognition signal was the rolled-up sleeves of her black pajamas—no country woman ever rolled up her sleeves. She turned me over to another guide who led me to a house in Xom Ca, a fishing hamlet that was part of Vung Tau. There I waited for developments, meeting with people and preparing banderoles, signs, and leaflets for the moment when we were ready to take over the city. We were filled with happiness and excitement over what was happening, but we didn't relax a moment in our preparations. The slogan we used was Ho Chi Minh's saying, "The nearer the victory, the greater the danger!" We applied this strategy right to the end. It was true about the danger. There was no law at that time—nothing but chaos, and anyone could get killed.

After Duong Van Minh [last president of South Vietnam] ordered the surrender on April 30th, I was there to meet the first military commander who came in to officially liberate the city.

Trinh Duc's story continues on page 197.

LE THI DAU (TRINH DUC'S WIFE): *Vietcong Nurse*

I JOINED THE REVOLUTION WHEN I WAS FIFTEEN. MY MOTHER HATED the idea. She told me to think about marriage, think about having a family. I told her I had other things to do. I did, too. Of course I ended up in prison. They arrested me at the Con O factory when I was sixteen. I was in prison for six years, five prisons in six years—Chi Hoa, Catinat, Giadinh, Phu Lam, Phu Loi. Phu Loi was the worst—so little food, no water even to wash yourself.

When I got out I went to school to become a nurse. After that I worked in Saigon for a while. Then I left for the jungle, to be trained at COSVN. This was at the end of 1965 or the beginning of 1966. My first assignment after COSVN was as a nurse in Bao Binh village. I was told that our first mission was to win the people's sympathy. If we helped them as much as we could we would win them over. After we won them over, they would help us.

When I got to Bao Binh I opened up a little infirmary, myself and two assistants from the village. One of the problems at first was that the people were illiterate. They weren't used to Western medicine at all. They relied mostly on prayers and superstitions, so we had to educate them. I took care of minor health problems, taught basic hygiene, baby care, things like that.

I was friendly with almost all the women I treated. Since I was constantly traveling from hamlet to hamlet I didn't get to make many very close friends, but I did have some. The ones who had husbands in the main force were under terrible stress. ["Main force" refers to regularly constituted guerrilla forces that operated independently. Their opposite numbers were the "local forces," guerrillas who lived in their villages and operated as Vietcong primarily at night.] They never knew if their husbands were dead or alive. The Party didn't inform them, and they had to live with the constant uncertainty.

Many of these women suffered from chronic depression. Mostly they kept it to themselves. But my good friends would talk to me about it. I couldn't really do anything to comfort or console them—just let them talk, give them sympathy and someone whom they could talk to freely about what they were going through.

When I had my first child, my husband sent me back to Saigon to live with his brother. He thought it would be better not to try to raise the child in the village, that it was too dangerous. But I was unhappy about leaving. I felt a terrible guilt about going back to safety myself and leaving my friends. But of course my husband sent me, so I had to go.

The war was horrible. But it excited me too. I liked the adrenaline. I had originally joined the revolution when I was young because it was exciting, interesting. It gave me something to do that was out of the ordinary.

NAM DUC MAO

As far as war deaths went, they affected Northern women very much as they did those in South Vietnam's liberated areas.

NAM DUC MAO: *Messengers of Death*

MY HUSBAND WAS A FISHERMAN. HE DIDN'T WANT TO GO INTO THE army because he was afraid of dying in the South. But since he was an ethnic Chinese, he didn't have to go.

Starting in 1968, they began sending men from our village to the South. If someone didn't want to go, he had his rations cut off. My sister's husband went. In 1970 my mother found out that he had been killed. My mother was an officer of the court, so she found out through friends of hers in the government. She told me, but neither of us was able to tell my sister. It was too risky. Nobody was allowed to talk about deaths or rumors of deaths, not until the official death notification came from the army. Up until then, if you talked about things like this it was considered anti-state, you were undermining people's morale. You would get into trouble or be sent to jail.

But it was very hard, because sometimes the wives didn't hear officially for years. But news would come indirectly that somebody's husband or son had been killed. It would come from messages sent by friends who were in the army or by other soldiers from the village, or in some other way. So sometimes a woman knew that her husband was dead, but she couldn't mourn out loud or she and the rest of her family would be in trouble with the police.

That's why my mother and I couldn't tell my sister. But I tried to keep her from hoping that he would come back. I especially wanted her to move out of her parents-in-law's house. I tried to persuade her to leave her husband's family and to live as if her husband were dead, even if she didn't know for sure that he was.

But I wasn't successful. My sister told me, "I'll wait for my husband to come home." I'd say, "It could be a terribly long time."

HAN VI

MUSICOLOGIST, CULTURAL CADRE

He showed me a picture of himself at the age of twenty-four. Slim good looks, with the intense eyes of a born performer and a nonchalant air that must have been deadly to the opposite sex. He was, in his own words, "a free spirit," trekking through almost all of South Vietnam as a propaganda and culture cadre during the French war.

Later he studied music at the Shanghai Conservatory, where he met his wife. Looking at their diplomas I saw that hers had the seal of the conservatory and the four smaller seals of the conservatory's directors. His had only the large conservatory seal. He had graduated two years after she did. By that time, the Cultural Revolution had consigned the four directors to oblivion. That was one of the experiences that started Han Vi thinking.

HAN VI: *A Single Will*

AFTER I LEFT SOUTH VIETNAM FOR THE NORTH, I WAS TRANSFERRED from my propaganda unit into a regular army outfit, as a political cadre. Like all the other Southerners, I was evaluated for class background and revolutionary credentials. I ended up with four different classifications: intellectual, Southerner, wounded veteran, and foreigner (because of my Chinese origin). After a few months of learning how to march, drill, stand at attention, and salute everybody in sight, I was sick of it.

I had spent the entire French war without doing any of these things. Basically I was a free spirit. I loved the propaganda work—living in the countryside, putting on performances, getting to know people, motivating them—that kind of thing. But the regular army life was something else entirely. Eventually I really did get sick, and they sent me to a rest and recuperation area.

I was there when the land reform movement started. Like everyone else, I had to analyze the way my thinking had developed, especially how it had been influenced by my class background. It turned out that my services over the past eight years weren't enough. First of all, my family was held against me. My father was a traditional doctor who also owned a kind of pharmacy for Chinese medicines. So I was from the merchant class. Before, no one knew who came from what class, but now we had to be organized by background before we could take another step. None of us was happy about it, but what could you do?

While this was going on, the village land reform had also started. All the *bo dois* [soldiers] were sent to live with poor peasants in the village. I was staying with a fifty-year-old widow and her son and daughter. At the same time we were having our meetings, the whole village was being mobilized.

To do this, the Party sent in a team of land reform cadres. They had a system for putting a village through land reform. A series of steps. The first step started with the land reform cadres moving into the cottages of the very poorest peasants. They made friends with these people, then they set up meetings with other poor people. At the meetings they'd have people tell their stories, talk about how badly they lived. They'd get them worked up and excited about how poor they were, and they'd explain to them about why they were so poor. They molded these people—the bottom proletariat—into the driving force in the land reform. They turned them into the strongest element in the village.

The next step was to classify the entire village—the poor peasants did this for them. There were different definitions they used for the classification. For example, a "landlord" was anyone who didn't work himself but who hired someone else to work for him. Anyone who owned more than the average share of land was also called a landlord. "Rich peasants" were those who worked the land themselves but also hired others to work for them. "Middle peasants" were those who rented land and had their own means to farm it—their own buffalo or ox, and farming implements. They owned their own means of production. The middle peasants consisted of two groups, upper and lower. Upper-middle peasants produced enough for themselves to live on and a surplus in addition. Lower-middle peasants produced just enough to survive, or not enough, so that they were always in debt.

Once the village was classified, the lower-middle peasants were included with the poor peasants—the real proletariat. These people lived a life of utter poverty. Their children were forced to work to help pay off their parents' debts. It wasn't unusual for the poorest peasants to give their children to the landlords or to have to sell them off. The majority of the peasants in the village lived their whole lives in this kind of debt.

So the second step was classifying the village. Once that was done, the land reform cadres formally took over the village administration. They had the authority to fire the Party chief. They kicked him out and they kicked out the whole Party administrative structure. Temporarily, they held all the power. The whole right to govern was in the hands of the land reform team. Then they were ready for the last step—the denunciations.

When they were ready, they gathered all the poor and lower-middle peasants together in a mass outdoor meeting. The rest of the village—the upper-middle and rich—were confined to their homes. The land reform cadres stood behind a table and told the people about the government's policy of punishment and land redistribution. Then some of the people began coming up to the front—the ones who had the worst stories. As they told them, people were crying and getting really warmed up. Some of them were shouting, "Down with the landlords!"

Then the cadres brought in the richest landlord. He was standing at the front with his head down. People walked up to him, accusing him and screaming at him. They forced him to admit to every crime. Some woman accused him of rape. He said, No, he didn't rape her. The crowd exploded in anger—everyone did. Even his relatives had to parade up to denounce him.

When all of the denouncing was over, the cadres evaluated who were the worst landlords and they sentenced them to death. They had a quota they had to fill. Even some Party members suffered, people who were revolutionaries but who came from the upper classes. The woman I was living with appeared to be quite pleased by it all. All the poor peasants were happy with the land reform—at least at first when land was distributed to them. Later when they were forced into collectives they weren't happy at all.

In our own army meetings it wasn't the same as the villagers' land reform. The main thing was that we had to confess our own errors. My problem here was that in my opinion, my behavior had been beyond reproach. I had always been completely dedicated to the revolution. When we were operating in the highlands among the Montagnard I had even filed down my teeth and learned to live in their way. Of course everybody else in my propaganda unit had done it too. But the point was that I couldn't think of anything about my conduct over eight years of making revolution that I could criticize.

On the other hand, they were taking this self-criticism business so seriously that I knew I would have to say something. I was afraid of being trapped somehow, and I wanted to demonstrate my sincerity and honesty. So I decided to confess my love affairs.

While I was wandering all over the South—from 1946 to 1954—I had met many girls. I had fallen in love with some of them, and some of them had fallen in love with me. I was a young man, a singer and musician, so it was a completely natural thing. I had never thought about any of these affairs in terms of the revolution. But now I realized that they could—from one perspective—be considered antirevolutionary. They certainly demonstrated that I wasn't thinking about the struggle 100 percent of the time. And from a revolutionary point of view, they showed that I had a "decadent" way of living.

Of course none of that was exactly earthshaking, especially when you saw it in the context of everything I had done, so it looked like the perfect thing to confess. It showed off my sincerity and my determination to improve. And it wasn't likely to get me into too much trouble. So I drew up a complete list of all the girls I had slept with. Then when they started badgering me to tell them the whole truth, I added quite a few more, for good effect. The entire list came to one hundred and eight names.

But what I saw as relatively trivial, the interrogators jumped on. Once you mention what you see in yourself as wrong, they use that as the basis for accusation after accusation. Many of my girlfriends had come from landlord families. So they attacked my class way of thinking. My own family was from the "exploiting classes" and here was a new and vicious example of my antirevolutionary, bourgeois habits.

When it was all over, I wasn't feeling well. One afternoon—I remember it very clearly—I was playing volleyball when they called me into the office. The division commander and a political officer were there. They announced that I was being expelled from the Party. They said the decision was based on the views I had expressed in self-criticism and in the land reform sessions. My views on land reform were particularly deficient.

I had to leave all my army clothes behind and all my mementoes from the French war. All I was allowed to take was the pair of shorts I was wearing. A bit later I learned that I wasn't alone; people from all the regiments had been arrested. It was a big purge. A few had committed suicide. Others were in jail.

Instead of putting me in jail they sent me to a little village in Hoang Hoa district to work with the peasants. I was given a small plot of land to cultivate and a cow to take care of. I didn't mind so much. The peasants were friendly to me. I also did a lot of thinking about the Party. I had been sent to the countryside for rehabilitation, so I figured that if I worked well enough, after a while I could begin a campaign to get myself reinstated. I worked like hell for six months. Then I wrote a letter directly to Ho Chi Minh.

In the letter I told Ho about my contribution to the revolution. I gave him my whole résumé, explained that I was a Chinese who had come to Vietnam to follow the spirit of the Vietnamese Revolution. I told him how I had sacrificed myself during the French war and how I had been admitted to the Party in 1946. I told him that through all the years when I was fighting nobody had ever asked me anything about my class background. Why was it that after our victory, they began to be so upset about it? In conclusion, I asked Ho to do one of four things with me. The Party could send me back to the South, they could send me to China, they could let the ICC decide on my case [the International Control Commission was the three-nation body established to supervise the implementation of the Geneva Agreements], or they could restore my honor—accept me back and compensate me for my sacrifice and humiliation.

After fifteen days I received a short letter over Uncle Ho's signature. It said simply: "I have read your letter. I know of your situation. I hope you will persevere in your tasks." Two weeks after that I was released and sent back to the army. The commander welcomed me back with a profuse apology. They gave me back everything they had confiscated. And they gave me the salary they hadn't paid me for half a year. I was told that my case had been a mistake committed by the Party. They hoped I would understand and continue to be a loyal Party member.

After they took me back they assigned me to be the political officer in the traditional orchestra for Zone 5. Of the hundred people in the orchestra, only ten were Party members, and being the political cadre put me in one of the top positions. My job was mainly to act as an adviser and friend to the orchestra members, to help them through whatever problems they might be having. I was also under pressure to be a model of proper behavior and to always volunteer first if there was some difficult or unpleasant job that had to be done. That was what a Party member had to do.

I liked that job, and I did it well. I also didn't take any chances. During the "Hundred Flowers" campaign, when they asked cultural cadres to freely criticize the government, I kept quiet. At one of the meetings I drew a little cartoon for my friend sitting next to me—a man's face in profile, with a padlock through his lips. I was saying that we'd better shut up. After the campaign was over, a lot of people suffered for the criticisms they had made when things were supposedly open. Even nationally known figures, party members. The atmosphere then was terrible. Many artists went to jail for what they had said. Other people humbled themselves or denounced friends to keep their positions. But I hadn't said a thing. So I just kept working at my job, up until 1960.

In 1960 I was sent to China to study at the Shanghai Conservatory. I was there until 1966. Then when I came back, I was appointed political officer for the Vietnamese School of Music [North Vietnam's leading music institute, later renamed the Vietnamese Conservatory of Music]. My main responsibility was to act as censor for all the music that was being written. I was the one who decided whether or not a composition was fit for public consumption, if it could be broadcast on the radio for example.

I was supposed to ban anything that showed Western influence, even some of the Russians—Stravinsky, for example. We couldn't teach Stravinsky because he had gone to live in the United States. Debussy? Debussy was considered a realist.

The compositions that were acceptable were the ones that conformed to the official structure: introduction; situation; optimistic, upbeat conclusion. The motivating impulse was always supposed to be the "class struggle." But real music has to have a natural, liberal character. In my own work I struggled to embody my outlook, my individuality—within the prescribed forms. I cultivated the art of writing music that appeared acceptable, but in subtle ways gave expression to feelings that didn't conform. These kinds of problems could only be discussed with my closest friends. As far as the students went, I presented the straight Party line.

Living with this kind of ambiguity depressed me more and more. If you were a Party member, you were always at war with yourself—your human feelings versus your duty to the Party.

This feeling—that my human nature was at war with my duty—even started me toward developing an aesthetic that I eventually taught in my classes. At least I taught part of it. I had spent decades as a Vietnamese, but I was also Chinese. My foreigner's perception of the Vietnamese was that they are a sentimental people, much more than the Chinese are. They are a people of great feeling and personal warmth. They put a high value on trust and loyalty and other personal attachments. The sentimentality comes through in their traditional music, which also shows great flexibility and variation and subtlety. Reconciling extremes, maintaining balance, emphasizing nuances—these Vietnamese personal traits also characterize the way they express themselves artistically. All of this runs in direct contradiction to the orthodox Party mentality, which demands rigidity and impersonal loyalty above everything. So I came to the conclusion that my own feeling of being torn between the Party and my humanity wasn't just personal. It was something the entire culture was struggling with.

As far as the war went, it didn't affect me personally very much. I just hoped it would end. I thought that eventually there would have to be a negotiated settlement. I thought that especially after 1970 when Nixon went to visit China.

Of course it wasn't possible to just ignore the war. We had to move the conservatory to Bac Giang, about twenty miles outside Hanoi, because of the bombing. We held practice sessions in different houses and we had to find places for the big classes. We even built a large bunker that became our main classroom. From time to time we would see bombing, but we ourselves were only hit once. I saw it when it happened. I saw the plane come down and I saw the bomb hit the pagoda that was another place we used as a classroom. Seven Laotian students were killed. After that almost all the rest of the Laotians wanted to go home. In 1969 we moved back to Hanoi, but in 1972 we had to go back to the countryside, to Phu Hoai.

Up to then, most of the conservatory students weren't too worried. They had their exemptions. But later on in the war the students in general began to get very scared. That was especially true after the 1972 bombings. They scared everybody.

Of course the government propaganda tried to motivate everybody to believe in victory. All along they had done what they could to keep morale high. One of the devices was to send the wounded soldiers to separate areas and isolate them. These soldiers were a real threat. They had sacrificed a lot, and they couldn't see that it had been for anything. They talked a lot against the government. They had big mouths that they weren't afraid to use. One of the things they were angriest about was that the university kids and the children of high cadres didn't have to go. So they were kept in special camps.

You see, the art of propaganda during the war was to paint the society as having a single will. There we always thought, not about the truth, but about the appearance of truth, and about how to manufacture it, how to stimulate patriotism.

Of course that was exactly what I had spent the first war doing as a propaganda cadre—stimulating patriotism and exciting hatred for the enemy. It was easy to do because the people relied on us. Out in the countryside we were their only source. Sometimes we would have to invent things. For example, if we had lost a battle we would say that we had won, and we would show off all the arms we had captured. We had a supply of previously captured arms for just these situations.

I did this kind of thing regularly, and with a good will too. If I had told the truth all the time, the people would have been disillusioned. Our purpose was to defeat the enemy. Any means to doing that were okay. Any dishonesty was allowable if it was for the benefit of the people. That's not contrary to the conscience of a revolutionary. I wasn't making propaganda for my own benefit. Had I done *that*, I would have felt guilty about it. But the crimes of the French were horrendous. They had mutilated the country. It was okay to do anything at all to them. For the Hanoi government, the American war was exactly the same. Anything at all was all right if it motivated the people and kept their morale up.

As far as I was concerned, the South Vietnamese regime really was just a continuation of colonialism. But I felt a lot of ambivalence about the Americans, and so did many of my friends. I hated their invasion of the South. But I had a lot of admiration for their standard of living, and for their history. There wasn't any colonialism in their history. As far as China went, I wasn't thrilled by what I had seen of it under Mao. And I couldn't see much to like about the Russians either. So as the war progressed I found myself in a confused state of mind about a lot of things.

MY real disillusionment with the war began to grow because of the conflict between China and the USSR. That wasn't possible for me to ignore. It brought too many problems.

After Ho Chi Minh died [September 1969] there were some signs of anti-Chinese feeling. I put them out of my mind, tried to suppress it. Tension between the ethnic Chinese and the government began in 1972. At least that was the year the campaign began. It was done covertly at first, disguised as an opportunity for certain groups of cadres to retire early. Anyone sixty or older was included—that meant all of them who were trained or heavily influenced by the Chinese. After the Paris Peace Agreement [January 27, 1973] they allowed people fifty-four and older to retire. The public rationale was to give them more time to enjoy themselves. Those with medals and honors, they could retire at fifty-two. Everybody had medals and honors.

I understood all this for what it was. Most people didn't know. I knew. I knew that Hoang Van Hoan [the leading pro-China voice in North Vietnam's politburo] had lost his power. He was no longer an effective counterbalance to the pro-Soviet faction in the politburo—Le Duan, Le Duc Tho, and Nguyen Co Thac. As I saw it, the pro-Soviet group was submerging the pro-Chinese and also people like Vo Nguyen Giap [minister of defense] and Truong Chinh [the leading politburo theoretician] who wanted to steer a middle course between China and the USSR, as Ho Chi Minh had done. By 1975 they were eliminating pro-Chinese elements from the Central Committee, using the pretext that room had to be made for Southerners.

It was clear as day what was happening. At the conservatory they began cutting the ground out from under me. First I lost my position as censor. Then I lost the big, prestigious courses I had been teaching. I was limited to scholarly activities—research—along with a course or two on traditional music. When China attacked Vietnam in February 1979, my wife and I wept. We knew it was the end. One night as we were eating dinner, a public security officer came to our house and said, "Now it's time for you to leave." We packed our most precious things into our suitcases and took our three children. Then we left.

HOANG HUU QUYNH

The future engineer and school administrator witnessed North Vietnam's land reform when he was ten years old.

HOANG HUU QUYNH: *Blood Debt*

THAT DAY THOUSANDS OF PEOPLE GATHERED ON THE VILLAGE SOCCER field, not only from Lam Son, but from all the villages around. The children were dressed in white shirts and blue shorts. They had red scarves and tambourines. There was a jungle of flags and banderoles painted with slogans.

Mr. Thuoc, one of the landlords, had been arrested a few days before. Some soldiers brought him up to the dais in front of the crowd, carrying him tied up like a pig. When they got near the dais one of them put down his end and they dragged him along the ground. Then his granddaughter came up to denounce him. She yelled that she wasn't his granddaughter and that he had killed his wife so that there wouldn't be any witnesses to his crimes. Every time she said something, he said, "Yes, yes."

I couldn't imagine such a thing happening, a granddaughter accusing her grandfather. I thought I would vomit. From time to time some *bo doi* in the crowd would yell, "Down with the landlord!" or "Down with the brutal reactionary!" Sometimes people shouted, "Blood debt paid by blood!" After an hour or so, they pushed Mr. Thuoc in front of the table to sign a paper.

The next day, the whole crowd gathered again. The judge read a statement saying that Mr. Thuoc was a brutal reactionary who had committed many blood debts against the peasants. He declared that the sentence for these crimes was death.

Immediately, a cadre standing behind Thuoc took a small towel and stuffed it in his mouth. The crowd shouted and rattled the tambourines. They shoved Mr. Thuoc in front of an open grave and tied him to a pole. Some *bo dois* stood about three meters in front of him. Then they shot him and he fell down, still tied to the pole. Then they kicked his body into the hole.

HUYNH LIEM

ARTIST

Stocky, with bunched muscles. He makes his living at a factory job in Connecticut. His real work is displayed on the walls and tables of the small apartment on the second floor of an old two-family house—paintings, lithographs, wood carvings. He opens a photo album, pointing with special pride to the plaster Buddhas he has made for various Buddhist temples.

HUYNH LIEM: *Life in the North*

I HAD WANTED TO BE AN ARTIST FOREVER. I HAD ALWAYS BEEN GOOD at it, at drawing and painting, always the first in my class. I enjoyed it so much. On weekends I would go out to the countryside to sketch. When I was seventeen I went to art school. It was 1954, the year of the Geneva Agreement. In my family we weren't political people at all. It never occurred to us to leave for the South.

In art school I studied every branch of art: drawing, painting, sculpture, design—everything. Here too I enjoyed it and did well. I was still decidedly nonpolitical. As one of the better students I was approached by the cadres about joining the Party. But I deflected them. I told them I wasn't progressive enough yet, that I needed time to improve myself. In fact I didn't want to have anything to do with it. It didn't seem very likely that the Southerners were going to march into Hanoi. And I wasn't particularly eager for the country to be united under the Northern government. So I just refused to think about it.

In 1962 I finished my studies and went out to my first job, as an exhibition display designer and painter. I can't say that I was happy; it wasn't exactly a creative situation. You did what you were told, painted what you were told—and most of it was propaganda. I felt as if I was squandering my talents.

But the army wasn't a problem. I was ethnic Chinese, and not many ethnic Chinese were being called up. There was even a lot of propaganda directed at us about how the Saigon regime was drafting Chinese, but our government wasn't. From what I could see, there was enthusiasm for the war at first. But by 1965 or so the situation had changed. In the city anyway, people wanted to stay out. In the countryside, you know, they weren't able to get out of it. But for a lot of the city boys it was a different story. There were different methods of avoiding the draft. You could take a job far away from your home and stay out of the hands of your local officials. Of course then you'd have to be careful about visiting home. Sometimes cadres could be bribed. Tobacco leaves were another favorite method. Chewing raw tobacco leaves sends your blood pressure straight up. If you did it before your induction physical you were a sure bet to fail.

But I didn't have to worry about any of this. What I had to worry about was making a living. I did a variety of jobs. Life was rough outside Hanoi where I was evacuated to after the American bombing started. When I got married and started having children, it got even rougher.

By 1972 we were back in Hanoi. I had a tiny photography shop that the local officials had let me set up. It just about kept us alive, and what income we did get from it was very unsteady. Sometimes I'd supplement what I was making by going on a black market run to Lang Son on the Chinese border. I made the contacts through my relatives up there. There were people who would get the goods through the border area. I would make arrangements to meet one of these guys and buy different kinds of things from him—wool and cigarettes were two good items. I would buy goods worth about twenty dong on the Chinese border and take them down to Thai Binh, about forty miles southeast of Hanoi, where I could sell them for a hundred and fifty dong. I could carry a maximum of about sixty kilos [a hundred and thirty pounds] on each trip. I traveled in trains, old buses, sometimes by bicycle. I learned how to avoid the control points. I wasn't scared. I thought, Our stomachs come first—I have to feed us all. So how could I be frightened?

MRS. HUYNH: I was scared to death while he was gone that he would be arrested or caught in the bombing. Once while he was away a whole section of Hanoi was destroyed by B-52s. I had five children at home at the time. What would I have done without him? As it was, I had to take care of the kids and help earn our living too by working in the photography shop.

We lived in a two-room apartment. Our running water came from a tap in the yard. The kitchen was shared by the four families that lived in the building. So was the two-hole outdoor toilet. As the war went on, that became a real horror. The holding tank was supposed to be emptied regularly by city workers, but by 1972 it just wasn't a priority anymore. Or maybe all the carriers had been sent to more important jobs. Sometimes the tank would go for three months without being emptied.

I'd usually get started at six in the morning. It was my job to buy the wood for the stove. I'd go down by bicycle to pick up our ration of sticks. Wash had to be done every day in the yard under the cold water tap. Clothes I either made or bought. In either case we were allotted four yards of cloth per person per year or its equivalent in storebought clothes.

Food was a preoccupation. There was never enough. After 1972 the ration was lowered to five kilos of rice and seven kilos of flour per month for each person. There was no meat, but often I could get some kind of vegetable to go with the rice. On occasion I'd be able to buy a little extra from the black market.

We lived on a subsistence level. None of it had to do with being ethnic Chinese, though. My husband is Chinese, but I am ethnic Vietnamese. There were never any problems, or any real feeling of difference. Both of our families were happy enough about our marriage. It wasn't until 1970 that a bad feeling began to creep into things. That's when the first anti-Chinese campaign began. Whispering campaigns were started against the Chinese. At soccer games, fights began to break out between Vietnamese and Chinese in the crowds. You could feel the animosity.

Personally, I had no hopes for the future. We were living at such a low level, and there was no way it could change, no way to escape from it. The only thing I hoped for was that my children would survive. That's all.

THE BOMBING

In the North it started on August 4, 1964, in retaliation for the Tonkin Gulf attacks, and kept on steadily until March 31, 1968, when Lyndon Johnson called a moratorium. Richard Nixon renewed the assault in response to North Vietnam's Spring Offensive of 1972. Then, in mid-December of that year, he unleashed twelve days of terror over Hanoi and Haiphong. The object was to get the North Vietnamese back to the Paris conference table.

The strategic and tactical results of the bombing were mixed. But there was no question about the psychological impact: fear among the soldiers, fear and hatred among civilians. A captured North Vietnamese sergeant talks about the reaction in Hanoi to civilian deaths caused by careless flyers. A Haiphong teenager describes what happened when a pilot whose plane was hit parachuted into his backyard. The other side of the coin is here, too. Air Force Commander Richard Stratton tells what it was like to have to parachute into the yard of someone you have just been bombing.

The North Vietnamese antiaircraft battery officer who speaks was captured himself. He may have been tempted to emphasize the negative for his interrogators. The Northern infantryman in Laos who helped capture a downed pilot wrote his account for Nhan Dan (The Party Daily). *Predictably, his memories of NVA performance against Americans have a more laudatory ring. It is likely that both accounts are essentially accurate.*

NGUYEN VAN MO, *Master Sergeant, NVA: Hanoi Under Attack*

THE PEOPLE IN NORTH VIETNAM HATED THE BOMBING. THEY WERE enraged about the air raids. In the beginning, the Americans carried out their attacks very carefully—the attacks on the Long Bien Bridge, for example, and the Gia Lam Airfield, and on Van Dien. We used to watch them, to see how accurate the bombers were, and to judge how good the pilots were at avoiding antiaircraft fire and rockets. We had to admit that during the early attacks they hit proper military targets and that their flying techniques were pretty good. If they hadn't been, our ground fire would have shot down a great number of them.

But later—and I didn't understand why—the Americans dropped bombs all over the place. The people in Hanoi had already gained a lot of confidence in the accuracy of the bombing, and large groups of them would gather to watch the attacks. At one point the pilots dropped a couple of beehive bombs on the Bach Mai and Hung Ky Street area, in the vicinity of the "Eighth of March" factory, and on Hue Street. These beehive bombs contained hundreds of little steel balls. A large number of civilians were unexpectedly killed. After that people began to hate the Americans. If the local authorities hadn't intervened, they would have beaten shot-down American pilots to death.

In my opinion, in the early days, the Americans didn't have any intention of bombing populated areas. Later, because the antiaircraft fire had gotten so heavy, the pilots had to escape themselves, and they dropped their bombs carelessly, without paying any attention to the lives of the people. They were afraid of dying, and they didn't think about the adverse political effects.

TRAN VAN TRUONG: *Bombing in Haiphong*

IN THE SUMMER OF 1967 I WAS FIFTEEN YEARS OLD. THERE HAD been a lot of bombing already, but by that time everyone was prepared for it. We had a bunker dug into the floor of the house underneath the heavy divan. It was an excavation about four feet deep in the dirt floor, with the opening next to the divan, which served as a roof. That was a common kind of arrangement. Some families even slept in their bunkers during the worst times. But we never did that, even though I lived in a dangerous area, less than a mile from the harbor.

All of the students had also gotten training in school about how to treat wounds. Every house had a supply of bandages, alcohol, and cotton for first aid.

There were a lot of casualties. Friends of mine were killed, especially by the *bi* bombs. That means "gravel" bombs, the kind that shoot out thousands of bearings when they explode. During the bombings I began to hate the Americans, really hate them. But I hadn't started out hating them. My family was classified "bourgeois." My father had been a small-scale merchant who bought and sold all kinds of goods. After the Communists took over it was very hard for him to make a living. Since I came from an unacceptable family background, I knew they wouldn't let me go to the university. So what kind of future would I have?

No one in my family liked the government. Of course you couldn't say anything to anyone about that. But inside the family we could be a little freer. I knew my father hated them. None of us would have minded at all if the Saigon army had invaded the North and liberated us from them. If the Americans were helping Saigon, then we thought that maybe they really would come someday.

But when the Americans started attacking Haiphong, I began to hate them. Before my mother got hurt in the bombing, in the summer of 1967, I was part of a crowd that captured one American pilot who was shot down. I saw the whole thing from the beginning. I was watching the planes attack and I saw plumes of white smoke streaming out of one of them. Then the parachute came open and he began to come down, almost as if it were coming right at me.

In fact he landed in the open area next to my house. I ran to see along with all the kids in the neighborhood. When I got around the house the pilot was standing up pulling the parachute in. While he was doing that some adults came up, including a couple of self-defense people who pointed their rifles at him. Everybody was gathering around him shouting. Some of the people tied his hands. Somebody took his pistol and somebody else took his watch. I was struggling to see everything. They took off his shoes, too. I don't remember if they told us in school, or where I had heard it, but it was common knowledge that Americans couldn't run without their shoes on.

People kept running up, and a lot of them were trying to tear up the parachute cloth, so they could take pieces of it home. While they were fighting over that, the kids began to throw clods of dirt and stones at the pilot. I don't know who started it. None of the adults were doing it, but all of us kids were. I knew it was prohibited, but I didn't care. I was trying to find good rocks so I could really hurt him.

After a little while the *bo dois* came and took the pilot to the district office. They yelled at us to stop throwing things, then they threatened us. So after that we stopped, and then we walked along behind them down to the district to see what would happen. But nothing did. They just took him inside and that was the last we saw. Later, one of the neighborhood women and two kids got a letter congratulating them for helping to capture the pilot.

That happened before my mother was hurt. I was in the house with one of my friends when we heard the roar of the planes. By that time it was too late. If you didn't hear a warning, but just heard the roar, you didn't have time to get into the bunker. We jumped into it just as the bombs began exploding all around. Then I heard my mother screaming. She had been in the back of the house and didn't have time to get to the bunker. I was so scared I couldn't think of what to do, but then I ran out to her.

By that time she had stopped screaming. She was sitting on the floor looking at the blood running all over her leg. I pulled her pants leg up and got the bandages and antiseptic while my friend ran to the Viet Tiep hospital to get my brother-in-law who was a doctor there. I cleaned the wound, then bandaged it, the way I had been taught in school. Later my brother-in-law came. He changed the dressing, but he said we didn't have to take my mother to the hospital. She had been hit by some of the "gravel" from a *bi* bomb. But it wasn't too bad. She was lucky.

THE CAPTURE OF COMMANDER RICHARD STRATTON

"I REMEMBER TRYING TO MANEUVER THE CHUTE. THERE WAS JUST one house down there and I was trying to land on the seaward side of it.

When the plane exploded, it looked like I could reach out and touch the sea. I was that close. I'm willing to bet I wasn't three miles from the water. A minute and a half by air from the water. I could have touched it. I could smell it.

"There was only one tree down there, too; one tree in a whole twelve-square-mile area and I landed in it. Not a mark on me. There were two persons waiting for me that I could see, a very old guy and a younger one probably anywhere from 18 to 22; the old guy, jeez, he was 102.

"Jesus Christ, the old guy had a gun that big. I could look right down the muzzle and see his teeth, look right into his belly button.

"The young guy had a machete. I got out of the chute sling; they didn't say anything and I didn't have anything to say. I was scared shit-less. They were scared shitless, too. All of us standing there scared shit-less.

". . . out of nowhere comes another one, a kid, and in an instant he had my watch. I still don't know how he got it off. The last I saw of him, he was hightailing it toward Hanoi, I guess.

"The kid with the machete stripped me with that knife: whoosh, whoosh—even the boots. Sliced all the laces and never marked the tongues. They piled up the clothing and I stood there in my skivvie shorts."

. . . the scene suddenly crowded with people: men, women, children came out of the ditches, out of the earth, out of nowhere, a curious brown gaggle of Vietnamese Lilliputians gazing in awe at a groggy American Gulliver. They kept their distance. Little talk. Just looks.

. . . By means unknown, word of the American spread quickly. By the time Stratton and his captors passed through a small hamlet not far from the scene of the crash, the crowd following had increased by perhaps a quarter to a third. Eyes found tongues and it was no longer a silent sea. It was loud and angry . . . an old man took off one of his sandals and threw it at Stratton. Then the other. It probably was his only pair. More sandals were flung, and lumps of dirt and angry words, and by the third hamlet Stratton and his captors were moving quickly, pushing and pulling each other through the ditches, over hillocks, along the paths. The crowd pursued and the air was filled with sandals and clods and words and stones and cooking pots, some of them complete with contents and hot off cooking fires. The barrage was so heavy many of the missiles missed their target and struck other Vietnamese. There were yells and thumps with hands and shaking fists. The crowd grew large and kept following.

NGUYEN VAN THANH, *Lieutenant, NVA:*
Antiaircraft Battery

THE WORST DAY FOR MY UNIT WAS AUGUST 19, 1968. I WAS COM-
manding a battery that was providing air defense for a supply area. We
had fifty-two men on duty. At 0900 we were attacked by F-4Hs and F-
105s. By the time it was over forty of my battery personnel were dead,
including two platoon leaders and the company executive officer. The
political officer and I were both wounded and three of our four guns were
knocked out.

My battery had been deployed right at the center of the attack and we
had taken all the fire. The 26th Battery, which was on one of my flanks,
had seven killed. The 38th Battery was at my rear. They had one killed
and three wounded. The 27th off to the east took five wounded.

The guys commanding these batteries had been playing tricks. In principle, the moment Battalion gave the orders, we were all supposed to
open fire at the same time. But the other companies had withheld their
fire for a couple of seconds. With that kind of delay, the target might
have been out of sight. If you delayed just one or two seconds, you could
conceal your position. The unit that opened fire first would be pin-
pointed. Of course the other units would be identified as well, but they
wouldn't be considered the main objectives. So it was my battery that
was identified, and we got all the bombing and shelling.

I complained about this to the battalion officers, but all I got out of it
was a reprimand for "lack of vigilance in leadership." I was lucky I wasn't
subjected to disciplinary action. Battalion didn't realize what was going
on. So from then on I used the same tricks myself.

VAN ANH, *NVA Soldier: Capturing an American Pilot*

IN JUNE 1964 FLEETS OF AMERICAN JET PLANES STARTED APPEARING
in the Laotian skies. Often they'd come twice a day, at about nine in the
morning and then at three in the afternoon. They seemed like tiny arrows, white against the blue sky. Behind them they left a white line of
smoke and a jet sound that excited the curiosity of people like us who
had lived for a long time in the jungle and had never seen any jets before.

Word was passed around that these jets didn't actually bomb, they only
observed. We believed that, and many of us were less than prudent.
Sometimes we came out of our huts in white shirts to watch them fly by.
It was exciting to watch and safe enough. But if the older T-28s came

close we hid. We were located on a mountain, and we cleared an area for an observation post high enough to observe the planes when they appeared. At that time our unit had no antiaircraft guns. With our ordinary weapons, we could hit a plane only if it flew nearby and low to the ground.

One day, at noon, we heard the sound of antiaircraft fire from Xieng Khoang, a nearby town. The sound alarmed us, and we positioned all the guns in that direction. This time we didn't just watch. Suddenly an F-101 jet appeared, very low. We didn't even hear its sound before it was on us. We were all shooting, without stop. Then the plane was on fire and we saw something come out of it. Somebody said, "Look, two parachutes!" But we saw only one pilot; the other thing seemed to be his chair.

The pilot came down into the jungle about three kilometers [two miles] away. We ran, struggling against time to get to the place where he fell before his comrades could get to him. About fifteen minutes after he parachuted, the sky was full of jets, helicopters, and an L-19 spotter plane. We climbed the mountain, past the waterfall while they circled around, looking for him in the wrong place. It took us almost six hours to find and capture him, but by then the sky had clouded over, and the planes couldn't see anything underneath.

At six-thirty in the evening, we listened to BBC radio reporting the loss of the jet and that bad weather had prevented rescuers from finding the pilot. It said that rescue efforts would begin again the next morning. At 9 P.M. Voice of America broadcast the same news. None of them knew that the pilot was in our hands.

The pilot's belongings consisted of a small flare gun to signal searchers, a flashlight that gave off a very strong line of light that could signal in the dark, and a life jacket that could filter seawater into drinking water. We knew that this pilot might be someone important and dangerous. The battalion commander told another comrade and me to write down the interrogation. This was the first time in my life I had met an American. When I entered the room, the pilot was struggling with fleas, moving around close to the fire to try to get them off. Here in the mountains of Laos, the popular song said, "Yellow flies, fleas and wind in Pha-Ka are most dangerous and impossible to stop." The only way to keep these flies and fleas off was to heat your clothes up. Then they would jump off. The fleas would always attack strangers. We used to burn jungle leaves to keep them off, but it didn't help much.

None of us could speak English well, so sometimes it was as if he were mute and we were deaf. We wrote down only what we needed to know, in our broken English. Our purpose in this urgent interrogation was to know the code words he would use to contact his friends when they tried to save him. Dr. Ngoc was the only one who acted as an interrogator.

After we got everything we needed for that moment, I went into the staff headquarters cottage to discuss plans. The atmosphere was serious. No one was in favor of moving out to escape the American search teams that would be coming the next day. We all wanted to wait to take some counteraction against them. We discussed over and over a plan and all the details. Then we called in all the company commanders to give them their orders.

Outside the cottage the soldiers were excited about this capture. They were all awake, talking about the first American they had ever met, and they were all happy about the victory.

According to the plan, Comrade Hoang De, the battalion chief of staff, would play the role of the American pilot. Hoang De was tall and fat, maybe the largest person in the whole force; he would wear the pilot's clothes and use the code signals to attract the teams that would come searching. He would lie down in an area of the Doi Tron Mountain that would be most advantageous for us. I would be closest to him, to give him support or to rescue him if it was necessary. Two B-40s [hand-held rocket launchers] were positioned to cover the area. Other big guns and automatic weapons were also zeroed in.

The next morning at about seven a spotter plane appeared, then two groups of T-28s flew in and rocketed around the mountain. Thirty minutes later, two units of jets came in to rocket and bomb. Now we realized that the jets could certainly attack, not just observe, and they could attack a lot more powerfully than the T-28s. Finally, two helicopters appeared. I hid myself in the brush and gripped my AK.

Hoang De was wearing the black pilot's uniform and his red hat with a visor. The hat partially covered his eyes and face, so that they wouldn't recognize that he was Vietnamese. He ran into an area where the spotter plane could get a clearer view of him, about a hundred and fifty meters away from me. Then Hoang De shot the flare gun to signal them, first one shot, then two more.

The spotter plane saw it and immediately flew in toward Hoang De to get a closer look. From where I was I could see the pilot very clearly. I was afraid he would see that Hoang De wasn't the right person. Then the helicopter lowered down, looking like a dragonfly. Hoang De half-walked, half-crawled, as if he were wounded. It was partly an act, but partly it was because he was wearing the pilot's shoes. Now he was only about fifty meters away from me. I kept thinking about his shoes, that if something happened he wouldn't be able to move quickly.

The helicopter hovered there, lower, lower, about thirty meters from the ground. The jets circled around to give support. Now Hoang De was in a totally clear area. I could see two Americans in the helicopter with their hands on their guns, ready to shoot. Hoang De stood up slowly and with difficulty. The helicopter lowered a long cable toward him. Then a head emerged from the helicopter—a red face, high nose, and brown hair. The man shouted something at Hoang De. I thought, Oh my God, Hoang De can't speak English. And even if he could, how could he reply without showing that he is Vietnamese?

I was really scared. It was the first time I had faced the American Air Force—helicopter, jets, spotter plane, everything. We didn't have enough weapons to counter them. I didn't have any idea what to do.

Suddenly Hoang De ran forward a few steps and fell down. The white bandage he had wrapped around his leg was clearly visible, and he lay there as if he were dead. I thought, What a reaction! What a great idea! They wanted him to answer, maybe they suspected something. But there he was, unconscious.

The American with the red face stuck his head out as far as he could to look, then another American stuck his head out. I wondered if they would set the helicopter down or if they would leave. But it still hovered there at the same height, no lower, no higher. They hesitated to make their decision.

Hoang De knew this was the crucial moment. Maybe he thought they had found him out, or that they would get away. Suddenly he shouted, "Fire!" The two B-40s roared. The helicopter was hit and exploded, then fell to the ground. Hoang De and I ran as fast as we could to hide. We were safely inside the bunker when the jets bombed the area. But after a while they left.

While the air strikes were hitting around the bunker, I was thinking of the scene. We had had many options. We could have forced Sa [the pilot] to call the rescue team and have them land. But we could have done that only if the pilot had agreed. But there were no guarantees. He might have agreed, then when they came in he could have changed his mind and told them the truth. How could we know? We couldn't stand alongside him to guard against it.

As it was, we didn't expect that the rescue team would try to speak to the pilot to check. But they were smart enough to do that. So Hoang De's quick decision to fall and pretend to be unconscious was a wonderful resolution. And when Hoang De shouted, "Fire!" it was at just the right moment. Who could tell if the rescue team was about to find out that he wasn't the right person?

VENERABLE GIAC DUC

In the early 1960s, life in the South was marked by an intensifying conflict between Ngo Dinh Diem's government and the Buddhists. During this period, Giac Duc emerged as one of the political strategists of the Buddhist movement. His story continues.

THE VENERABLE GIAC DUC: *Buddhists and Catholics, the Showdown*

AT FIRST THE ONLY THING WE DID ABOUT THE FORCED CATHOLIC training was to prepare arguing points. We wrote up a few pages of answers to the most objectionable doctrines and we circulated them. At least we hoped that Buddhists who had to go through these programs would be better prepared to stand up to the criticisms they were hearing.

But the pressures on non-Catholics who wanted advancement in government or in the army kept getting worse. Ngo Dinh Nhu [Diem's brother and chief adviser] had started his own political party called the Can Lao. And practically the only way you could get anywhere in public life was by joining it. There was tremendous pressure to become Catholic so you could get ahead, and we began hearing about a lot of secret conversions.

More than anything else, that was what got me involved in politics in a serious way. I was incensed by what was going on, and I felt it was dangerous. We had to take steps so we could keep informed. Also, we had to devise some kind of counterstrategy to what we saw as an officially imposed Catholicism. There's no question that we were afraid of what Nhu was trying to do.

One of our first actions was to insert some of our people into Archbishop Thuc's *Nhan Vi* program and Nhu's Can Lao Party. One of our men even became Nhu's secretary. So after that we were kept aware of what was going on. Our next big step was to establish the Committee to Propagate Buddhism [*Hoi Dong Hoang Phap*], which we did in 1960. Thich Tri Thu was the chairman, Don Hau was vice chairman, and another monk and I were the secretaries.

Our idea was to develop a corps of itinerant preachers who were especially trained in social psychology and in the dangers represented not just by the government but also by the Communists. These people would circulate through the country lecturing and teaching and counteracting the influence of the Can Lao and the Communists. They would be able to work politically with Buddhists in the local administrations and they would teach the people, to strengthen their beliefs and to drive home the point that Buddhism and the nation's life were inseparable. Buddhism was part of the Vietnamese sense of nationhood. Neither Can Lao nor communism could make any claim of that sort.

The monks we chose for this job were all mature people, masters in their own right and accomplished preachers. In the training, we sharpened their awareness of the different kinds of audiences they would be lecturing to. We focused on adjusting the style and content of their sermons and their answers depending on whether they were preaching to peasants or educated people. We taught Buddhist thought, but we taught them to emphasize tradition rather than spirituality. The national life and Buddhism were one, inseparable, like milk and water. We encouraged them to make ancestor worship a center of their attention, since that was one of the built-in national customs that was excluded from Catholicism.

At that time we trained about sixty or seventy monks. All of them were effective people. They'd go out on the road, in the towns and villages and cities. They'd preach and give classes at the local pagodas or the village meeting places. They'd advise and teach local Buddhist leaders how to deal with the government pressure and with the Communists in their villages. Their work always had a spiritual basis, but there's no doubt that what they were doing was political, too. That's what they were supposed to be doing.

I was in charge of training for the committee. The monks we chose would come to us for training, then go out on the road. After a period of time they'd come back to discuss their experiences, the problems they had had and what they had learned. I also went out myself, so I would have firsthand knowledge of what they were facing. I wanted to get a feeling for what was going on. I went to the cities to lecture for intellectuals. I went to peaceful areas in the countryside, and also to places that the Communists controlled. Some of the areas I visited were so remote even Buddhism hadn't really penetrated the way of life—places like Ba To in Quang Ngai Province where they didn't know the term *thich* [venerable], but called me *anh* [brother].

When I'd get to a village, most often I'd send out word through the Buddhist laypeople that I'd be teaching at such and such a time. Crowds would always come, sometimes only a couple of hundred people. But in the cities there might be ten thousand or more—it depended on the place. I'd talk to them about popular Buddhism. I'd tell them, "Look in the past. Look at the first century, the second century. Who helped the people? Then and always. The monks! The Buddhists! Buddhism and the nation are one—like milk and water, like space and light, like figure and shadow. You have to help each other and love each other! You have to love the people! You must not kill the people with bombs or shoot them with guns."

So, you see, it was patriotic—but anti-Communist and antigovernment. The people loved it. They would clap and get excited. I'd say, "Stand up! Close your eyes!" The whole crowd would stand up with their eyes closed. I'd say, "Put your hands in the lotus position! Let us all have the wisdom not to fall into the hands of foreign ideas! We must love one another! No one else will love us, so we must love ourselves. We must have compassion for each other."

This was, of course, politics, mass psychology, and religion at the same time. I felt as if I had two burdens on me—a spiritual burden and a political burden. It was one thing to *have* compassion, but you also have to *realize* your compassion. You have to teach spirituality, but you also have to motivate people to struggle against what will destroy their spirituality.

I have to say that in reality we were not involved in a religious fight between Buddhism and Catholicism. There was no religious conflict per se. The conflict came about because Diem and his brothers were using Catholicism as a tool of political control. Thuc, the archbishop brother who was later defrocked by the Catholic Church, was the keystone, since allegiance to the Church meant allegiance to the Ngo family as well. So political pressure and religious pressure went hand in hand.

Another of the Ngo family's attempts to use Catholicism this way was the Dinh Dien Movement that started in 1959 and was especially strong from 1960 to 1962. Ostensibly this was a policy to give land to poor peasants. But actually what they did was to ship stubborn people into virgin land areas where they were completely dependent on the government rice ration in order to live. These areas were mainly in Quang Duc and Phu Bon provinces. If the people were compliant, they'd have the right to buy rice. They were completely at the mercy of the government. The result was that there were mass conversions to Catholicism.

To resist this we organized missionary committees to visit the Quang Duc and Phu Bon areas. But when the missions got there, they found that each of the families' huts would have a crucifix in front, and that people would be afraid to talk to them. I went to Quang Duc myself to see what could be done. The mayor there, Ngan, was a Northern Catholic who was an old friend of mine. When I accused him of organizing the terrible oppression that was going on, he said no, it wasn't his doing, it wasn't his policy. Eventually I prevailed on him to let me lecture in public and to drive through the streets in an official sound car to announce it. So people weren't afraid to come.

Overnight we set up a temple. Then we organized a group of lay Buddhists who were willing to help people keep their faith. At the first public lecture I asked everyone in the crowd who was a Buddhist to raise his hand. They all raised their hands. Afterwards we distributed cards certifying that the individual was a Buddhist. Then we sent the lay volunteers around to help remove Catholic artifacts from the houses.

At the same time we were helping individual Buddhists reassert their faith, we were also finding ways to fight the government. Free markets were set up to help break the rice monopoly. We used the local officials' corruption to get assurances and protection from them. We also threatened the national government with massive opposition. Our strategy at that point was to keep the conflict level low, but to make it clear that we had a lot of leverage—83 percent of the population was Buddhist. They had to know that we wouldn't be afraid to use this leverage.

At one meeting I had with Thich Tri Quang [later to become the chief Buddhist opposition leader] I explained to him my approach to building political consciousness and strength. I told him that without adversity we wouldn't have any strength. We wouldn't be able to create an effective movement. We had built the Bo De high schools because the people wanted them. They wanted to assert their Buddhist identity, partly because the government was against it. That was what motivated the people. So let them have feelings against the government. That would strengthen us. The government was threatening and pressuring, that was fine. Confronting the government would help us build a Buddhist mass movement. It would give us coherence and would make us strong for the real fight we saw in front of us—the fight against the Communists.

IN 1963 Buddha's birthday fell on May 7–8. Unfortunately, that year the day of the Lady of La Van coincided with it. [At La Van there had been a vision of the Madonna, and the place had become a Catholic shrine.] Also, on that particular day there was a visiting delegation from the Vatican that was investigating Archbishop Thuc's candidacy to become a cardinal. As usual the Buddha's birthday was being celebrated with flags and marches. But because of the Vatican delegation, the minister of the cabinet, Quach Tong Duc, proclaimed that only national flags could be flown. All the Buddhist flags had to be taken down.

Of course there were confrontations about this all over. But the most active ones were in Hue, which was the center of Buddhism in South Vietnam. Thich Tri Quang and Thich Thien Minh [the Buddhists' chief political planner] refused to have the flags taken away. They were at the great Tu Dam Pagoda for the holy day celebration and none of the Buddhist institutions in that area would take their flags down. So the police were trying to get rid of them, and the people and monks were putting them back up.

Early on the morning of May 8th Tri Quang began to preach to the crowds at Tu Dam—two hundred thousand people or more had gathered there for the celebration. He told them he was speaking on behalf of the supreme patriarch. He said that Buddhists had no political demands to make of the government, but that we insisted on religious freedom. We especially insisted on equal status for Buddhism under the law. You see, at that time Buddhism was included under Article 10 of the Constitution which regulated clubs and private organizations. That meant we were under close government control. We had to get permission for any meeting or celebration we wanted to have, and we had to report all of our funding. We had the same status as sports clubs. Tri Quang explained our demand that the Buddhist Church be removed from Article 10 and our demands for equality. Then, when his teaching was over, a giant procession marched through the streets.

All the time tension in Hue was rising. The mayor was a Buddhist and was sympathetic to us. But the military chief was Major Dang Si, strictly under Diem's control. And the real power in Hue and the whole center was Ngo Dinh Can, another of Diem's brothers. So the conflict between the police and military on one side and the Buddhists on the other was sharpening.

What set the explosion off was an incident at the radio station. Every year by tradition the radio station would broadcast the Buddhist ceremonies. But this year there was no broadcast. So the mayor and Tri Quang went down to the radio station to ask why. They were there in the open lobby of the station building with a crowd of people when Major Dang Si moved up troops and armored cars and attacked. There's no doubt he was out to assassinate Tri Quang and the mayor. But instead eight innocent people were killed and the ones he was after got away.

Less than two hours later, Radio Hanoi was broadcasting news of the government's attack on Tri Quang. The next morning the BBC took up the story, and right after that the Voice of America did. It was an international incident. Meanwhile Dang Si had launched a propaganda campaign against Tri Quang, sending sound trucks all around the city to denounce him. That precipitated demonstrations by the Buddhists in the city and army counteractions. In a short time, Tri Quang and the whole Buddhist hierarchy in Hue were surrounded in the Tu Dam Pagoda, in a state of siege.

While all this was happening I was in Lam Dong Province. The first reports I heard came in on Radio Hanoi. When it was clear what was taking place, I made immediate arrangements to get to Saigon. I knew something had to be done to support the Tu Dam monks in Hue, even though I hadn't figured out exactly what that could be. But I did know it was only in Saigon that we could organize any kind of effective action.

As soon as I got to Saigon I went to the Giac Minh Pagoda, where I met a Vietnamese UPI reporter who had been in Hue. He gave me a tape recording of Tri Quang's talk and a photograph of the people who had been killed at the radio station. When I had these I called all the monks of Giac Minh together to look at the picture and listen to the tape. Once we had heard it, we all agreed with the demands Tri Quang had made—he had tremendous influence among us. We also agreed that we had to begin a struggle in Saigon immediately. Otherwise the government would just destroy the movement in Hue.

The first step was that the leaders of the Giac Minh monks wrote a public letter. It said that all monks, all nuns, and all laypeople should stand behind the Buddhist struggle. We needed to fight for the very survival of Buddhism. We mimeographed ten thousand copies of this letter and distributed them all over Saigon. Then I took the letter, the tape, and the picture to the An Quang Pagoda, which at that time was just a monastery. It wasn't yet the center of the Buddhist movement, as it became later.

I gave a talk to the monks there—about three hundred of them—explaining what had happened and giving them details on the background of the struggle for religious rights that had been going on against the government. I wanted to move them to struggle in support of Hue. But even though there was a lot of sympathy for my point of view, the two heads of the temple weren't sure about it. They said that whatever was done should be done religiously and "smoothly." They weren't in favor of any struggle, though they would go along with something that was "quiet." I said, Okay, in that case we would express our support quietly, in a religious way. In the end, we agreed to pray for the salvation of the victims who had died in Hue. Every Tuesday we would have public prayers for that purpose.

I had the same problems at Xa Loi Pagoda, the other chief temple in Saigon. There too the leaders didn't want to move, they didn't want to do anything drastic. Meanwhile the temple in Hue was still surrounded, without any food or water coming in. Nobody knew what might happen there, especially without a clear demonstration to the government of our strength and the support among the people.

Fortunately, one of the leaders who was in favor of struggle was Tam Chau, the head of the Buddhist Intersect Committee. This was the umbrella organization for eleven different Buddhist sects in the country. He felt strongly that something had to be done, and he called a meeting of the intersect leadership so that I could address them. I explained to them as forcefully as I could the need for an organized struggle, and I told them that we had to set up a permanent committee to direct it. By the end of the meeting, we had done exactly that. Tam Chau was elected president of the committee and I was elected head of organizing and training.

Meanwhile the government was busy raising the level of confrontation. They refused to take responsibility for the murders in Hue, and the government radio began to denounce Tri Quang as a Communist. There was no sign of the seige letting up. I felt we were on a collision course. We were riding on the back of the tiger, unable to get off. I couldn't see the future clearly at all.

By this time we were all afraid of being arrested and had begun to stay in the Xa Loi Pagoda compound. From there we sent out letters to all of the provinces in South Vietnam calling for demonstrations in support of Tri Quang. Every day I'd give lectures to monks and laymen, at first inside the pagoda, but then as more and more people came we moved outside. I'd speak from the balcony to the laypeople and high school and university students who gathered in the streets in front of the pagoda. What started as relatively small talks grew within a week or so to lectures before ten or fifteen thousand people.

We had also become quite aware that the foreign news services were interested in what was going on. Thich Duc Nghiep was in charge of foreign affairs, so that was his side of things, to see that news got out regularly. He spoke English well and was an effective strategist. By this time, the three of us—Tam Chau, Duc Nghiep, and I—were running a countrywide movement that was putting more and more pressure on the government.

Of course the Communists wanted to use the situation for their own benefit, too. One sign of their intentions was a telegram we received from Vo Nguyen Giap [North Vietnam's defense minister]: "We support your struggle. We have requested the International Control Commission to investigate the evil actions of the Diem regime in persecuting our Buddhist religion." He actually said "our Buddhist religion."

The telegram was delivered to me by one of the ICC's Indian delegates. When I read it to the leadership, at first we were all confused about what to do. Everyone understood that Giap was trying to use us, and we were all anxious not to be associated with the Communists in any way. Finally I composed an answer: "Thank you for your message. But this is none of your business." But the others thought that showed too much friendliness. So we crossed out "Thank you for your message." The text we actually sent simply read "None of your business!"

In the middle of all this activity, one day an old Xa Loi monk named Quang Duc came to me and said he wanted to burn himself as his donation to the struggle. The first time he said this, it didn't make any sense to me. It was just some bothersome old monk disturbing me in the middle of a hectic situation. I dismissed him without thinking anything more about it.

But the old monk was persistent. Each day he would come with his request that he should be allowed to burn himself. He even went so far as to kneel down in front of Tam Chau, Duc Nghiep, and me praying that we would permit him to make this donation of himself to Buddhism.

The whole thing was very strange. Self-immolation had been practiced during the Ly dynasty in the eleventh and twelfth centuries. It was also described in the *Lotus Sutra* as an act someone might perform who had achieved complete mastery over his mind and was beyond the cycle of birth and death. There was even the ancient story of the monk who had spent three years gathering wood for his self-immolation, then had burned himself in one hour. *"Kiem cui 3 nam thieu I gio"* had even become a proverb—"Collect wood three years, burn it in an hour."

But the idea was exotic and horrible. Tam Chau didn't even want to be involved in listening to the old monk. I felt pretty much the same way. But Duc Nghiep didn't say anything at all about it. He just kept quiet.

One day after Quang Duc had been making his entreaties for a while, we were told that he had prostrated himself a hundred times in front of the great statue of Buddha in the main chapel and that he wasn't eating. He had told the other monks that he was fasting and praying for us to open our minds to him.

When I heard this, I began to see his focus differently. I decided I had to talk to him about it. When I confronted him, the first thing I asked was whether he hated the government. He smiled and said, "No." Then I took his hand and pinched it. When I asked if that hurt, he answered that it did.

While we were talking I noticed that his eyes were very bright, but that he had a calmness about him that I hadn't seen before. He seemed completely relaxed. I asked him why he wanted to do this thing, and he said that he had told me many times already. He wanted to make a donation of himself to the "three jewels"—the Buddha, the Buddha's teaching, and the Church.

I asked, "Are you a Boddhisattva revealed?" He just looked at me, like a father looks at a son he loves—with smiling, compassionate eyes. He answered, "No, I'm not."

As I walked out of the room, I had the conviction that I hadn't treated him well before, when I had been so brusque with him. When I saw Nghiep I told him, "Brother, there's something divine about him." Nghiep said, "Yes, we could do something to help him fulfill his vow." As soon as he said this, I knew Nghiep wasn't asking for advice. He had made up his mind.

After that I went to Tam Chau and told him that Nghiep apparently was willing to go along with it, that he had made his decision. Tam Chau's reaction was immediate. He said, "I won't be involved in this." My feelings were the same as his. By this time I had come to see Quang Duc in a different spiritual light, but I still couldn't bring myself to take part in what he was planning to do. I told Tam Chau that, and I told him that I would leave the temple for Lam Dong, so I wouldn't have to be there when it happened.

After I made my arrangements to leave, I put on my formal robes and went to see Quang Duc. I bowed in front of him three times. I said, "Boddhisattva, sir, I beg you to receive my bows as a token that we will see each other in the future life." When I said this, he put his hand on my shoulder and looked in my eyes, but not the way a subordinate looks at his superior. He said, "Yes, I will see you." Then after a silence, he put his hand on my head—that's something only a master will do to his disciple. I remember his words very clearly. They were the last I heard from him. He told me, "You do not know. Many Boddhisattvas and Buddhas surround us. Can you see them?"

Then I left. I believed then and I believe now that Thich Quang Duc was a Boddhisattva. I left Saigon on Monday for Lam Dong, where I helped organize the struggle. On Tuesday Thich Quang Duc fulfilled his vow to burn himself. Afterwards I came back to Saigon.

When I returned to Xa Loi the first person I met was a young monk who was one of my students. He looked at me and said that he was going back to the countryside, that he couldn't take part in the struggle anymore. He felt overwhelmed by what had happened. Nghiep himself was also in awe. He told me that after I left he had bowed down before Quang Duc and said that he would help him fulfill his vows. When Quang Duc knew he would be permitted to perform the immolation, he sat down to write—three letters, all in *chu nom,* the Chinese-style character script. He hadn't known how to write modern Vietnamese.

The first letter was addressed to the Church. It expressed Quang Duc's hope that the Church would be unified forever. The second letter was to his disciples. It read, "Nothing lasts forever except compassion. The physical body is temporary; the spirit is eternal. There should be no tears."

The third letter was to Diem. To the president, Quang Duc had written, "Before I pass through the Buddha gate, I pray the president will treat his people with compassion so that he may maintain the treasure of the nation forever." This last letter Nghiep had had translated into modern Vietnamese.

Every Tuesday there was a religious procession. The Tuesday after I left it started at An Quang Pagoda, stopped at Phat Buu Tu for the service, then started toward Xa Loi. The route went right past the Cambodian Embassy. But the procession stopped there—three to five hundred monks with Thich Quang Duc in the middle.

Then Quang Duc sat down while the monks gathered around him in a circle, all of them praying. Quang Duc picked up the can of gasoline and poured it over himself. But he could get only one side wet, so he asked for help to get the other side. Then he took his lighter and tried to set himself on fire. But the lighter didn't work—the mechanism had been too soaked by gasoline. He tried for nearly five minutes until someone threw him a box of matches. Then the fire started. For ten minutes he sat there, burning.

Nghiep told me he was in such awe that he was squeezing his palms together with all his strength the whole time. He said he felt as if he had lost his mind—that he couldn't do anything but kneel down in the street and pray while Quang Duc was burning. He believed as I did that the old monk was a Boddhisattva. Everybody around him bowed down—all the monks, the laypeople, even the police. Students came running out of the high school that was near there, and they were bowing down too.

When the fire finally went out, they carried Quang Duc's remains back to Xa Loi. That day, June 11th, the government lifted the siege of the Tu Dam Pagoda.

AFTERWARDS the government agreed to a number of our demands. Buddhism would officially be considered a religion. Buddhist flags could be flown in celebrations, although they couldn't be as large as national flags and they had to be flown lower. They also agreed to stop all anti-Buddhist actions and to punish the people who were responsible for the deaths in Hue, though they refused to admit that the government was guilty in any way.

My feeling was that the government's offers were acceptable and that the struggle was basically resolved. But it was only a few days after the joint government-Buddhist communiqué was issued that we could see we were going to have more trouble. Arrests started up again among lay Buddhists. Madame Nhu [Diem's sister-in-law] continued to make speeches denouncing the Buddhists. There was a massive, spontaneous demonstration against the government in Saigon where more than a million people had gathered for Thich Quang Duc's funeral. A nun in Nha Trang burned herself in protest over police action against Buddhists there. There were problems everywhere.

Then, in the first week of August, there was a massive wave of arrests all over the South. That forced us to the wall. Practically the entire leadership agreed that a second movement had to be launched to get the government to carry out the terms of the joint communiqué. We began to make plans for a struggle that would bring pressure against the regime by Buddhists within the government itself and that would start a great nationwide general strike.

On August 20th most of the leadership was at Xa Loi Pagoda discussing and planning for the confrontation we saw in front of us. Then in the evening we got a message that the police were planning to attack all the major pagodas in the country that night. The initial warning was delivered by friends of ours who were close to Nhu. But shortly afterwards it was confirmed by other contacts. Nghiep quickly got in touch with his American friends, who offered to help the leadership escape from what was about to happen.

I advised that anyone who wanted to escape should, while there was still time. Personally, I couldn't. I was the chief public spokesman for the movement, so I was responsible. There was no way I could leave the monks by themselves. All the others felt the same way. It must have been about ten-thirty at night when we made a group decision to stay. We would simply endure whatever happened.

At that point we asked all the laypeople who were still in the pagoda to leave. Then we organized the five hundred or so monks who lived at Xa Loi. I told all the younger ones I wanted them outside with me on the big second-floor balcony that overlooked Ba Huyen Thanh Quan Street.

The older ones I wanted inside the main chapel where they would be protected. They all sat down there, around the supreme patriarch, who seated himself on the floor in front of the great Buddha statue. All of them were very calm. At that time the patriarch was one hundred and two years old.

My idea was that when the police started gathering on the other side of the street across from the balcony I'd talk to them. Once or twice before in similar situations I had been successful in preventing police attacks, so I had experience with this kind of thing. I thought that if I was calm and reasonable, but strong at the same time, I could cut through the anger and the craziness the police worked themselves up to in this kind of confrontation. I knew them all anyway, and all the police knew me. So I was confident I could do it if I handled things properly.

A little after midnight special riot police and soldiers started surrounding the pagoda compound. I was standing on the balcony with all the young monks watching them form up on the other side of Ba Huyen Thanh Quan Street. When I thought it was time I picked up the electric bullhorn and started to speak to them. I tried to arouse a struggle in their consciences—telling them not to attack us, that we were the same people. I truly thought that I could win them over—I didn't think they'd dare to attack.

But after I had been talking for about fifteen minutes I saw Colonel Le Quang Tung drive up in his jeep and begin shouting at them very angrily. Almost immediately after that things began to happen. Hand grenades were thrown over the wall and there were explosions in the courtyard. Then they started firing at the balcony. I saw some of the young monks falling; the P.A. speaker I was holding was shot out of my hand. I bent down to pick it up—I don't know if I still thought I could speak to them or exactly what I was thinking. But when I raised it to my mouth it wouldn't work. Then there was an explosion at the front gate and soldiers were running into the courtyard. Some of the monks were lifting up the big flowerpots on the balcony to throw at the soldiers, but I shouted at them to get back, to get inside.

The main shrine took up the entire second floor. When we ran in from the balcony we closed the great iron door behind us and I told all the young monks to sit down with the older ones who were around the patriarch at the far end of the hall. I waited for the soldiers in front of the door. As I was looking at it there was a big explosion on the other side and the door just fell in. The huge iron door of the shrine. The police ran in right over it. But when they saw the shrine with the great Buddha statue they just stopped. I stepped toward them with my hands out, telling them, "*Hay thong tha*"—"Take it easy, slowly. This is a holy place, you must respect it. Our supreme patriarch and all the leaders are sitting quietly before the statue. What do you want? Speak to us."

The police stopped where they were. For a moment they didn't move. All the monks were sitting silently with their legs crossed in the lotus position watching the policemen. When I asked, "What do you want?" one of the police walked up to me with tears in his eyes and said, "Please understand, we have to do our job." Then he put my hands behind my back and handcuffed me. Other police were walking through the sitting monks and handcuffing them too. But when they saw the supreme patriarch, they were frightened, afraid to touch him. Instead they invited him to go with them, using the most respectful language they could.

ON THE HO CHI MINH TRAIL

The first infiltration routes to the South were opened up on August 20, 1959, by a handpicked unit from North Vietnam's 301st Division. A feeling for the times and the difficulties—and the heroism—comes through in a short panegyric and two personal accounts, all three from Nhan Dan *(The Party Daily).*

THE HO CHI MINH TRAIL

(From Nhan Dan, November 22, 1984)

ALL OF OUR RESISTANCE MOVEMENTS HAVE BEGUN WITH WONDER-ful, great, fiery, martial operations which impelled the people forward. We recall in the old days the waves of Vietnamese pushing forward into the South. The roar of cannons echoed everywhere in the Southern mountains, warming the entire country as we dashed forward into the South to kill all our brutal foes. We recall the massed soldiers slicing through the Truong Son Mountains to save the country, singing their songs:

> The guns' sound spreads over the Southern land.
> It warms our beloved country.
> I want to fly to the South
> To kill all the barbarous foes.
> I climb the Truong Son Mountains.

My feet abrade the rocks and stones.
Rocks and stones don't hurt them at all.

The army comes, the army returns to the homeland while the wind blows.
These are our warlike operations.

NGUYEN DANH: *Opening the Ho Chi Minh Trail*

IN MAY 1959, THE 301ST DIVISION WAS STATIONED AT PHU HO VIL-
lage in Vinh Phu Province. [The 301st Division was made up of Southern Vietminh fighters who had regrouped North after Geneva.] The brick
houses of Phu Ho dotted the mountainside, creating a beautiful romantic
view. I was enjoying this view when I received an order to report to the
division commander. In the sitting room of the headquarters, Comrade
Duong, the division's political chief, introduced me to a colonel who was
with him, Brother Vo Bam of the Army Command Staff.

Colonel Vo Bam then informed me that the Army Command Staff and
the Army Political Committee were creating a special unit whose task
would be to transport matériel to the Southern provinces. At this, Comrade Duong said that in fact the special unit had already been formed.
Three hundred and eight *bo dois* from the division had been chosen for it.
My friend Chu Dang Chu had been appointed as the unit commander,
and I was to be the political chief. I was told that the existence of the
unit was to be kept completely secret. No one other than those who had
been selected could know about it, including the senior officers in the
division and in the Hanoi command staff.

At the end of May, the special unit embarked by train at the small
station near the 301st Division's headquarters. It seemed like quite an
ordinary movement—there were no goodbyes, no parties, just a different
posting for three hundred and eight of the division's *bo dois*.

The train took us to Thanh Hoa Province. From there we were driven
by truck to Vinh Linh, a border town on the 17th parallel. Vinh Linh was
the headquarters of the 341st Division, a defensive border guard outfit
whose men were mostly engaged in hard woodcutting work. We inte-
grated ourselves into this division, pretending to be doing the same kind
of work. But in reality, we were preparing for our mission.

At first we weren't sure exactly how to go about it. We had been given
the task of opening a road to the South, but no detailed instructions had
gone along with the order. We would have to draw from our own experiences and our own resources.

In June two comrades were ordered across the Ben Hai River [the natural border between North and South Vietnam] to collect firsthand intelligence. They reported back that they had contacted the Quang Tri Party boss [Quang Tri was the northernmost province of South Vietnam] and that he would furnish all the logistical support he could. But he had also insisted that no one who crossed the Ben Hai could have anything on them that might be traced to the North.

This simple necessity turned out to be a major problem, especially for me. If you looked at the *bo doi*, everything about him came from the North, from his pith helmet to his uniform to his belt, shoes, flashlight, and cigarettes. The only thing not Northern was his Southern accent. We had to reequip each of our *bo dois* from head to foot. And we didn't just reequip them, we gave them new names as well, and new biographies in case any of them were captured. Unable to handle this job alone, I went to my own chief for help, then to the Party boss in Ho Xa, a neighboring district.

Within several days we had everything we needed: black pajamas, the floppy-brimmed Vietcong hats, everything to give us the appearance of real Southern guerrillas. We scraped out the names on our Northern-made flashlights, got rid of our Northern cigarettes, and left behind every photo, document, or letter that could give anyone away.

A much more difficult job for me was learning the new names and biographical details of the three hundred and eight men in the unit, among whom were one hundred and sixty Party members whom I had to know especially well. Minor things took on major significance, mail for example. The unit couldn't just disappear from the face of the earth. So we instructed the men to write letters, as they ordinarily would, but not to include descriptions of the countryside or any mention of where they were. When we got to the South, we collected the letters once a month and took them to Quang Binh [on the Northern side of the 17th parallel] to be posted. The return address was also c/o postmaster Quang Binh.

By the first week of June we had drafted a plan for Road 559 to go through the central region of the country south of the parallel. We had decided to establish nine stations, two in the region north of the Ben Hai and the rest in Zone 5 to the south. But as we were working on it, we got a report that Comrade K, a cadre from South Huong Hoa village, had disappeared. He had participated on the planning staff, and we didn't know if perhaps he had been arrested or if he had rallied to the Saigon side. For several days we called a halt to our work, then took it up again, making some adjustments in the plans.

On June 10th, we crossed the Ben Hai and proceeded to set up all of the stations. The Quang Tri Province secretary and our own ranger group reported there was no evidence that we had been discovered. On August 20, 1959, our unit transferred the first weapons and ammunition to the Party branch in Zone 5. Each man carried four French made Max 36 rifles bundled together or a twenty-kilo box of ammunition, in addition to their own gear. Comrade Van, a member of the Zone 5 secretariat, received the first official aid and infiltration from the North to the South.

For the next three years we lived in the jungle preparing the road. Our life during that time was unimaginable. Our food was rice with salt. We created "stations," which were in fact just rendezvous areas, no housing, no roofs. We'd cover the jungle floor with leaves for sitting down or sleeping, then restore the area completely before we left, so that no trace would be left for the Saigon Special Forces to track us. Although at that time there were no air strikes or heavy attacks, still we had to be extremely careful. Worst was the rainy season. Then we had only a piece of plastic to cover ourselves with, and we'd stay under it while we ate, slept, or talked.

At first we planned to take the road past Khe Sanh, but when our local contacts advised against this, we went eastward instead. Crossing Route 9 we had to move between the enemy army posts and avoid their patrols. Evening was the best time, at dusk. During the day of course we would be visible, and at night they had their patrols out. But in the evening they ate dinner and prepared for their night activities. It was then that we'd cross the roads. First we'd send a small reconnaissance party over. If it was safe, the rest of us would follow, laying a piece of plastic down on the surface to keep our muddy footprints off the road, then pulling the plastic after us when we had passed. Other times we'd use the big culverts under the roads, though the green algae on the stones would be disturbed by our footsteps. So we'd turn the stones over before we went through, then turn them again once we had passed.

At the beginning of 1960, a reconnaissance patrol of three men was trapped by the Saigon Special Forces. Two escaped, but Comrade Truong, who covered their withdrawal, was wounded and captured. According to the report I received later, he was tortured, then killed, without having revealed anything. If I'm not mistaken, he was the first to die on the Truong Son Trail.

SAU THUONG, *Political Officer, NVA: The Road to the Motherland*

IN 1959 I WAS IN DIVISION B38, ALL OF WHOSE SOLDIERS WERE Southerners who rallied to the North in 1954 and were stationed in Hoa Binh. One day in the fall of that year several friends and I were called to present ourselves at the Political Military Department headquarters in Hanoi to receive orders for a new mission. Since only several of us among the thousands in the division were called to Hanoi, it meant that something important was happening. I felt that it could be about going back to the South, and my heart was beating so strongly that I couldn't sleep for nights before the meeting. Others who heard that I was going to Hanoi, perhaps to go South, were jealous, but they shared my happiness with me.

Every minute, the Southern *bo dois* in the North thought about their homes in the South. In 1954 they expected they would return home two years later. We heard about the suffering of our relatives under the yoke of the French and then the Americans. So now I could not put into words the happiness my friends and I felt.

After we arrived in Hanoi—before we were actually given our assignment—we had to be checked by a group of doctors. It was a thorough examination, and at times we thought that maybe we were being sent overseas to study. We certainly weren't happy with that idea; we were determined to go South.

Unfortunately, after the examination I was ordered back to the division. I was so angry I asked why, and the doctors said that I still had a piece of bullet in my lung from an old wound. The doctors hadn't been able to get it out then, and it will never be taken out. But by that time I knew that this mission was definitely to go South, and I couldn't give that up for any price. I couldn't let this happiest moment of my life just slip away. So I stayed in Hanoi, making an effort to see the top leaders. I managed to see Le Duan and General Giap, and I told them I was determined to go South despite my wound. In the end, they gave way to my pleas, and I stayed in Hanoi to prepare for the journey.

Ours was one of the first trips South. Our unit had twenty-eight members. Comrade Bui Thanh Van was head of the unit, and I was Party secretary [Bui Thanh Van is presently a four-star general]. All twenty-eight of us were young Southerners.

First we were sent to a mountainous area in Hoa Binh Province for military and political training. All the top leaders visited us in the training center—Uncle Ho, Uncle Ton Duc Thang [chief of state], Comrade Le Duan [Party chief], Pham Hung [politburo member in charge of the South], and General Vo Nguyen Giap [minister of defense]. They all came, and they themselves taught us political lessons. It was something we were proud of, that we never forgot. It indicated the great honor and warmth the Party, the government, and the whole people accorded to those of us who were going South.

I remember one cold evening, the mountain and jungle cold of North-eastern North Vietnam a cold that cut the skin. Uncle Ho came to visit us then. We were thinking that we wouldn't see him for a long time because who could know when we would win and greet him in the South, or when we might return to the North. So this was like a final meeting.

But Ho surprised us again a few days later, just before our departure, when he and other leaders came back to wish us farewell. When he appeared, everyone was so surprised that we couldn't speak for a moment or move. Then we went to him and embraced him. He hugged each of us as if he were a father hugging his sons. His final words brought tears to our eyes: "All the brothers going South should give the Southern people my best wishes and greetings. There is no doubt that one day I will come to see our Southern blood brothers." We answered that we would give our best, including our lives, so that the sacred mission would succeed, so that we would see him in the South.

In November we left, passing Nam Dinh and Thanh Hoa, then beginning our trek along the Truong Son range. Each of us was carrying thirty kilos. Aside from a pair of black pajamas and a small quantity of medicine, most of the rest was weapons and ammunition. These were the first guns given by the North to the South. We also brought a small quantity of gold with us to assist with the organizing effort.

About two weeks into the trip I began having shoulder trouble. At first I thought it was due to my pack, and I tried to readjust the belts. But the pain continued and I began to vomit blood. It was obviously due to the wound in my lung, which had worsened during the journey.

The Party branch of the unit had an urgent meeting about the situation and decided to send me back for treatment. But I objected to the decision, and since I was chief of the branch I convinced them to let me continue. I would rather have died in the mountains than have to go back and face Uncle Ho and the other leaders without having finished the mission. The others understood my determination about this, and they decided to approve my objection. But I had to agree not to carry anything, so my pack was carried for me.

The farther south we got, the worse our situation became. Finally we were down to a few kilos of rice, which we decided to save for the last extremity. For two months we ate what we could find in the jungle— leaves, roots, animals, jungle birds. When we finally arrived in the Baria area the unit stopped while I attempted to make contact with Bay Tham, the province Party chief.

When I eventually succeeded, I couldn't believe the circumstances Bay Tham was living in. He and three others were the only people we had in

Phuoc Long Province. The four of them had been living in a bamboo jungle, starving. Bay Tham told me that they had barely eaten for a month, that there hadn't even been corn, let alone rice. He and the others looked like skeletons, pale and malaria-ridden. We embraced each other, crying. As we did, Bay Tham said to me in a hesitant and trembling whisper, "You've come from the North, the base, give us some rice."

When I rendezvoused back with my unit and told them the story, we decided to give all our remaining rice to Bay Tham. Along with it I gave him a piece of ginseng that Le Duan had sent along, telling him that it was the gift of the Central Committee to the brothers in the South.

Several days later we arrived in Ma Da—formerly Special Zone D, one of the home bases of the resistance. We were overjoyed to be there. I took a bath in the Dong Nai River, drinking as much of it as I could, as if I were embracing the South, my motherland. I felt fresh, as if I had been reborn.

Meeting with the comrades in that area, Van [the head of the unit] and I told them about the journey and relayed Ho's message to the South. Then we gave them our weapons, the gold, everything we carried—the first aid from North to South. It was a moving scene. Some of them were crying.

A short time later, in July 1961, these twenty-eight men from the North were part of the group that formed the first regular battalion in the South. Bui Thanh Van commanded the battalion and I was the political commissar. This battalion later was built up into the Binh Gia Division, one of the most heroic units during the Spring victory over Saigon—fulfilling the promise we made to Uncle Ho and Le Duan in Hoa Binh back in 1959.

HUONG VAN BA

The Southern artillery officer who regrouped North in 1954 began his own trek down the trail almost a decade later.

HUONG VAN BA, *Colonel, People's Army of North Vietnam, NVA, Regroupee: Back Down the Trail*

I LEFT FOR THE SOUTH MYSELF ON MAY 24TH, 1964, AFTER HAVING trained other infiltrators for the previous two years. Forty-five men in my artillery unit went as a group. Our leader was a man from Nghe An

[Ho Chi Minh's home province, in the center of the country] who had spent nine years in the South fighting the French. I was deputy commander, and we also had a political officer with us. Our weapons—artillery, rockets, mortars—were transported by a special team, so there was no need for us to carry them. At that point I was a lieutenant, but just before we left I was promoted to captain.

We drove in covered trucks from Thanh Hoa Province to Dong Hoi on National Highway 1. The trucks were covered for the same reason we had trained in civilian clothes—to avoid raising people's suspicions. We made our stops only at deserted places along the road. When we arrived at the Vietnam-Laos border, we were given a day's rest. At that point we traded in our North Vietnamese army uniforms for black pajamas, to give us the appearance of Southern peasants. We were asked to carefully go over all our gear and possessions to make sure we weren't carrying anything related to North Vietnam or to other Communist countries. We were invading, but we did our best to disguise ourselves as native liberators.

We left the trucks at the border and began to walk. It wasn't an easy trip. There were no roads, hardly even trails. We just cut out across the jungle carrying seventy-pound packs on our shoulders. We crossed the Ben Hai River and began to climb. The most difficult part of the route was right at the beginning—a treacherous mountain called Hill 1001, part of the Truong Son range. On the peak we rested. In the morning the sun shone hot. By afternoon it would be raining. It was always either wet or humid. I didn't see how my health would be able to hold up for the entire trip.

At first we would walk about eight hours a day. But with the climbing and the jungles, it was slow going. When and where we rested depended on the guide and our leader. Any place that was clear and safe would do. But even the way stations were not like some stopover in the city. There was nothing to shelter you from the rain, no beds. You just put up your hammock and slept in it.

The way stations had been established by our predecessors on the trail. They were supposed to supply us with food and water. But they were often short. So each individual learned to save his own food and water. The farther along we got, the worse the hunger we faced. As food grew scarcer, comradeship broke down. People became more and more intent on saving their own lives.

As we came closer to the South, we were also exposed to enemy action. Passing near Pleiku and Kontum we crossed wide fields of thatch, camouflaging ourselves to avoid being spotted by enemy planes. Several times jets flew right over our heads. We saw droves of wild buffalo, but we didn't dare to shoot at them for fear of giving ourselves away. My unit never came under attack, but ARVN rangers operated in the area and occasionally did ambush groups of infiltrators.

Somehow I never got sick during the whole journey. But a great number of people contracted malaria, and many died of it. There were never any official statistics. Losses of any kind were always kept secret for morale reasons. But information would spread among friends and acquaintances. People died despite the antimalaria tablets we carried. My close friend Captain Tran Chanh Ly was among them. His death was sudden, as we were resting at one of the way stations. He just never got up.

But although I wasn't sick, I stepped on a punji stake that had been planted by a local guerrilla. My foot got infected and swelled up painfully, so I was forced to stay for a while at a way station for treatment, along with some of my friends who were sick. Of the forty-five men in my unit, maybe seven or eight made it. The rest had to stop here or there along their way. Some never got through. Sometime in late August I arrived in Tay Ninh. I had left the North on May 24th. At the reception area I was allowed two days rest before some people from the artillery command came to take me to my first assignment.

At first I was assigned as an instructor in artillery unit V-60 in "R." ["R," standing for *rung* (jungle), was shorthand for COSVN, the command headquarters for most of the South.] Then in 1965 I was transferred to the Saigon/Giadinh region. That was where I was from, so they assigned me to the local leadership group there.

At the time my unit moved out of "R" to our local assignments, the Americans were carrying out military operations in Cu Chi. We were moving almost a thousand men from village to village through underground tunnels. Parts of the tunnels had collapsed under bombing by the B-52s, and we had to crawl through narrow holes like snakes. The tunnels were so crowded and so short on air that I fainted and had to be carried out.

My other experiences with B-52s weren't any better. The first time I was attacked was in Ben Cat. We were eating in our bunkers when they came, two groups five minutes apart, three planes in a group. It was like a giant earthquake. The whole area was filled with fire and smoke. Trees were falling all around. My shelter collapsed on me, although it hadn't been hit—I felt as if I were sitting in a metal case which someone was pounding on with a hammer. I was sure I was dying. An image passed through my mind quickly—of my mother giving me a checkered scarf the day I first joined the army. It was terrifying.

Up through 1966 I was in a lot of battles against the ARVN. The last important one was at An Nhon at the end of that year, when we destroyed a regiment of the ARVN 5th Division. After that we were mostly engaged against U.S. forces from Cu Chi to Trang Bang. The Americans fought better than the ARVN. But you can't fight really well without hatred. Still, according to the Chinese, the VC needed one division to destroy one U.S. battalion. But Nguyen Chi Thanh didn't think so [Thanh was commander in chief of revolutionary forces in the South until 1967]. He argued that if we needed a division to fight against each American battalion we ought to just quit fighting the Americans because we'd never have enough men for it. He believed that we could fight them one on one.

But in order to fight the Americans, you had to get close to them. You couldn't fight them from a distance. The best way was to attack them while they were on the move, or at night when they were stationed together. So our tactics were different from theirs. Their idea was to surround us with ground forces, then destroy us with artillery and rockets, rather than by attacking directly with infantry.

Usually we could get away from that, even when they used helicopters to try and surround us, because we knew the countryside so well and we could get out fast. That happened at Soi Cut, where they destroyed three villages while they were trying to catch us.

The Vietnamese Communists and the Americans had very different ideas about the war. When the Americans came to Vietnam, they didn't bring with them a hatred for the Vietnamese people. But we had it for them! Stalin said, "In order to defeat the enemy, one must build up hatred." We had been thoroughly exposed to anti-Saigon and anti-American propaganda in the North. We had seen pictures of the South Vietnamese people being beaten, arrested, and tortured. We had seen documentary movies of Ngo Dinh Diem's cruel suppression of the Buddhists, of people being shocked with electricity and women being raped. These pictures had built up our rage and our determination to liberate the South.

We had such hatred for the enemy and such devotion to the noble cause of liberating our suppressed people that we felt we could overcome any difficulty and make any sacrifice. We didn't have any kind of humanitarian feeling about it, as the Americans did. We were defending our country and our people and punishing the aggressors. The point is that we had faith in the cause we were fighting for, and that this faith was reinforced by effective propaganda.

Maybe not everyone believed the propaganda completely, but since they were locked into the Communist orbit, it was very difficult to see things differently. Besides, the overriding moral principle, the cause that justified the war, was the liberation of fifteen million South Vietnamese people. To save fifteen million people was the highest moral obligation. To kill a few dozen people in the fighting was nothing important.

Of course sometimes we were deeply touched by certain situations. I remember after one battle where I had killed many men of Saigon's 38th Ranger Battalion, I found a picture on one of the dead puppet officers of his wife and his children. When I saw it I thought for a moment about how his wife would feel when they told her he was dead. I even kept the picture with me for a while and finally asked some local people who were going to Saigon if they could try to return it to his family.

But aside from personal feelings and human conscience, we had political ideals and revolutionary objectives. These had become deeply rooted in our minds and they were intensified by our Party indoctrination. So this kind of emotional sensitivity was aroused only once in a while and very quickly disappeared.

Of course we still had problems and conflicts, regardless of our ideals. There were minor conflicts between Southerners and Northerners. When we were in the North after regrouping, the Party had had a policy of special treatment for the Southerners. If there was a conflict, the Southerner would always be right. But the situation was reversed when we were in combat in the South. Then, if there was some kind of confrontation it was the Southerner who was likely to be disciplined or maybe expelled from the Party. But these conflicts were mostly minor.

We also felt resentful on occasion when someone like Nguyen Huu Tho [president of the NLF], who didn't have any fighting record at all, was assigned to a high leadership position while we who were fighting and facing death every day got nothing. But the Party's strategy was to attack on three fronts simultaneously: political, military, and propaganda. It was explained that individuals were used according to the needs of the revolution [Nguyen Huu Tho was a moderate intellectual whose appeal was primarily to the South's intellectuals], and that the victory of the Party was the most important priority.

More substantial conflicts were between the military command and the regional Party committees. The military people often had good knowledge of local situations, whereas the regional Party committee would get its orders from the central command and would often carry out these orders without consulting the local units. The only ones who dared oppose the Party committee policies were military people who were Party members trained in the North.

The Tet Offensive was a good example. Most of the military cadres didn't agree with the offensive at all. But since it was the Party's order, it had to be carried out. The Party said it had studied the situation carefully and that there would be strong support from the people. But most of the military didn't believe it.

Before the battle there was a lot of confusion. At that time I belonged to the E 268 regiment. Our primary objective was the Tan Son Nhut airport. But we didn't have liaison people to bring us in and we were forced to stop at Go Vap, where we were hit by rockets. After we broke through the Saigon defense perimeter, the great force of the "R" IX Corps was supposed to follow us in. We moved into the outskirts and tried to break through for three days. We expected that the IX Corps would arrive to help us break through the defenses and occupy the city. But they never came. We had to stay where we were, just waiting to be killed. We were under orders just to hold on and wait.

Many couldn't hold out and surrendered, even Lieutenant Colonel Tam Ha also gave himself up. After that I withdrew the regiment and waited.

When the Tet campaign was over, we didn't have enough men left to fight a major battle, only to make hit-and-run attacks on posts. So many men had been killed that morale was very low. We spent a great deal of time hiding in tunnels, trying to avoid being captured. We experienced desertions, and many of our people filtered back to their homes to join local guerrilla forces [instead of staying with mainline units]. We heard that in the North there were more young people trying to avoid the draft. When they were arrested, they were put into the army but were assigned to labor and transport units.

From that low point, news that the United States was withdrawing was like a resuscitating medicine for us. It raised our spirits. After that, the Party argued that it was due to the victory of our Tet Offensive campaign that the Americans were being forced to withdraw.

In May 1970, when American and ARVN forces carried out their thrust into Cambodia, all the forces in the area where I was stationed had to disperse to avoid their mopping-up operations. All the main forces split up to join the local organizations. It was at that point that I was captured. I was trying to make contact with a local hamlet liaison agent to get a message to the regional Party committee. I was caught in a small store where I was supposed to make the connection. Some Saigon soldiers had seen me go in. I saw them coming and ran, but they caught me and tied my hands. They kept me for a day, then sent me to the American 25th Division at Cu Chi for interrogation.

I had been fighting for twenty-five years. It isn't something I ever had nightmares about. Maybe we had a different view of killing. We were killing enemies and aggressors to regain our independence and save our country. It wasn't like the Americans. When they killed they thought of the Vietnamese as human beings.

THE BATTLE OF DONG XOAI

In the spring of 1965, infiltration from the North was countered by the intervention of American land forces. Up till that time, the Northern polit-buro and its NLF allies in the South had conceived of the war as a political conflict with a military dimension. But with the Americans in, the armed struggle took center stage.

In this new phase of the war, the revolution's military commander in chief, Nguyen Chi Thanh, advocated a strategy of conventional, large-unit con-frontations, to complement ongoing guerrilla actions. It was an approach that resulted in a series of bloody losses for his command.

Dong Xoai was one of the first battles in which large regular units of the Liberation Army pitched themselves against a massed South Vietnamese enemy. In Vietcong veteran circles, the engagement remains one of the best known, and most controversial, of the war. Argument still goes on about whether the South Vietnamese and their American advisers had advance knowledge of the attack. Tran Van Duc, many of whose recruits died at Dong Xoai, was sure they did.

The account is from the war memoirs of a Vietcong political cadre who rallied after the battle.

VU HUNG: *The Battle of Dong Xoai*

THE ATTACK WAS SET FOR JUNE 10, 1 A.M. HANOI TIME. REGIMENT Q762 was the main unit, Q761 was positioned to stop any relief col-umns, and Q763 was held in reserve. A battalion from Phuoc Thanh Province was supposed to attack the airstrip on the west side of the base, and a heavy artillery battalion attached to COSVN had been brought up to reinforce the artillery units of the three regiments.

In the general attack plan, Q762 was located to the east of Dong Xoai, Q763 to the west, and Q761 to the north. Ambushes were prepared at various places where it was anticipated that relief columns would try to break through.

The medical team prepared equally well, projecting the number of casualties and equipping itself to handle them. The famous doctor Tan Hoa, also attached to COSVN, had been assigned to Dong Xoai especially for this battle. He had fought against the French and afterwards had gone to study in the Soviet Union.

Four days before the attack, the Party committee for Regiment Q762 [the main attack unit] had issued a resolution which it had sent to the Party committee in charge of the Dong Xoai campaign. "We promise to eliminate Dong Xoai within one hour and thirty minutes." The Party committee for the campaign gave them an additional hour.

When I lived in Saigon I used to hear the propaganda of the Saigon government about how the Communists used special drugs before battle to make them fearless. But that wasn't true. Instead the emphasis was on preparing everybody psychologically. They believed that this kind of preparation was the most significant factor in winning.

On June 8 they gathered all the troops of Q762 for speeches by several eloquent Party leaders. They explained the purpose of the campaign and the duty of the soldiers, and they spoke about the honor of the regiment. General Hai Chan (Le Van Tuong), the Party boss for the campaign, also gave a talk, presenting the regiment with a victory flag. Then a representative of the regiment read a resolution expressing the determination of all the fighters.

Advanced headquarters was established near the Dong Xoai base. The bunker was equipped with a complete communications system, including telephone networks and radio communications. All the lines to the regiments and battalions were tested out. There was a lot of talk about the coming victory.

At about ten-thirty on June 9, two and a half hours before the attack, a telephone call came in. It was taken by Nam Thac, the colonel in charge of communications. Sweat began to drip off him when he answered it. He was saying, "What's happening? Yes, yes." Others in the bunker were asking him, "What's going on?"

Nam said that Q762 had come under fire from the base. They had said the west side—the airport side—was still quiet but that the telephone line to the airport side had been cut. When he heard this, General Hai Chan hit the table saying, "They know the plan."

Colonel Nam answered that that was nonsense. It was probably just harassment fire. If they knew the plan, the helicopters and jets would have already been here.

The atmosphere inside the bunker was tense. Everybody was gathered around looking at the maps when the telephone rang again. The operator reported that the airport unit was now under fire, too. We could hear the sound of artillery. It had only been about thirty minutes since Q762 had deployed, not enough time for them to have dug in. From outside, the artillery fire increased. We could hear 60s, 81s, 75s, and 105s—all of them.

At first we thought that only Q762 was under fire, then Q763 (the reserve) reported that it too had been attacked. Inside fifteen minutes we had reports of nine dead and twenty-three wounded, with casualties increasing by the minute. The command staff couldn't decide if this was a preemptive attack or not, or how to respond to it, since a response would give the positions away.

Before another fifteen minutes had gone by, the commander of Q762 called, asking for permission to attack, saying that if he didn't get the order he'd be a sitting duck. Nam told him to wait a few minutes, then he'd get an answer.

Then the Party committee met on it. Nam said he didn't believe the plan had been given away—security had been too tight. "Let's wait," he said. "It's just harassment fire." But Hai Chan was afraid that the *bo dois*'s morale would break if the situation lasted much longer.

While they were meeting on this, the telephone kept ringing. At one point the call was given to Nam and he shouted, "My God! The artillery unit has already attacked. They didn't wait." More calls came in—another unit said that it had to attack, the artillery had given the whole thing away, they couldn't hold back any longer.

At that Hai Chan ordered over an open radio line, *"Ceb tab! Ceb tab! Ceb tab!"*—"Attack, attack, attack!"

The battle was joined. Hardly anything happened according to plan. We had thought there were only two tanks in Dong Xoai, but it turned out there were four. At one point all the communications lines were cut and we had to rely on runners. Reports of heavy casualties kept coming in. By early morning, Q762 had lost two battalions but had managed to take four posts on the perimeter.

By 5 p.m., the fighting had become sporadic. In the relative quiet a call came in from Q762 reporting that they totally controlled Dong Xoai. When he heard that Colonel Nam shouted, "We've won!" Shortly afterward the telephone rang with the message that a relief column had been ambushed by Q761, just as we had planned.

Suddenly, there were explosions all over the place. At the phone, Nam said, "My God! It's brutal, brutal." A fleet of jets had come in to bomb the whole area. The bunker was shaking, its lights swaying back and forth. Colonel Nam said, "Oh my God, what's happened to 761?"

THE MINE SAPPERS

General Thanh, the Northern architect of confrontational warfare, died in 1967. Some say he was killed in a B-52 raid, others that he had a heart attack. Whatever the case, by the time of his death, the bloodied Liberation forces were ready to shift into a war of attrition. They had recognized the futility of battling American and South Vietnamese firepower and air strength head-on. Now their object was to kill as many of the enemy as possible at the smallest possible risk to themselves.

To carry out this strategy, the "special operations" men came into their own—miners, who could lay a bewildering variety of deadly land mines; and sappers, skilled at sneaking through rows of barbed wire to blow holes in defenses and let in the attack, or to appear suddenly inside a post and wreak havoc. A successful sapper attack might trade several dead for substantial casualties among surprised defenders. If unsuccessful, only the members of the sapper team would be lost.

These men, who developed a sixth sense for detecting and disarming mines, had the war's most dangerous job. South Vietnamese interrogators recorded the first three stories. Afterward, Captain (now Colonel) Stuart Herrington describes the experience of surviving a sapper attack.

NGUYEN VAN MO, *Master Sergeant, NVA, 40th Mine Sapper Battalion*

AFTER I CAME DOWN FROM NORTH VIETNAM, I WAS ASSIGNED TO A mine sapper unit. As soon as I got this assignment I was sent for training in sapper techniques and tactics. These mine sapper tactics allowed us to gain the advantage. The Americans were fighting a modern war, with artillery, air support, and helicopters. But mine sappers specialized in the tactics of hand-to-hand combat. In this kind of close fighting, artillery and air power were relatively useless.

The training was elaborate. We learned how to crouch while walking, how to crawl, how to move silently through mud and water, how to walk through dry leaves. We practiced different ways of stooping while we walked. In teams of seven men, we practiced moving in rhythm to avoid being spotted under searchlights, synchronizing our motions, stepping with toes first, then gradually lowering heels to the ground, very slowly, step by step.

Wading through mud, we were taught to walk by lowering our toes first, then the rest of the foot. Picking our feet up, we would move them around gently [to break any suction], then slowly pull up the heels to avoid making noises. If you just pulled them up, without first moving them around gently, you'd make sounds. The same thing would happen if you didn't put your toes down first. We used the same methods for walking through water. On dry leaves, we'd sling our weapons over our backs and move in a bent-over position using hands as well as feet. We were taught to move the dried leaves away with our hands, then pull our feet up underneath our palms so that we wouldn't step on the leaves. We'd keep moving that way until we reached the objective. Time made no difference. In training it might take two or three hours to crawl like this through five fences of barbed wire.

We trained constantly with various types of weapons. We learned how to use the AKs most effectively at short distances. We practiced rapid firing and shifting the fire from left to right. We became familiar with B-40 and B-41 rocket launchers, bangalores, grenades, explosives. Against concertina-type wire, we would insert the bangalores into the middle of the fences. After lighting the fuse, we would have to rush out and lie flat a few meters from the fence. As soon as the bangalores exploded, the sapper would rush through to assault the objective. We conducted exercises to familiarize ourselves with real combat situations, simulating attacks against trenches, buildings, and tanks.

In an actual sapper operation, we would prepare the battlefield beforehand. That meant getting as close to the objective as possible—say a fortified post or a fire base—so that we could observe the enemy blockhouses and other positions we were going to hit. To do this we would first have to crawl through the barbed wire, but without cutting the wire or removing mines—we couldn't leave any traces. We were supposed to tie the wire up with string and mark the mines on the route we were following.

After penetrating into the post and observing, we'd return to our base and make a sand table model for the assault troops to study. During the attack we'd come in as slowly as we could, following the route we had marked out during observation. To avoid making noise, we wouldn't clip the barbed wire, only cut it two-thirds of the way through, then break it with our hands, holding the wire firmly so that the fence wouldn't move. To detect mines we used our hands, feeling the ground ahead of us very carefully, bit by bit.

The worst part was reaching the inner fence around a position. I was always scared to death at that point. Even after I was a veteran of these attacks I would still start trembling. If the Americans discovered you at that point, you were certain to be killed. There was no chance of getting away back through the fences under machine gun fire.

In June 1969 my unit was engaged in a battle in the Duc Pho district of Quang Ngai. Our objective was the Go Hoi airstrip, defended by the 11th Brigade of the Americal Division stationed on Vang Mountain. There were American technicians quartered in the area, and the facility was lit by floodlights all night long.

I had accompanied the platoon leader to prepare the battlefield. We had crawled through five barbed wire fences and across a stream, and had marked the sentry posts, the technicians' barracks, and the vehicle park. After we got back from the reconnaissance, we constructed the sand table to develop a plan of attack. Battalion decided to use the first platoon, which was the top unit in First Company. Most of the sappers who were chosen were cadre; only two of the eight who would be going were enlisted men.

When we got to the first fence one of the enlisted men was too frightened to go on. The rest of us were also scared, but we couldn't give up the attack, even though we knew what the chances were of getting back. We had been specially chosen for this mission and we could hardly go back without doing anything.

Halfway through the fences the assistant company commander pulled out. He told us he had to go back to deploy the B-41 gunners and that we should go ahead according to plan. The fact was that he was afraid for his life and didn't have the guts to go all the way in himself.

But the rest of us managed to get in without being spotted. We got all the way to the barracks and the vehicle park. According to the plan, I was supposed to make the deepest penetration and fire a signal for the attack. Everything went off exactly on schedule. As soon as I fired the signal cracker, the others began to attack the blockhouses with explosives and grenades. A couple of the blockhouses were destroyed in the first minutes, which eliminated a lot of the Americans' firepower, so they weren't able to get a counterattack going. Then we attacked the technicians' barracks. They didn't have any weapons and ran wildly in different directions. When we went into the barracks there were two Americans with M-16s. The AK gunner with me killed them both instantly. Most of the Americans were running into the trenches. It seemed to me that they must have thought they were under mortar attack.

I found the generators and fixed the explosives. When they blew, all the lights went off. I kept on, setting charges to trucks and more buildings. Meanwhile the sappers deployed in the outer area had been successful in silencing the American machine guns. While we were getting out, one of our people was killed. But the other six made it. We didn't know what the American casualties were. Division reported that we had killed over seventy. From what I saw, we got some of them, but hardly that many.

After this battle the unit held meetings to study our success and to commend us for our achievement. Seven of us had attacked a large American force inside an installation surrounded with defenses and flooded with as much light as if it were daytime. Three of us were awarded third-class medals and were praised for being outstanding American killers. I was one of them.

The next assault on the airstrip was conducted by the Second Platoon, about two or three hundred meters from where we had launched our attack. Of the seven sappers in that unit, only one survived.

HOANG TAT HONG, *Sergeant, NVA*

THE EXPLOSIVES WE USED WERE TNT, PLASTIC, AND C-4 chemical substances. TNT had to be carefully maintained and always kept dry. Each bar was about twelve by five inches. We used it against bunkers, fortified emplacements, trenches, and buildings, operating it by detonators or blasting caps.

Plastic had the same effect as TNT, but it was easier to maintain and transport. In particular, it was extremely thin, only about one to one and a half inches, and it could be bent, so you could carry it around anywhere. Plastic could also be soaked in water up to seven hours and it would still be usable.

C-4 was as soft as rubber and had an explosive capability much greater than TNT or plastic. You could soak it in water for a week running. We used it to attack bridges, culverts, and other damp targets.

We had different types of mines, like the claymore, DH-5, and DH-10. The claymore was an antipersonnel weapon. The DH-5 and DH-10 were used against wire fences. A DH-5 could completely destroy five rows of barbed wire. When it exploded, the wire would melt and twist, opening up a hole four to five meters wide. The DH-10 had twice the capability of a 5. Both were detonated electrically. It was rare to see them on the battlefield though. Newer tactics called for the sappers to crawl in through the fences, then use explosives to destroy the primary targets.

We had three types of hand grenades: locally made, Chinese-made, and the American M-26. We only used them in critical situations, when we had to protect our positions. If a sapper was not discovered, his job was to get as close to the target as possible, then use explosives to destroy it. He used his grenades or AK-47 only after his position was known.

We were also trained in camouflage techniques for three basic situations—planting mines, covering trails, and body camouflage. In planting mines, the basic requirement is to make the mine emplacement identical to the surrounding terrain. If a mine was planted in open ground, the top layer of earth had to be preserved. After planting the mine, you would replace the top layer of earth over it, so there would be no visible sign of new earth. But if the emplacement was out in the open, with no trees or grass, there was no way to camouflage it from air observation.

Where there was grass it was possible to hide an emplacement completely from both ground and air detection. But the sapper had to be extraordinarily careful. Before he began digging he had to be sure to preserve the grass from the top of the hole. When he had planted the mine, he would fill in the hole with the earth he had dug, then carefully cover up the emplacement with the grass layer that had been preserved, making sure that no different colors were showing. If he did it well, the emplacement couldn't be discovered.

For trail camouflage, a unit would move in single file, each person in turn stepping in the footsteps of the man in front. The last man in the line would be responsible for eliminating whatever tracks there were.

Body camouflage was a time-consuming affair. During an operation a sapper would wear only a pair of shorts; that wouldn't cause him any trouble while he was crawling under wire. Before an assault the surroundings would be studied closely. Afterwards we would prepare body camouflage to make ourselves blend in with the color of the locale. For example, if the target was in a grassy area, the sapper would have to disguise himself with an identical green. Where there was no grass, leaves would be ground and mixed with dirt, then plastered over his body to make him indistinguishable from the ground. It might take them a couple of hours to do all this. If an attack was scheduled for 10 P.M. the sapper team might start their camouflage preparations at 7.

VAN CONG VAN, *Company Commander, Deputy Chief, Special Operations, Ben Tre Province*

THE DEATH OF A SAPPER IS DREADFUL. WHEN HE DIES HE IS WEARing only a pair of shorts, his body camouflaged green to blend in with the battlefield. When he dies his corpse is most often left on the road, or in some hole or canal. Often the ARVN will expose his body so that his relatives passing by can see it. The people in general admire and praise the special operations men. But their parents, wives, and children are afraid. They try to persuade them to quit or go home, or transfer to some other kind of unit. They know that in every battle the special operations men have to lead. And they know that when they die, their corpses will be left behind.

Through nine years of fighting I trained so many sappers, for every special operations unit. I knew thousands of them. Today, so few of them are left alive. As a commanding officer I witnessed the deaths of my men. The peasants whose sons were in my units regarded me with hostility. They were unhappy that their sons were pushed into danger. And I, the commander, was still alive, while my fighters—their children—were killed.

At the beginning of June 1970, I was on my way back to my headquarters when I was caught in a B-52 bombardment at Luu Phu village. The two reconnaissance men with me were killed. Blood was leaking out of my ear from the concussion. I thought, This war has been going on long enough. The liberation struggle has brought death and misery. Nobody wants to continue it. Many young men have lost their lives on the battlefield. Those who died have not been properly buried and their families have received no information about their deaths. The higher officers and the Party haven't paid attention to the lives of the fighters.

I thought of my own special operations training in September of 1962. Mo Cay district sent seventeen of us to the course. Now all the rest are dead. Only I am still alive. The special operations course will die with me.

CAPTAIN STUART HERRINGTON: *The American Side**

IT WAS ONE A.M. ON MY LAST NIGHT IN DUC HUE WHEN THE MORtar rounds began to fall in our compound . . . I pulled on my boots and

---

* From *Silence Was a Weapon* by Captain Stuart Herrington (Novato, Calif.: Presidio Press, 1982).

reached groggily for a knapsack full of grenades. The "crump" of the exploding mortar rounds was punctuated by the heavier "boom" of demolition charges as we rushed to our bunkers. Satchel charges! That meant we were under sapper attack. Close by, the "whoosh-bang" of enemy B-40 rockets could be heard, along with the sporadic chatter of at least one AK-47 rifle. A distressingly weak volume of M-16 fire was coming from the perimeter. Major Nghiem's troops had been caught napping.

My bunker mate and I unlimbered our .50 caliber machine gun. If the enemy tried to cross the river anywhere to the north of us, he would have to contend with us. If he came from anywhere else, our weapon would be useless, since it could not be turned around. Aerial flares lighted up the landscape like day, but we could see no Vietcong on the perimeter. Fifty meters to the south of us, a tremendous explosion went off next to the Phoenix office. An enemy sapper had hurled a satchel charge and scored a direct hit on the Vietnamese mortar position. The explosion ignited the weapons' ammunition stockpile and killed the three-man crew.

By this time we had our .50 barking out long bursts of tracered ammunition at the opposite river bank. The tracers cut a spectacular orange swath through the night, a reassuring sight in spite of the fact that we couldn't see anything to shoot at. After firing off several hundred rounds this way, we had to cease fire because of the cordite fumes in the bunker. . . .

We called for artillery illumination from Bao Trai, and helicopter gunships from wherever we could get them. The enemy mortar barrage subsided, but the sky was lit up by the secondary explosions from the mortar positions where the district's mortar crew had met their end.

Soon the gunships arrived on station, putting on their own impressive display of pyrotechnics. The helicopters were armed with rockets and "miniguns," and they passed low over our compound as they delivered their ordnance on targets we called to them. Actually, by then the enemy sappers had already withdrawn, leaving behind the body of one comrade. The best that the gunships could do was to saturate the tree line to the south of our compound with fire in hopes of inflicting some damage on the enemy sappers and mortarmen as they withdrew. I spent the rest of the evening crouched in the bunker, selfishly thanking God that the Vietcong's target for the evening had been the Vietnamese portion of the compound.

The enemy had come and gone in not more than thirty minutes. The brief mortar barrage had forced our troops into their bunkers and given the three attacking sapper squads the opportunity to cut their way through the barbed wire undetected. Luckily, only one of the attacking elements had succeeded in penetrating to its target. In the compound of the militia company, several sappers had managed to toss satchel charges into an empty building. It was this squad that had lost one man in the brief firefight that had followed. His body, clad only in a loincloth, had already been laid out at the crossroads by the government troops. The second enemy squad had attempted to penetrate our perimeter near the mortar pit. It was this group that had tossed the tear gas cannisters as they tried to create enough confusion to allow them to break through to our ammunition storage area. The third sapper squad had fought a fierce battle with the soldiers of our small artillery unit and had failed to break through to their target. The score for the evening was five friendly troops killed and eight wounded. It could have been much worse.

VC ASSASSIN

Terror was an effective weapon in keeping the Southern government's local administrators off balance, intimidating the weak and eliminating the strong. Assassinations were also used to maintain discipline among revolutionary soldiers who might be considering defection to the government side. The following is from an interrogation of a Vietcong assassin.

NGUYEN VAN THICH, *VC Ranger Platoon Leader: VC Assassin*

BEGINNING IN MAY 1967, MY UNIT WAS ASSIGNED TO DO ASSASSINA-tion missions in the Soc Trang City district. It was explained to us that assassinating and kidnapping GVN officials would help South Vietnam be liberated even faster. Destroying the government infrastructure would help the Party mobilize people to fight. The General Offensive and General Uprising was approaching, though we didn't know when it would be. The motto we used was "Kill the Wicked and Destroy the Oppressors to Promote Mobilization of the People." That was our guideline.

At first our targets were policemen, informers, and hamlet or subhamlet chiefs. In April 1970, Hoi Chanh [VC who had rallied to the Saigon government], who were working for government armed propaganda teams, were given top priority. These were people who knew our procedures and tactics very well. They were quite harmful to our own infrastructure. If they weren't annihilated they'd give us all sorts of difficulties. Liquidating them would also cut down on defections. People wouldn't be so eager to rally if they were afraid of retribution.

When we'd get an order to kill someone, we'd begin keeping tabs on that person's activities. We would also set up a network of agents inside the area where the assassination was supposed to take place to give us an understanding of the everyday goings on there. These agents were expected to give us a plan of the area, a description of GVN forces that were there, and so on.

After we had understood everything thoroughly, we would draw up an operation plan. On the day we put the plan in motion, the network people would lead us in. Most often these agents were women—women rangers. They usually didn't have legal government identity papers. But since they were women, they could sneak into the city and operate there much more easily.

If there were special difficulties, sometimes it might take us a couple of months to complete an operation. Inside the city we had hidden cellars which we could use for operations there. We called staying in these places, "clinging to the pole." That meant living underground waiting for the chance to surface and complete the assignment.

Altogether I participated in about thirty killings, mostly of policemen and hamlet chiefs. The first were two policemen who were guarding the Cau Quay Bridge in Soc Trang. An intelligence agent from inside the city came out to lead me and the other two guys in my cell in. We snuck up to the bridge and shot them. One was killed, the other badly wounded. We grabbed a pistol and a carbine and got out along our escape route.

After that first killing I had nightmares, anxieties. Later I got used to it. My buddies felt the same way. I was trusted with this kind of mission and indoctrinated with the necessity of killing. I never had any regrets. I couldn't tell myself who was good or who was bad. Regardless of what a person might be like, the order came from above and I carried it out. If I didn't, I would have been severely criticized and given a hard time.

But I did feel sorry for the victims' relatives. In December 1968 we killed the chief of Kho Dau 11 hamlet, a man named Ro. It was a difficult assignment. We had gone into the hamlet three times without getting it done. Finally, we were ordered to do it during the daytime. At 9 A.M. Tuan, Hung, and I walked into the hamlet from the ricefields and saw him in the marketplace. We saw him go into a shop and dashed towards him. Hung and I stood guard outside. Tuan asked, "Where are you going?" Ro answered, "Are you looking for me? Who are you?" At that Tuan said, "I've come here just to kill you." And he pulled out his knife and stabbed Ro. Then we took off running towards Tan Thanh village.

Two weeks later we were back in Kho Dau 11 on a propaganda mission. After dark we got all the villagers out to the hamlet meeting area and spoke to them. We told them that Ro had been a government henchman and that he was a wicked person who had committed many crimes. We pointed out that it was because of him that the GVN [government of Vietnam] was able to oppress the townspeople. We explained that the Liberation forces had eliminated him to liberate the village so that they, the villagers, could enjoy more freedom. The villagers kept quiet through all this. They were very frightened of us. They didn't dare to say a word.

At about midnight, when we had finished with the propaganda session, we went over to Ro's house. We knocked at the door and told his wife that we were Liberation men. When we asked her about her husband, she said, "I'm not resentful at the Liberation forces for killing my husband. But I have been miserable since his death because I can't afford to raise my children." When I realized that Ro had come from the poor class, as I do, I felt very unhappy about it. By that time I had learned that his wife worked as a small peddler to make her living and that she had five children.

The other case I was unhappy about was a young girl named Thuy. She was twenty-one and had worked for the VC as a liaison agent. We had previously lived in the same area and knew each other well. She had been arrested by the GVN and had denounced people in her network, including three city committee members. Because of her cooperation, the government had given her Hoi Chanh status. Meanwhile, the VC sentenced her to death, and the sentence was given to my cell to carry out.

Thuy was living near the electric company in Soc Trang City. Around midnight one night we broke into her house. Her husband, a GVN soldier, wasn't at home. She was sleeping and was obviously pregnant, near term. But I couldn't afford any indecisiveness. I had orders to kill her. So we woke her up. At first she didn't recognize us because we were wearing GVN uniforms. She asked, "Who are you? Why are you here at this hour?" I told her to shut up and follow me, that we'd shoot her if she screamed. Once we got her out into the open I told her, "You have harmed the Liberation Movement a lot. The people have sentenced you to death and I have been given the job of executing you. Before, you were my friend. But now you are my enemy. If I spare you, I will be killed myself." She didn't say a word. Then I asked her if she knew she deserved her death. She replied in quite a normal voice, "Yes. I realize I will die. Go ahead with your mission." No begging for mercy. We took her over to the road and stabbed her in the chest. She slumped down without a moan. She knew that it was a consequence of what she had done against the Front.

That was in April 1970. I regret that I killed her while she was pregnant. I should have waited for her delivery.

BUI VAN TAI, *NVA Assistant Platoon Leader: The B-52s*

AFTER THE SWEEP OPERATION AGAINST US IN AUGUST 1968, OUR previous base in the Hon Tan Forest was occupied by U.S. and ARVN troops. We had to retreat deeper into the hills. It took us two months to finish building new shelters and installations for our rockets. Then we began to deal with the food shortage, concentrating on bringing in rice supplies from Dien An, which was about a six-day round trip from our new base. As soon as we had gotten enough food stored, our camp was spotted.

The whole year—from the second half of August 1968 to the second half of August 1969—we kept busy avoiding the enemy, building new installations, and looking for food. Moving an artillery unit around isn't as easy as moving infantry. Our rocket tubes were 2.2 meters long and weighed 30 kilos [66 pounds], the tripods weighed 35 kilos [77 pounds]. It's not so easy to carry them around in the jungle, especially after your health has been shattered from ten straight months of fighting. After the August '68 sweep, we weren't able to stay more than a month at any one place—we were on the move all the time. Our health and fighting ability got worse and worse.

Eventually, about November 1968, the U.S. and ARVN troops withdrew from the Hon Tan Forest. Afterwards the whole area was bombed by B-52s. All the way from Son Phuc to Deo La and from Son Hiep on there was no place to hide. It just became bare. Fortunately, my unit never got hit. But morale was terrible.

Once we were on the Cay Khe road on our way back from a food supply run. At various places on the communications routes we would build resting places—two vertical bamboo posts with a bamboo pole tied across horizontally. The horizontal pole was for people who were carrying heavy loads. You could lean back against it for a while, taking the weight off your back. You could use it to prop up your rice pack, backpack, and ammunition belts without having to take them off. At a rest stop near

Hon Tan there were five dead men standing against one of these poles. They had been killed by shrapnel from a B-52 attack that had hit a long way off. They hadn't fallen down because their packs were propped up over the resting pole.

TRAN VAN TRA

The Vietcong colonel general describes his feelings about the battlefield.

TRAN VAN TRA: *Comradeship*

I WAS ABOUT TO RETURN TO THE GREEN JUNGLE [FROM HANOI], where the battlefield was on fire with fighting, back to my combat units. I was eager and happy to get back. These spontaneous feelings allowed me to understand something I had had inside me for a long time. I discovered that I regarded the base as my home. The battlefield was my native district. The cadres and soldiers . . . were my family.

I had felt anxious and nostalgic when I was assigned to the Four Party Joint Commission in Saigon [in 1973]. I had had to leave the battlefield and I thought that I wouldn't be returning. It had been like bidding a sad farewell to my home. Now that I was about to return to the base and the battlefield, I was as happy as if I were coming back to my old village and my loved ones.

Maybe it was the decades I had lived on the battlefield. [Tra had been in almost continuous action for twenty-nine years.] The jungle birds and fish, the wide open spaces, and constantly changing scenery had conditioned my soul to respond only to the green jungle. Or maybe it was because I had yearned all my life for independence and freedom and had pledged to bear arms and fight until the final objective was reached. So my life had been tied in with the battlefield.

But these things were not the whole story. Now I understand even more clearly the sentiment behind the life and society of the soldiers during the many long years of war. How beautiful and noble is the sacred comradeship created by the goal of liberating the homeland and the people. During the hard days of hunger and thirst we shared each piece of jungle root, each bit of firewood, each apple, each drink of spring water we had brought from the other side of the mountain. Every year on the Truong Son route [the Ho Chi Minh Trail] after months of exhaustion, we shared each spoonful of sugar or bit of salt, or offered each other the last quinine tablet to help each other get to the goal.

Each human life was precious and the homeland needed each soldier. But we analyzed our joys and sorrows. If someone heard that someone else had won a battle and had done a better job, he would enthusiastically study the other's example. If someone heard that someone else had been defeated, he would be worried and look for ways to help him out. Everything was for the common cause. Everything was for the revolution. One for all, all for one. That was life in the "green jungle."

That was the way life was for comrades in arms during two wars of resistance—in Duong Minh Chau, War Zone D, Dong Thap Muoi, and the U Minh Forest. The love one had for one's comrades and fellow fighters, for the jungle and the streams was unlimited, immense. That was the love we learned from Uncle Ho, from his vast love for the nation and for the workers and fighters. That love transcended space and time and was the same everywhere and at all times.

Anyone who had lived such a life would be sentimental and nostalgic. It wasn't that the battlefield had captivated me, but that my heart and morality had bound me to it.

PART THREE
RESOLUTION

APRIL 30, 1975, WAS THE DAY VIETNAM'S THIRTY-YEAR WAR OF INDE-pendence finally ended. For most of the victors it was a moment of intense elation. Some years later, General Tra recalled, "There are few moments in life when one is so happy one wants to cry. I suddenly felt as though my soul were translucent and light . . ."

But the war ended in different ways for different men—and at different times. Over the years of struggle, perspectives shifted and evolved. The battlefield camaraderie that General Tra loved, the brotherhood and alliances engendered by warfare, had begun to break down well before the final victory.

As the nature of their partnership revealed itself by stages, nationalist independence fighters became disillusioned with their Communist cousins. Many of them began to think, as one of their leaders expressed it when he rallied, "They had credulously stepped into an adventure that they have been and still are regretting."

By 1970 also, many Southerners began to understand that victory would lead to their domination by the "Tonkinese"—the men of the North. Party as well as non-Party cadres were alive to that uncomfortable eventuality. By the April 30, 1975, victory it was far too late to do anything about it.

Another group that had run out of time by then was the "Third Force," South Vietnam's opposition factions. Having spent years fighting Saigon's succession of dictatorial regimes, they now found themselves with no leverage for a struggle against the new rulers. Their steadfast pursuit of democratic reforms brought them a particularly bitter resolution.

But it was no more bitter than it was to be for ethnic Chinese, both North and South. Some of the more politically aware among them had sensed a worsening in their situation since 1969, when Ho died. But none could have guessed what a nightmare would unfold for them within a few short years of victory.

XUAN VU'S STORY: *Back to the South*

BY 1964, THERE WAS A REGULAR PIPELINE TO THE SOUTH. ALL SORTS of units were going—soldiers, medical people, journalists, artists. The buildup started then and got more intensive after the American intervention [1965]. I heard through the grapevine that they were talking about sending me. But I also knew that I wasn't completely trusted because of my mistake with the ICC years ago. Finally I was called in for a talk.

The tone of this meeting was "Let's forgive and forget." That is, my bosses were willing to forgive and forget about the ICC. What they wanted in exchange was a major piece of propaganda. At this point all of the Northern and NLF strategy was based on what was called *Dong Khoi*—"The General Uprising." The idea was to coordinate a large-scale military offensive with mass uprisings in all the big Southern cities. The Saigon government would never be able to handle both at the same time. The Americans would be helpless against mass demonstrations. Civilian and military chaos would topple the regime, and we could expect negotiations that would lead to a new coalition government.

But for all of this to happen, the Southern people had to be prepared to rise up. People's Uprising Committees were formed. Mass organizations covertly controlled by the Party were mobilized. And, of course, a huge propaganda effort was in the works. I was supposed to be part of the propaganda effort. The idea was for me to write a historical novel or group of short stories about the resistance in Ben Tre Province. Ben Tre was one of the historic hotbeds of revolution. It was also my home province. The theme would be Ben Tre Then and Ben Tre Now—the heroic continuity of the anti-French and anti-American resistance. I'd go back, gather material on the anti-American war, put it together with my earlier writing in a book, then make a movie out of it.

Here was my chance, they said, to make up for my errors. I thought, Here is my chance to get back home. I told them that I would write a great book, something really extraordinary. I meant it, too.

The next thing I knew, I was sent to a special training camp for people going South. I was there for three months—three months of eating, sleeping, and exercising. Exercising meant hiking—with a load of bricks on your back. My unit was all artists of some sort: writers, musicians, photographers, painters, dancers—even some Western-trained ballerinas. All of us were being trained to go South down the Ho Chi Minh Trail. Like everybody else we would have to climb along the Truong Son Mountains. So we practiced by carrying bricks in our backpacks. At the start we would trudge along with six bricks that felt as if they weighed a ton. By the end we were carrying thirty kilos of bricks. We'd load them up and start hiking at nine in the morning. From nine to eleven, then from two to five. After we got used to it, they added a nightime hike, from seven to ten.

A lot of people never took their packs off. They would even eat with those goddamn bricks on their backs. The camp motto was, "More sweat" (here), "Less blood" (there). We were also trained to shoot AK-47 rifles, but most of the time we spent lugging around bricks. By the end of the three months I weighed sixty kilos [one hundred and thirty-two pounds] myself and could carry another thirty kilos. That was the required standard. If you couldn't carry thirty kilos around indefinitely, you weren't considered fit enough for the Ho Chi Minh Trail. I was in the best shape of my life. If they had required fifty kilos, I would have trained myself to carry that. I would have become an elephant if I had to.

Most of us felt the same. Morale in the camp was really high, at least among the Southerners. We were dying to go back. Some of the Northerners weren't so sure. But everyone was motivated by the idea of the great General Uprising. Among us were some of the finest young artists in North Vietnam. Most of them were being sent to help celebrate the great victory. That by itself was worth all the hazards. Everyone felt it: victory must be just around the corner, like all the newspapers were saying. Why else would they be sending a group like this? Shortly after Tet my unit was ready to leave, about thirty of us altogether.

In camp I had become very close to one of the dancers, a beautiful girl from Quang Nam [a central province, part of South Vietnam], a ballerina. We started off huddled together in the back of a military truck, one of the two that carried our group. We drove by night—it was as if we were starting a great adventure. I couldn't have been happier. After a decade I was going home with my first real love riding next to me.

The trucks followed a military road toward the 17th parallel [the border between North and South Vietnam], then left us off in the foothills of the Truong Son range at the Laotian frontier. From there we walked up into the mountains along a little footpath. We crossed the source of the Ben Hai River, sometimes leaving the trail to cut across country. At night we slung our hammocks up and arranged our canopies and mosquito nets over us. In our packs we had quinine, snakebite antivenom, water purifying pills, and flints for our lighters that maybe were the most precious items of all.

After three days of climbing, everyone was so footsore they could hardly walk. Our rubber sandals weren't the ideal footwear, but it was impossible to go barefoot. Even the most calloused peasant feet would be cut to shreds on the jagged stones we were hiking over. On that trail your sandals were your life. You learned to sleep with them under your neck so they wouldn't be stolen. My sweetheart's feet were cut and became infected and swollen. She was distraught about it, not only because it was so hard to keep up, but because she was a ballerina. Every night I washed them carefully. But there was no place to stop and really take care of it, and no antibiotics for something like this. We began to shake our heads about how they could have sent us on this kind of trip without even the most basic facilities to take care of people.

For two weeks or so we just climbed. Everywhere work gangs were building bridges and new trails. We met other groups, teachers, nurses, soldiers, all of them going South. Each night we would stop at a way station where there was supposed to be a store of rice. At first there was. But as we got farther along the trail, the food became scarcer. Sometimes a station would have no rice at all, nothing—after we had been walking all day. Then we'd search the forest for edible roots and leaves.

About a month into the trip I got sick. I could feel it coming. We had been moving through a constant downpour for what seemed to be days. There was no way to keep dry. During the day we wrapped our squares of vinyl around us like raincoats. At night we'd sling them up over our hammocks. But the water always found a way to sluice down over you. I began to feel achy and feverish. But I knew there was no place to stop, that I'd just have to fight it off and keep with the group. One night I put my hammock up and collapsed into it. The next morning I couldn't get up.

I had already said goodbye to my sweetheart. She had taken the trail off toward Quang Nam some days before. Now I said goodbye to the rest of the group. They had to go. There was no way they could stop. Some had tears in their eyes because they felt sorry for me. Some of them were indignant about having to leave me there. I knew I was alone, burning with fever. I couldn't open my eyes. At times I would wake up and know that I had been unconscious, but I had no idea for how long. At one point, two men came by. I could hear them talking, but my eyes hurt so much I couldn't open them to see. I sensed that they were standing right over me. They must have opened up my canopy to take a look at who was inside. These guys were liaison agents, trail guides who would lead groups from one way station to the next. I listened while they discussed my case. "This one's had it," one of them said. "Yeah, nothing to do for him," said the other. Then they left and I slipped back into unconsciousness.

I don't know how long I stayed in that hammock. In the times I was awake, I knew that I'd been delirious. Two lines from the poet To Huu kept running through my head.

> What's the use of regretting it; it's enough now.
> I've been struggling in life for so many years.

To Huu himself had seen us off when we left the training camp. It was as if he were still talking to me. I could see the Van Dien cemetery six kilometers south of Hanoi, a place I had been to a couple of times to say goodbye to friends. It was a place where Southerners were afraid to be buried. I escaped from the Van Dien cemetery—that was one of the things I was thinking when I left. Now I imagined what my grave would look like here—puddles of yellow water next to a mound with incense sticks stuck into it, without a gravestone.

The rain kept falling. It followed the strings of my hammock and wet my back first, then the whole hammock. I remember thinking about the rain in the Mekong Delta that I used to listen to draped in a warm blanket, reading a book on the porch of my house. Not like this evil Truong Son rain.

When I finally woke up, it might have been a day later, or maybe a couple of days, I don't know. I could see the sunshine. I heard birds singing and a waterfall rushing somewhere nearby. I felt as if all my bones were disconnected. I had no strength to get up, even to move. I looked down. Underneath the hammock was my cooking can, with a potato in it and a note from one of my buddies: "This is for you. See you at the next station."

I struggled to get up from the hammock but couldn't do it. Finally, I managed to fall out. I lay there on the ground for ages staring at my cooking can. I thought I would try to light a fire and cook the potato, but I couldn't move. Getting back in seemed impossible, even though the hammock was hanging only a foot or so off the ground. Eventually I got up the strength to heave myself back into it, first my upper body, then my legs.

Lying in the hammock shivering, I began to feel bitter. I was thinking to myself about how awful I felt, and that there was no one there to help. My sweetheart and I had been talking about just this earlier on. She had told me, "Look, this isn't the way to treat people. It's like throwing your own children out." Now I found myself thinking about what she had said, and thinking that she was right. They had thrown me out, like a piece of garbage.

Whatever I had was some kind of periodic fever. I'd get chilled, then hot, then very hot, sometimes delirious. When the crisis passed I'd feel better, but very weak. I had the uncanny sensation that all my bones were disconnected, as if the tendons and ligaments holding them together had dissolved. In the periods between crises, I cooked some of the rice I had saved and ate a little.

Gradually, I began to get my strength back. In the pool next to the waterfall where I got my water, I could also look at my reflection. The first time I saw it I almost cried. I couldn't believe the gaunt, cadaverous face in the water was mine.

But now I was feeling better every day, and eventually I got strong enough to start walking again. I hooked up with two other stragglers who had also been sick and had left several of their buddies dead, burying them under brush and rocks at the side of the trail. They had been too weak to dig graves.

Alongside the path, we began to see discarded weapons and ammunition—base plates for 81mm mortars, and sometimes the mortar tubes themselves. I understood it. When you're sick with jungle fever you felt lucky if you could lift yourself up, let alone something like a mortar. Every piece of extra equipment you had to carry was excruciating. But you only stopped when you were so sick you couldn't move. Once you stopped, there was a good chance you'd never get up. And there was no way of going back.

Food was a constant problem. Way stations were always low or out, or else the rice had gotten moldy from sitting too long. But occasionally we'd be able to trade with the tribal people who lived in the mountains. You'd see them from time to time along the trail—men and women wearing loincloths and nothing else. We would talk to them with gestures; they only spoke their tribal language. They were after belts, shirts, pants, any kind of trinket. What they valued most were needles and flints. They loved those flints. They were like treasures. Their usual way of making fire was by striking two rocks together. They would trade a chicken for one flint. Sometimes they would offer fish or dogmeat. They even raised pigs, and they'd let one go for a watch. After some business with these people we would have plenty to eat for a while. Then nothing again.

Several times we went down into their villages to trade. It was frightening, but exotic. These were Tai tribespeople. They filed their teeth down, sometimes to the gum line. The women wore huge bamboo disks in their ears. Young girls had small plugs, which they replaced with larger ones as they got older. The adult women's ears were so stretched out you could hardly recognize them as ears. The men hunted with poisoned arrows. We weren't exactly afraid of them, but it was eerie. These were real Stone Age people.

It was as if we had bumbled into a prehistoric place. Every night hanging in your hammock you would hear the roars of tigers. They filled the jungle. As far as I know, they never attacked anyone, but it was common knowledge that they ate the dead bodies that were left along the trail. Listening to them every night and thinking about them was enough to scare you to death, like the Tai and their poisoned arrows. It was primitive, and it aroused all your primitive fears.

As we walked South we'd meet different people—sometimes intact units, sometimes people who had gotten separated. There were deserters, too—guys who left their groups and were staying alive any way they could—hunting, trading, stealing, hanging around the medic stations. Anything to keep from going South. Here and there you'd see hammocks slung up near the trail, maybe just one, but sometimes whole clumps of them—people who were sick, or just couldn't go on. It would look like the forest was loaded down with giant cocoons swinging from the trees or packages that some monster spider had wrapped up.

Not too long after I had gotten over my first fever, I passed a hammock that was hanging very near the trail, covered by the usual canopy and mosquito net. I went over to tell the guy inside to move farther away. I thought I'd help him sling it up out of the traffic if he was too sick to do it himself. When I lifted up the vinyl and the netting I was staring at a corpse. Ants were crawling all over the body—its eye sockets were swarming with them. I ran as fast as I could screaming inside my head, That's me, that's me!

My own fever came back sporadically, sometimes worse than others. Everyone came down with some variation of it, or with malaria. We called it "the jungle tax" or "your closest friend" because you knew the fever would stay with you even after your buddies were long gone. When it hit there was no choice. You'd sling up the hammock and stay put, hoping you could stay lucid enough to nurse yourself back to health. Sure as hell nobody else was going to do it for you. Several times I was too sick to move for weeks, hanging there with the other fever cases, and the dead, and the stench of decomposing bodies.

When I was healthy and walking, I'd think to myself over and over how awful this whole thing was. It was simple murder. I was amazed that they could put so many people through it. But I still knew that I was going to get back to my family. Nothing was going to stop me from doing that.

I could tell when we started to get close to the Vietnam border from Cambodia. We could hear the rumble of bombing in the distance. Everybody stopped to listen to it—a dull continuous roar. A surge of fear went through everyone in the group I was traveling with. I was sick and half-starved and scared to death. But I was near home. It had taken six months to get here—where, I didn't know exactly. The discipline was, "Don't ask!"

From the last station they took me directly to the Front organization that controlled literature and art. There were lots of people from the South there. It was a real homecoming. I was happy as hell. I stayed there for about a month, not really doing anything, just recovering and resting.

While I was there I began thinking seriously about the book on Ben Tre. I started getting excited about it. I had missed out on doing any really good work in the North and I was ready for what I thought was going to be my masterpiece. When they got the group together that was going south from Tay Ninh I was more than ready.

The way down there was through the jungle along the military trails. A commo-liaison agent would lead us from one station to the next, not much different from what it had been on the Ho Chi Minh Trail, except that the surroundings were much more comfortable. Sometimes we traveled at night, sometimes in the day, whichever the liaison decided. The whole trip took maybe a month. We never got involved in any fighting, though we did have one close call. There was a station where we weren't picked up in time by the liaison. Consequently we didn't get to the station we were supposed to get to until the next day. When we did arrive the place was a ruin. Just burned debris and lean-tos. Nothing left of it. It had been destroyed the previous night, when we should have been there. What happened to whoever was there instead of us I don't know.

When I finally got to Huong My I was ecstatic. Supposedly there were Americans there, so I didn't go in. But I sent a messenger to tell my parents where I was staying. I saw my mother as she was walking into the hamlet. We just stared at each other without saying a word. She was laughing and crying at the same time. I was too. This is what I had come home for.

It turned out that my father hadn't come because he was working for the Saigon army as a financial secretary. They had him living in a military compound. There were so many Vietcong in Ben Tre that it wasn't safe for him to come out at all. What an irony—I was right there and we couldn't see each other.

At that time—this must have been mid-1966—there were still a lot of VC-controlled villages in Ben Tre, but things were getting much harder than they had been. I realized immediately that all the Radio Hanoi and Radio Liberation news about what was going on was simply a lie. They kept trumpeting about how we controlled three-quarters of the population and four-fifths of the land. But that was ridiculous, pure propaganda for people in the North or in remote areas in the South.

The truth was that we were losing more than we were winning. The villagers supported the VC, but there wasn't anything like the high morale I remembered. Instead there was an unspoken feeling that we couldn't win now that the Americans were there. They were just too strong—helicopters, jets, B–52s. How could you beat them?

I got a sense that people were getting desperate. You could see it in the trickle of peasants who were leaving for safer areas, places where they wouldn't be bombed or attacked. That meant areas controlled by the ARVN. Young men weren't eager to go into the resistance either. You could see them trying to avoid the recruiters when the came through. None of that could possibly have happened before.

It wasn't exactly the most stimulating atmosphere to write an epic about victory. But I started gathering material anyway, interviewing VC soldiers about their parents and about their own experiences. There was a lot of good material from people whose fathers had been in the Vietminh. Some of their parents had gone North in 1954 and were still there. Others had been killed in the French war. Two generations of resistance fighters; sometimes two generations of martyrs. I was also writing stories occasionally for Radio Liberty and teaching some classes about how to write. Not how to write professionally, just how to record facts that had been observed.

In 1966 the liberated zone was shrinking. When I first arrived in Ben Tre it was possible to get through weeks at a time without being attacked. But after a year or so you couldn't do it. I got into the habit of cooking as soon as I got up and putting some of the rice into my bag so I'd be ready to leave. I spent more and more time moving around, trying to stay away from ARVN operations.

In Ben Tre it was mainly the ARVN 7th Division that was causing the problems. Most of the division was recruited from the Delta so they knew the whole area—ricefields, swamps, rivers, everything. They were as familiar with it as we were. If there was a bombardment nearby, you'd have to get out fast. Their usual method was to hit whatever area they were going into with artillery in the early morning. Then they'd circle it with their helicopters or bring in infantry. They'd close the circle tighter and tighter, then start searching for bunkers and hidden foxholes.

VC who were caught in the circle would hide underground or sometimes climb into the tops of coconut trees. The underground spiderholes were terrible. We built them so that they were really well camouflaged. Someone could stand right on top of one and not even know it. But being inside the holes would always give me claustrophobia. When it's closed you feel as if you're buried alive. One time I was caught in a sweep and had to hide in one with this other guy. The ARVN soldiers were so close we could distinctly hear every word they were saying. I felt as if I were suffocating. I was sure I was going to die in there. I tried to get up. I don't know what I was thinking. I was panicked. But my buddy grabbed me and held me down. He was whispering, "Don't, don't. Don't open it."

Somehow I stayed down there. I still don't know how. When night came we opened it and got away. Some people weren't so lucky. Occasionally the ARVNs would camp practically on top of a foxhole. When that happened the people inside would drown. In Ben Tre the groundwater would come up so high at night there wouldn't be any air left. Two cultural cadres from Hanoi University died that way. One was a young poet named Anh Xuan. The other was a literary critic whose name I can't remember.

By the time I had been in Ben Tre a couple of years, I was beginning to be sure I'd never write the book. I was on the move most of the time, traveling mainly by night. I think I was in every corner of the province, on both Bao and Minh islands [two large islands in the Mekong]. We'd move at night and meet at night. It took every ounce of energy I had just to stay alive.

I began to get very bitter, especially after my friend Hoang Viet was killed. He was a young composer who had come down the trail with me. He had studied classical composition in Bulgaria and was one of our few symphonic composers. His bunker took a direct rocket hit, all to himself. Afterwards they found a little hair and some scraps of flesh. That was how one of the finest young composers in Vietnam died.

The whole thing was a hoax. Our Southern people had been at war for thirty years and they hadn't gotten anyplace. I started realizing what they had done to us, what they were doing to us. The Northern leaders were sending their sons to Russia and Eastern Europe while our poets and composers were getting killed off wholesale. I thought, What kind of communism is that? What kind of equality is that? I hadn't liked the Northern leaders when I lived there, and I didn't like them now. I saw them as

ambitious bastards who were wasting their people. They wanted everything and they didn't care how many people they had to kill to get it.

I saw my own life slipping by, too. I was thirty-seven years old and I
didn't know what I had spent it on. I began thinking about quitting. But
that wasn't so easy. It was like a bad marriage. You didn't like it, but you
had roots and experiences together. You had suffered together. What
could you do?

That was until Tet Mau Than. When that was over we hardly controlled
any land at all. Every day we hid, watching for the helicopters. At night
we'd go back to the village and sleep a little. Sometimes they'd attack at
five in the morning, sometimes at night. You couldn't predict it anymore.
We felt like we were sitting around and looking at each other just waiting
to be caught. It was a nightmare.

The situation was so impossible they moved a lot of the cultural cadres
out. I joined a special group under Tran Bach Dang that was going back
to R for safety. We traveled through six provinces to the Cambodian border, then up to Tay Ninh. When we got there I was sick again, the same
as I had been when I was there the first time. But by then I had made my
decision. After I recovered I told them I needed to take a rest. They gave
me a pass to get into Cambodia. But I wasn't going to Cambodia. One of
my friends guessed it. He looked at me and said, "We're not going to see
each other anymore, are we?" I said, "That's right, no more."

Strangely enough, after I had been in Saigon awhile, I began to write
again, a book about the Ho Chi Minh Trail [*The Endless Road*].* The irony
of it was that I had to quit in order to do it.

NGUYEN CONG HOAN'S STORY: *The Communist Assembly*

THERE WAS NOTHING I OR ANYONE ELSE COULD DO ABOUT THE MIL-
itary disaster that developed in February and March of 1975. But I
thought that at least I should be with my people while it was happening.
So I went back with my family to Phu Yen Province.

The problems came like a tidal wave. There were streams of refugees
from the areas the Communists had taken, rivers of them. There was no
order in the cities, no authority. Food supplies were running out everywhere. The military could shoot anybody they wanted. It was chaos.

Then on March 30th Nha Trang was taken. Just before Tuy Hoa fell
my wife and children and I escaped by fishing boat to a small island off

---

* *The Endless Road* was awarded the National Prize for Literature and Arts in 1972.

the coast to wait until the fighting died down. We stayed there for a few days, then we went back.

In my office, everything had been destroyed. My files were scattered all over, and all the furniture strewn around. The place had been ransacked. So I went back home to wait. I didn't announce myself to the new authorities. I just stayed at home as if I were no different from anyone else. A few days later a North Vietnamese cadre came by to tell me not to move out of my house.

After a week or so, the authorities ordered all the students to start working, cleaning up and fixing things. They told me to go to the high school to lead the students in the cleanup. When Saigon fell on April 30th I was still at school, where I had set up an office to run the effort to clean up the city.

Here people began to come to me, telling me about their husbands or relatives who were being arrested or who had just disappeared. Of course there was nothing to do, so I just kept my mouth shut. Then my people in the villages reported that at Hoa Thanh and Song Cau there had been mass executions, that the *bo dois* [soldiers] had shot five hundred people in Hoa Thanh and two hundred in Song Cau. I tried to understand what had happened by having my people find eyewitnesses and relatives for me to interview. I talked with people who had seen the massacre sites and had claimed the bodies of their family members. In the end I was never able to ascertain how many had been shot, but there was absolutely no question that the executions had taken place.

When I was sure of what had happened, I went to the Military Management Committee to tell them what I knew and ask what they were going to do about it. They said they hadn't had any reports of massacres, and that retribution was not the policy of the revolution. The revolution was going to go forward, not back. They said they would "look into it."

I was dismayed by what had happened, but I can't say that I completely lost heart. I had seen enough during the war to know that the worst things could happen in battles or in really chaotic situations. And it was true that the Military Management Committee didn't seem to be out to terrorize people—that clearly wasn't their policy. So I still hoped. I said to myself that we just went through the end of the war. There were terrible things about it. But we were now at the beginning of something new. Maybe it would get better.

In June we heard that everyone who had been in the old government had to report for reeducation. I had to go to Saigon for this, but when I got there I found that I was one of the former opposition assemblymen who were going to be exempted from the camps. Instead we were going to be allowed to go through a short course of reeducation right in Saigon.

This course consisted of lectures on such subjects as why the revolution won, and the crimes of the former regime and of the Americans. After the lectures we had to write reports on what we had learned. None of us liked it, and we certainly didn't feel we had very much to learn on these subjects. But the whole thing was done in a friendly atmosphere. When it was over they gave us a "reeducation certificate" to prove we had passed the course.

When I was finished with my reeducation, I went back to the province and took a job teaching chemistry and physics in high school. I did this until May of 1976, when I got a call to report to the office of the chairman of the Phu Yen Province branch of the Fatherland Front [the Northern mass organization that absorbed the National Liberation Front after the war].

This was the time when the North and South were being reunified. All of the details had already been worked out by the Party, and now the process was going to be ratified by an Assembly elected from the entire country. When I got to the chairman's office he informed me that I should run for office in this unified Assembly. I told him that I didn't consider myself a candidate. I hadn't been a revolutionary and I didn't know much about the revolution or its goals. Besides, I had been having serious stomach problems and didn't feel up to traveling [the Assembly was to be held in Hanoi]. When he heard this the chairman got angry. He told me, "Look, your stomach isn't important. The Fatherland Front has decided you should run, so it's your duty to run. It's not a matter of wanting to or not wanting to."

So of course I ran. But the campaign was nothing like my previous campaign for the Saigon Assembly. Then there had been twenty candidates for two seats. Now there were twelve candidates for eleven seats. All twelve of us would be present at meetings and rallies. The Front official would introduce us in turn and give a kind of brief description of our backgrounds. Then he would give a speech about the victory of the revolution and about reunification. None of the candidates ever got to say a word. The audience had been forced to come, and so had we.

After the voting it turned out that I had won 94.9 percent of the votes. That made me eleventh, so I won the last seat. The highest vote getter had polled 99 percent, the second highest, 98 percent, the third, 97.9 percent, and so on.

But although the percentages we had been assigned meant nothing, the election had actually taken place. The votes were very carefully tabulated. In reality it was a kind of testing device that the Party used to determine its own strength. Of the twelve candidates it had chosen, a number of us were non-Party people. Since we had all been selected by the Fatherland Front and had been on the ballot, the people felt comfortable about voting for any of us. When the votes were in, the Party saw where candidates who were Party members had done well and where they had done poorly. It was a clever way of identifying the towns and regions where there was opposition to the Party, and these places would then be targeted for bigger propaganda campaigns and strengthened security.

The first unified Assembly met in Hanoi in July. For this occasion, the Southern members were treated with special deference. We were put up at the Thang Loi [Victory] Hotel, which was usually reserved for foreigners—even high Party cadres only dreamed about staying there. We were given shopping privileges at special stores; we were taken to model farms and factories and to sites of American bombings. They made an all-out effort to impress us.

But when the Assembly opened, it immediately put all the friendliness into perspective. The authoritarian nature of what was going on was obvious the moment I stepped into the place. In the Saigon Assembly, you could sit anywhere you wanted. So of course colleagues and allies usually sat together. Here, you sat in your assigned seat and you weren't allowed to move. It was like high school back in Tuy Hoa.

Much more significant, you weren't allowed to address the Assembly on issues. Instead, the entire Assembly was divided into groups, twenty or twenty-five to a group. Each group had a leader—always a high Party cadre—and the leader announced what issues we were going to discuss. At the end of the discussion session one of the group members would be appointed to write up a statement which would be delivered to the Assembly. Of course the statement had to be cleared with the group leader.

The chief of my group was Tran Quynh, who was then special assistant to the Party leader Le Duan [Quynh is now vice prime minister]. One of the first topics he put on the floor for discussion was the proposed name for unified Vietnam (the North had been called the Democratic Republic of Vietnam, while the South was the Republic of Vietnam). Quynh opened discussion by announcing that the new name, as decided by the Party, would be the Socialist Republic of Vietnam. Then he asked if anyone had any questions.

When I first heard the name, I didn't like it. I got the floor and said that the "Socialist Republic" would not be easily accepted in the South. Most Southerners weren't used to the idea of socialism. They didn't know exactly what the concept meant and they didn't trust it, so the name would cause a lot of unnecessary hostility. The country wasn't ready to be called the "Socialist Republic." It wasn't timely.

The gist of Quynh's answer was, "It was we who defeated the foreigners and won independence. Now there's only one road to building the nation, and that's our road. The Party leads the nation, and the Party has decided that this will be the name. The only question under discussion here is whether you have faith in the Party (he was looking directly at me as he said this), or whether you think that maybe you are more intelligent than the Party."

I was sorry I had opened my mouth. I was used to the attempts of the Southern regime to intimidate me when I was a representative in Saigon's National Assembly. But I had never experienced this kind of thing before. So I shut up.

That evening after dinner a Party cadre came up to my room for a visit. He explained to me that apparently I wasn't familiar with how democracy works under socialism—which is a lot higher than the way democracy used to work in the South. He told me that democracy under socialism is a democracy of the Party. In this particular situation, Le Duan and the Party leadership had made a decision. That decision was a national decision—it had become the national platform. I might have some ideas about how that decision could best be carried out, but not about the decision itself. He hoped that was clear.

He also explained to me about "freedom," which was another concept I might not understand. In order to have freedom, as he explained it, the first thing was that you had to know "the law of freedom." This "law of freedom" was like any other natural law, the law of gravity, for example. Those who didn't know the law of gravity, or the law of falling bodies, could easily endanger their own lives.

He said that, for instance, if I weighed a hundred pounds and jumped out of an airplane, I would need a certain size parachute to support me. But if I weighed two hundred pounds or a thousand pounds, I'd need a different size parachute. Someone couldn't just jump out of the plane if he didn't know these things, not if he expected to live. So, by the same token, I should understand that the more important a person's role is in the state, the more necessary it is for him to understand the "law of freedom."

As I listened to this, I was thinking to myself that the whole thing was unbelievable. This guy was just a thug. I couldn't imagine what I was doing there. Under Thieu there were plenty of thugs, but it had been much more interesting. At least there you were only bribed and beaten; it wasn't the immutable laws of nature that were demanding your obedience.

Anyway, that was the last time I opened my mouth. After that everything went according to pattern. The Party's decision on some issue would be announced to the group, there would be some perfunctory discussion, then somebody would write up a statement.

The single exciting incident that happened in the two weeks of the session was over adopting a flag for the country. The old flag of the North had been red with a gold star in the middle. The old flag of the Southern revolutionaries—the Vietcong flag—had been half blue, half red, with a gold star in the middle. The Party's decision was that the new flag for the unified country would be "a red field with a gold star." In other words, the flag of North Vietnam would now become the flag of the whole country.

When the chairman of the Assembly asked if the proposal was approved, he only expected yea votes from the different groups. But there was really a lot of emotion about this issue, not only from the Southerners, who were still learning to keep their mouths shut, but from the Northerners too. After all, they had been fighting for independence for thirty years and for unification for twenty.

At least one of the Northerners thought that the formulation "a red field with a yellow star" was an insult. It seemed somehow too neutral. The way he saw it, the new unified country should just forthrightly and explicitly adopt the flag of the Democratic Republic of Vietnam, which after all had done most of the fighting and had made most of the sacrifices. And he wasn't afraid to get up on the Assembly floor and say what he thought.

When they heard this, the Southerners began to boil. It was bad enough that the Northern flag was being shoved down their throats without their being able to say anything and with only this transparent technical description of the flag being provided to save their faces. And now this Northern guy wanted to take even that away. Hands went up all over the place and the level of noise began to rise. Truong Chinh, one of the top politburo people, was in the chair, and as soon as he saw this he shouted out, "Stop! Out of order! Out of order! We'll take the first formulation."

Along with the other Southerners, I found the episode humiliating. But then, the whole Assembly was humiliating. To put a cap on it, at the end I was assigned to write a closing statement on behalf of the "intellectual and urban movement of the South."

I couldn't write it. I just couldn't. It was all so depressing and unadmirable. So I wrote a terrible statement. Even that was like ripping my conscience out. After they read it they told me it wasn't any good and that somebody else would have to write it. At least that was a relief.

After that I went home and took up my high school teaching—Assemblymen had to have regular jobs, since their only real function was to be present for the Assembly sessions, which only lasted a couple of weeks. They certainly weren't supposed to represent their constituencies at home.

But I still made it my business to see as much as I could. Phu Yen's Cung Son district had become the site for a number of new labor camps where they kept former Saigon army officers—T–50, T–51, 52, 53, and 54. Hieu Xuong district had two big camps for Saigon politicians and other political prisoners. I managed to visit two of the Cung Son camps, T–50 and T–51.

I went to T–50 with a cadre from the Fatherland Front who was a friend of mine and whom I convinced to take me along. When we got there, there wasn't that much to see. Most of the prisoners were away from the camp either doing lumbering or farming. Those who were left inside were busy working with logs that had been cut, or doing different kinds of woodworking. The impression I got was of sullen, withdrawn prisoners doing hard physical labor. I was escorted around by the colonel in charge, so there was no way to talk to them freely. All I could do was give out my cigarettes and leave.

It was the same general story at T–51, except that this camp was in the deep jungle, really remote. I had gotten permission for one of my distant relatives to visit his cousin who was a prisoner there. It took us five hours by motor scooter from Tuy Hoa, then another hour by foot. Once we got there we were only allowed into the "guest house," which was outside the camp itself. Several prisoners were there talking to visitors, the inmates on one side of a long table, the visitors on the other. The prisoners were all unnaturally quiet, giving short answers to questions, as if they didn't dare to talk. They were emaciated and obviously frightened. When we left the camp, I had a very bad feeling about what was happening there.

But these two trips were unusual. Mostly I was limited to teaching school. I couldn't write, I couldn't speak in public. People in Phu Yen were even afraid to talk to me. Meanwhile, economic conditions got worse and worse. The rice ration went down substantially. Many families were distraught about relatives who had been shipped off to the labor camps, nobody knew for how long. There was mass suffering and there was absolutely nothing I could do about it, or even any way for me to protest it.

The second session of the unified Assembly was held at the beginning of 1977. I attended, but I was already making plans to escape the country by boat. I had decided that I could not live the life of a puppet. I hadn't done it under the dictators, and I wasn't going to live the rest of my life that way.

I had the idea at that time that after 1975 world opinion had ignored what was going on inside Vietnam. I knew that as an assemblyman I could speak with authority about the situation inside the country. Of course I talked it over with my wife. I wasn't too afraid about leaving her and the children. I knew there would be consequences for them. But I thought that the combination of outside pressure and the hostility toward the regime inside the country would force some changes. A lot of people had suffered for the country, so we could accept whatever happened.

NGUYEN THI TY (NGUYEN CONG HOAN'S WIFE):
Death in Absentia

AFTER HOAN AND I HAD DISCUSSED THE IDEA OF LEAVING THE COUN-try, we finally decided that he should go first. We had four children, so arranging for all of us to go would be a major business. There would also be much more of a chance that we'd get caught. Besides, I expected him to come back. I thought that if he made a lot of noise in Japan and in the West, conditions would get better, there'd be more freedom, and he'd be able to come back. But if worse came to worst, I'd find a way out with the children.

On the day he was supposed to leave, my youngest son came down with a fever. Hoan didn't want to go. He said he'd wait, that he'd be able to make other arrangements. When he told me he wasn't going, I got angry with him. I said, "Now the whole country's being lost and you're worried about leaving one sick boy. He'll be fine! You'd better go!" When I spoke like that to him, he just turned and walked out the door. I didn't even know if he was really leaving or if he was just angry at me. I didn't know where he was going or what he planned to do.

A couple of days later the BBC and VOA both reported that a Japanese ship had rescued a Vietnamese boat with thirty-four refugees on board. I guessed it might be Hoan's boat. There were a lot of reports in those days, but not many refugee boats were leaving toward Japan, and I knew that Hoan had wanted to get there. The following day the radio reported that an assemblyman had been on the boat the Japanese picked up. They got the name wrong, but I was sure it was Hoan. At that point I told my eldest daughter that her father was safe. It was the first she knew that he had left.

Over the next several days I got visitors from the Party and from the school where Hoan had been teaching. They all wanted to know where he was. I gave them the story we had planned, that he had gone to a hospital in Saigon to get his ulcer treated. Of course I didn't know which hospital. I told them he was planning to send me a telegram as soon as he was admitted.

Shortly after that the security police came and searched the house. They confiscated all of Hoan's things, including his pictures from the North showing him with Truong Chinh and other leaders. They took all his papers, diaries, notebooks, all his work. They were very interested in knowing if he had had any official documents at the house.

After the search I was uneasy, but nothing else seemed to be happening. Hoan had gotten away, but I thought maybe they weren't going to touch us. Then, almost six months after he left, the two oldest children were expelled from school. They were told they belonged to a "traitor family." Right after the children were expelled, the security police told me I had to get out of our house. The house belonged to the people. We were a traitor family, so we couldn't live in the people's house. We had to leave immediately.

That afternoon I packed all the luggage I could. We had to leave everything we weren't able to carry behind in the house. I hired two pedicabs, piled all the bags in, and left. It was terrible. They hadn't given us any time to find someplace else to stay, and we only had permission to live in the city district where our house was. That meant I wasn't able to go to any of our relatives or friends. I went to every district police chief to ask for living permits. The whole procession—pedicabs, baggage, and the four children, ages fifteen, thirteen, three, and one. None of them would give me a permit. We lived on the street for two days before one of them took pity on us and allowed us to stay in his district where we had friends who would put us up.

After that we lived in their house as if we were under house arrest. The security police followed us all the time. If I went to market or the children went out to play, we were followed. If we stayed in the house for a couple of days, a security man would come in to check on us. They stopped everybody who came into the house or talked to any of us on the street. Any friend or relative who was in contact with us was interrogated.

Then, about two months after we moved, I was invited to come to Nha Trang for my husband's trial. He was being charged with treason and they were going to try him in absentia. When I went to Nha Trang, a court-appointed defense lawyer from the North asked me a lot of detailed questions—what Hoan's plans had been, what he intended to do after he left, how he had gotten out, what he talked about before he went. I said I didn't know anything, my husband never told me anything. I said that as far as I knew my husband had left with a girlfriend— that was a report the Party had spread after he left to try and diminish the importance of his defection. Through all the questioning I maintained the same thing, that he had never told me anything at all about his plans.

After a couple of days the trial opened. There were more than five hundred people there. But I was the only one who was there for my husband. They hadn't allowed anybody else—not his parents or any of his relatives. At the beginning, the chief judge announced that the reason they had invited Hoan's wife to the proceedings was so she would learn about the crimes her husband had committed, some of which she might not know about.

Then the prosecutor got up and gave his statement. He railed at Hoan for about twenty minutes. He seemed enraged. Half the time he was looking directly at me, as if he could take out his anger on me. He accused Hoan of four crimes—against the Party, the nation, his profession, and his family. According to him, Hoan had committed high treason, he had betrayed national secrets to enemies, he was a bad teacher, and he had immorally abandoned his family.

After that they began to call the witnesses. All of them spoke in support of the prosecutor's statement. To hear it, Hoan must have been the worst person who ever lived. The only exception was one of the teachers from Hoan's school. He had the courage to say that Hoan's departure was a great loss to the school and to the students. When I heard him, I knew that the Party had miscalculated. The teacher's father was a high Party official, so they thought he would say what they wanted him to say. But it backfired. Instead he felt safe about telling the truth.

When the prosecution's case was finished, the defense lawyer gave a speech. I was surprised that he actually defended Hoan. He did the best he could. For example, one of the witnesses had accused Hoan of being a CIA agent during the time he was a student activist. The lawyer showed how ridiculous that charge was. When he was done, there was a fifteen-minute break. Then the chief judge came in to read the finding and the sentence. Of course Hoan was guilty on all charges. His sentence was death.

After that I was allowed to make a final statement. I said that I didn't know anything about my husband's political activities, but I accepted perhaps that he had abandoned us. Since he had, I asked permission to live in Nha Trang with my parents, so that I could take care of the children. Otherwise I couldn't do it, since I was alone and had no money and no job.

Then the judge said that the sentence was final, there was no appeal allowed. As far as my request was concerned, that was not the court's business.

Shortly after I went back to where I was staying I had to disperse the family. I sent Thuy, my fifteen-year-old daughter, to sell soft drinks on the streets. I sent Han, my thirteen-year-old son, to work as a fisherman. I went to work myself as a street vendor selling cut tobacco.

What I thought most about was the children's future. I had been thinking about that ever since they were expelled from school. I couldn't stand the thought of them growing up ignorant. Ever since that happened I had been ready to leave. Finally my uncle, who had a lot of contacts with the fishermen, was able to arrange our escape. When he got it organized, he sent my brother as a messenger to tell me to have the children ready. That's how we escaped, almost a year after Hoan.

TRINH DUC'S STORY: *The Purge*

AFTER LIBERATION I STAYED IN VUNG TAU AS HEAD OF THE HOA VAN [Chinese Department] Committee and director of the Vung Tau fishing fleet. I was also a member of the Vung Tau Party branch standing committee.

Most of the people on the standing committee were old friends of mine. They were people I had worked with for many years, like Bay Khanh, who was chief of the Party branch, and Ba Lan, the deputy chief. I had other old friends too, back in Long Khanh. My whole former network was there. I had spent so much time and had such unforgettable memories from Bao Binh and the other villages that it was like my home. I went back as often as I could just to visit and talk about old times.

Every time I went back it was an emotional experience. It was impossible for the people in Bao Binh not to show the feelings they had for me. I felt exactly the same way about them. I had fought for them and protected them for so many years. And they had supported me. I couldn't leave there without being loaded down with huge amounts of fruit and other gifts.

But starting in 1976 I began to hear open complaints about the way things were going. People weren't happy about the new taxes, and they weren't happy about the attitude of the cadres. The main thing they complained about was they couldn't do what they wanted with their land. They had to follow the program the administration got from the central government, a lot of which was absurd. For instance, they were ordered to grow more coffee on the land where they used to grow tea. But that land wasn't suitable for coffee, so it was absurd. Also, they had to sell their produce to the government at the official price. In return, the government was supposed to sell them fertilizer and tools at the official price. But the reality was that there were never enough supplies. So they had to go to the black market and buy what they needed at black market prices.

In the end they had less and less to eat. After the harvest they wouldn't have anything left for themselves. They didn't like being forced to study political lessons either. But they really hated not having control over their own work.

A lot of these peasants had supported us in 1968 and 1969. As far as I was concerned, they were heroes. They had smuggled rice to us in the bamboo handles of tools or in hampers with fake bottoms when we were starving to death. They had hidden cadres and transported guns for us. And that was at a time when no one knew if we would win or lose.

That was when I started getting unhappy with the way the government was handling things. The problems weren't only in Long Khanh either. The same thing was happening in Vung Tau. It didn't matter if the fishermen had supported the revolution or not. Their boats were all nationalized and they were forced to sell fish at the official price in return for fuel and nets and other equipment—the same kind of thing as in Long Khanh. In Vung Tau fishermen were beginning to leave. Sometimes they'd take their boats out in the morning and they wouldn't come back. I had a big fight with others in the fishing administration about whether to allow them to go out on the high seas or to limit them to the offshore waters. I argued that if we couldn't control their hearts we wouldn't be able to control their boats, no matter what we told them. If they liked us they wouldn't go, and if they didn't like us they'd go regardless. Besides, how could we stop them from fishing? Stopping them from going to where the fish were wasn't any kind of solution. Later we put police or security agents on the boats. Sometimes this worked. But sometimes the fishermen forced the agents to go with them, or bribed them. They even killed some of them.

Another upsetting thing was that Northern cadres were being appointed to high positions in the Vung Tau administration. This was going on all over the country, but in Vung Tau there was a real confrontation. It seemed as if every day there were quarrels and confrontations between Southerners and Northerners. Bay Khanh and Ba Lan felt they were being undermined by cadres who were being sent down from Hanoi. These new guys owed allegiance directly to their ministries instead of to the local Party branch, so they always had different ideas about how to do things.

I was one of the cadres who were trying to fight against the Northern invasion. When they sent me engineers for the fishing department, I put them on projects out in the countryside. These people didn't know anything about Vung Tau and they didn't know anything about fishing, but they had been trained in the Soviet Union and they thought they knew everything. They were impossible. So I sent them to work at some of our inland fishing lakes. It was like sending them into exile.

In 1977 the troubles started on the border with Kampuchea. That's when the Party began its campaign against the ethnic Chinese. Everyone in the Party heard rumors about the "Chinese brothers" who were betraying Vietnam by supporting the Khmer Rouge. By "Chinese brothers" they meant us, the ethnic Chinese. Supposedly we were trying to undermine Vietnam because the Vietnamese were refusing to do what China wanted them to. For example, Vietnam was refusing to follow certain Chinese policies such as making friends with capitalist countries. There were also stories about how the Chinese had betrayed Vietnam during the wars against the French and the Americans. The whole thing was a rumor campaign, stories that were circulating around, not actual propaganda publications. That happened later, in 1979.

The main result of these rumors was to poison the atmosphere inside the Party between Vietnamese and ethnic Chinese. It was a very uncomfortable feeling. People who had been friends for years suddenly began acting distant and cold. They would pretend not to see me if we walked by each other. They'd make a real effort at it. Or they'd look at me with strange expressions, as if maybe they really thought I had done things against the Party.

My bosses didn't take part in that though. Bay Khanh called me into his office and told me not to worry about it. He said that some Chinese might be bad, but not me. China's government was bad, but I was someone who had contributed to the revolution. I would always be a comrade and a friend. But the words sounded a little too sweet to me, as if they were wrapped around a poison pill.

I wasn't under any illusions about what was happening. They began to isolate me at my work. Fewer reports came across my desk. Not so many people came to see me. I still had my salary and position, but there was a lot less work for me to do. I didn't have the power I used to have.

Then they stepped up the pressure. Some of the mass organizations began to launch campaigns denouncing the "Chinese betrayals." The Youth Union, women's associations, and students all did. The object was to create a hostile public atmosphere between Vietnamese and ethnic Chinese. The rumor campaign had gotten it started inside the Party. Now they tried to get the people involved. But it didn't work well. It only worked inside the Party because inside, the Vietnamese officials were afraid for their jobs. So they felt they had to visibly show at least some hatred for the ethnic Chinese.

In private it was a different story. Vietnamese friends of mine would tell me how they really felt about what was going on, that they thought the Vietnamese Communist Party was betraying the ethnic Chinese, not the other way around. Some of them said they had been aware of anti-Chinese feeling in the Party since the early sixties, when Le Duan came back from a trip to Russia and had been so impressed with Russian advanced technology.

At the end of 1977 the arrests began. The first sign was when my direct bosses in the Hoa Van Committee were ordered to leave the country. (They are living in China now.) They had been working closely for years with the Chinese Communist Party, overseeing the supplies and aid that were coming from China. Then Chinese cadres were arrested as "Chinese spies." No one had ever heard that charge before. My uncle was arrested at that time. He had been working for the revolution since before I came to Vietnam, at least forty years. He had been awarded the First Rank Revolution Medal [*Khang Chien Hang Nhat*]. But it didn't matter, they arrested him anyway. Then they began questioning my brother.

When I heard this I went to Saigon, to the security officer who was doing the questioning. I asked him what he had to do with my brother, what had my brother done that would make him a suspect? I told the officer that if he wanted to do something, he should do it to me, not to my brother. The security officer told me, "No, there's notl.ing. You and your brother are our comrades and friends." There it was—"comrades and friends" again. That's when I began to think I would have to leave.

You see, during the war the Party needed to woo the ethnic Chinese. And they had to get assistance from China. At that time the Hoa Van Department was so important that we worked directly with COSVN. Afterwards, when they decided to get closer to the Soviets, they didn't need the Hoa Van anymore. When China became the enemy, people like me weren't wanted. We could easily turn into a fifth column. The other side of it is that when this happened, the ethnic Chinese didn't have any reason to stay in line with the Vietnamese. Unfortunately, there wasn't anything we could do about it. We were in their hands. We never foresaw the possibility of this kind of break, so we were completely unprepared for it.

The anti-Chinese campaign finally led to a purge in the Vung Tau Party branch. Some of the Southern cadres who had been our comrades in arms for a long time wouldn't apply the discrimination policy against us. That made the Northern-Southern conflict even worse than it had been before. Hanoi was in an uproar about it. They wanted to replace the Southerners with people who would obey orders blindly, what we called *Dao Chinh* [the coup]. Bay Khanh and Ba Lan disregarded the policy as much as they could—I still had a pretty good relationship with them.

Then in 1978 they refused to accept any more Northern appointments. They sent them back to Hanoi. After that it was just a matter of time. One day the security arrested both of them for "suspicious activities." Supposedly it wasn't clear if Bay Khanh and Ba Lan had always acted the way they should have. After all, during the hard years of the struggle many cadres from Vung Tau had been arrested by the Saigon government. But they had never been arrested—why was that?

These were the kind of charges that could never be answered. Because they couldn't be, they put an end to Bay Khanh and Ba Lan's political lives. Bay Khanh was replaced by someone who was completely subservient to the Northerners. All of us, all the Vietnamese and ethnic Chinese officials in Vung Tau, were outraged by the arrests. Of course we knew it was a purge, that the charges of "suspicious activities" were ridiculous. A few of my Vietnamese friends managed to retire then. Others were so scared for their jobs they just kept silent. After that I felt unsafe myself.

Finally I decided the time had come to get out. But I couldn't just abandon my people in Long Khanh and Vung Tau. I knew that when I left, they would be in great danger because of their relationships with me. So I organized an escape for the ones who wanted to go—two boats full from Vung Tau. Some of them are living in the United States now. They could tell you about it.

I arranged it out of Vung Tau. Since I was the head of the fishing fleet it was no big problem. There was a business going on in boat people at that time, an unofficial policy to let ethnic Chinese escape without being arrested—for a price, of course. That depended on each area and on who was going. The frontier police [*Cong An Bien Phong*] and the security police [*Cong An Noi Chinh*] were in charge of making arrangements. The boat organizer would have to contact them directly and negotiate about how many people would be allowed to go, where they would leave from, how much gold per head—all the details.

Although there weren't any public pronouncements, the business was completely legal. As head of the boat fleet, I had to sign the permits for people leaving from Vung Tau. The only people who were arrested in those days were the ones who tried to leave illegally, without paying. When they were caught, it would mean spending a few months in prison and having all their property confiscated.

When I organized the boats for my friends, we bought false papers for everyone who was going. I couldn't just buy places for them, as if they were ordinary ethnic Chinese. If I had there would have been a chance it could have been traced to me. That would have caused real trouble for my friends and their families, and for my relatives and me. After the boats had left safely, I went to see my friend who was the head of the frontier police in Vung Tau. Just for a talk, nothing unusual. When it was time to eat I told him I was tired, I'd like to take a nap on the little bed in his office. After he left I took all the papers on my boats out of his file. I didn't want to take any chances about them finding out it was mostly my network and friends who had left.

After that I sent my wife and children to Cholon to stay with my brother. Then I arranged to take a couple of days off from work. In the meantime, I made arrangements with friends of mine in Rach Gia [a port city west of Vung Tau] to get us onto a refugee boat that was leaving from there. It wasn't safe to go from Vung Tau, since I knew I was the next in line to be purged and I was sure they were watching me.

When everything was ready I took a day off before the weekend and disappeared to Rach Gia. That way they wouldn't miss me until Monday or Tuesday, or if there were problems I would be able to get back to my desk as if nothing had happened. But there weren't any problems. My brother brought my family and his family down from Saigon and we got out safely.

That's how we left Vietnam. I felt I had two countries—China, where I was born, where I learned how to be patriotic and to sacrifice for a cause; and Vietnam, where I spent all my young time learning how to die for a cause. It is painful for me that my two countries are enemies now. But I know who is right and who is wrong.

AFTERWORD
by David Chanoff

"HIM? HE'S A COMMUNIST, ISN'T HE? IF I SEE HIM, I'LL KILL HIM!"
That came from a shy, painfully thin Vietnamese immigrant who eight
years before was an officer in South Vietnam's air force. I was asking him
about someone who had been a loud opponent of the Thieu administration in the early seventies, an individual I was trying to track down for a
possible interview. The fact that after the war the ex-militant had spent
two years in prison and then had managed to escape the country by boat
hadn't exonerated him in the air force officer's eyes. What mattered was
that his actions had aided the Communists a dozen years earlier.

Most Vietnamese refugees wouldn't have been as outspoken as my
friend from the air force, but many would have felt the same. That's one
reason it's so difficult to get former Vietcong or North Vietnamese army
people to talk. They live in a sea of refugees as unforgiving of Communists (that is, anyone who abetted the other side) as are the most hard-
nosed Iron Curtain émigrés. These are people who have lost a country,
who have pulled off hair-raising escapes, who have seen loved ones die,
or have left them behind. They are not tolerant toward those they believe
contributed to their tragedy.

As a result, people who were on the other side usually prefer to keep
the past quiet. You approach them through connections, individuals they
know and trust, or usually you don't get to approach them at all.

And it's not just the people they live among whom they fear. They also
have concerns about their former colleagues. That is more true in France
than in the United States. In Paris, Vietnam has an embassy and, it is
believed, agents who circulate in the Vietnamese community. But even
in the United States, former revolutionaries who deserted the cause feel
they are at risk. As long as they live quietly, the risk is minimized. But
if they go public with what they know of wartime events, they aren't sure
what the consequences might be.

Those who were highly placed are especially afraid of direct reprisals.
A man who had helped train Cambodian guerrillas in the 1950s would

not talk to us for publication because he knew how efficient the Party's security apparatus is: he had run a large security organization himself. Others would agree to interviews only on condition that their real names not be used and that such traceable details as unit numbers, dates, and places would be altered. Where we felt such changes would not detract from the integrity of the story, we acceded.

Almost all the refugees are concerned about their relatives still in Vietnam. They feel that if they talk critically about the government, they may well bring harm to their families, or at least make it more difficult for them to eventually leave. I never heard from anyone that their families in Vietnam had been explicitly threatened. But fear for their relatives is an inescapable feature of everyday life for the refugees.

In terms of our effort to put this book together, these fears caused some immensely frustrating losses. We met people whose experiences revealed dramatic features of North Vietnam's wartime life—who talked about them freely, but not for the record. It is for that reason we weren't able to include a close description of the isolation camps that North Vietnam's government established for severely wounded soldiers. American veterans often came back to less than a hero's welcome, and those who had been badly hurt frequently felt a deep bitterness about the treatment they received. But homecoming for wounded North Vietnamese veterans was even worse. One nurse I met had been assigned to these camps for a time. I was shaken by her descriptions of the lives led by the amputees and paraplegics who had been lucky enough to be brought back up the trail. But though we ate together several times and became friends, her mother and father were still alive in Vietnam and she would not allow me to use her story.

Another chilling facet of North Vietnam's war story is the way combat deaths were treated. Nothing I can think of illustrates the difference between American and Vietnamese attitudes toward war as sharply as this. In the course of talking to a North Vietnamese field officer, I had mentioned that American commanders sometimes talked about how gut wrenching it was to write letters to families of soldiers who had been killed. When I asked how that kind of thing affected him, he looked at me as if I were crazy. "We never did it," he said.

He then launched into a comparison of Americans and Vietnamese that emphasized his own soldiers' willingness to sacrifice themselves. If you were dead, you were dead. You had watered the soil of the fatherland with your blood. Nobody could expect to do more than that with their lives. As far as the bodies went, if local guerrillas had been killed, there was an attempt to get them back to their families. If the dead were

Northerners or main force guerrillas from somewhere else, there was nothing to do, even if the bodies could be recovered. Notification of families wasn't important. If a son or father were killed, well, that was a sacrifice many families were making. Eventually people would be advised. Even this former field officer's own wife and children in Hanoi didn't hear from him from one year to the next.

He was telling me this in the nicely furnished living room of an intermediary's house, another North Vietnamese who had arranged our meeting. This individual's two younger children were on the floor playing happily with blocks. His wife had just come home from work and was preparing dinner with her mother. The high school–aged children had been introduced to me when I first came in, then had gone off to study. Except for the Vietnamese faces, it was a *Saturday Evening Post* scene from middle America. Several hours earlier we had picked the former officer up at his house, also stolidly middle American. Neat and newly painted, it nestled under the Douglas firs on a winding suburban street. Both men were doing well in their new lives, adapting successfully to American ways. But the idea that during war, notifying families of war deaths might be a priority—that American notion was unfathomable.

In France a North Vietnamese doctor said about the MIAs, "You Americans even want to find their bones, even *les os*." He said it with a sense of incredulity.

But he wasn't as coldly matter of fact as the NVA officer had been about the impact the war had on the home front. He had seen a different side of it in Hanoi's hospitals. He talked about the psychological effect of loneliness and uncertainty on the families the *bo dois* left behind in the North, particularly on the wives. Schizophrenia, he said, was especially widespread among women. "They had to bear it for many years by themselves. They didn't know if their men were alive or dead." He said that the worst was when they would hear through friends' friends or village grapevines about deaths. Then they would have to live with the knowledge, without being able to express their grief openly. The emotional consequences were staggering.

His story, though, the story of North Vietnam's hospitals and outpatient psychiatric care, was not for publication. He also had family in Hanoi.

But fear isn't the only reason people won't talk. There is also a "the less said the better" attitude among many who are now living in the United States or France after years spent fighting the French and Americans. For the most part these people, at least the ones who were truly revolutionaries, look back with consuming bitterness on lives they now see as having been sacrificed for what turned out to be ignoble purposes. They tend to think of themselves as idealists whose ideals were betrayed by their leaders. But the more introspective of them blame themselves as well. One high-level technical official who now lives in France whispered to me as he walked to the elevator in his apartment building, "I wasted twenty-five years of my life with them. My wife still won't forgive me." He was a Southerner who had chosen to cast his lot with the revolution after he finished his studies in Europe. As a young man he had made a conscious decision to go North. Now he was starting over.

Although gray-haired, this former cadre was still full of vigor—angry at the past, but raring to carve out a new career for himself. Others have less energy—the fifty-five-year-old busboy who had once controlled a province; the former propaganda chieftain who was assembling parts in a California electronics factory; an aged Party leader who had once been a top figure in the Vietminh. He had recently defected, but he wasn't going to talk to anyone about it. After more than forty years in the revolution, what would he say? A friend of his, one of the founders of the Vietcong, wrote to me that they had met and reminisced. "We have no regret for ourselves, but for our people . . . after thirty years of stoicism and heroism. But he goes on life in his way, and I in my own."

Beneath the resignation and iron endurance of such people, one senses they are having a hard time coming to terms with the strange twists their lives have taken. They are sitting on a volatile and complicated mix of emotions—emotions that are better suppressed or, if possible, buried. It's understandable that not many of them are eager to start turning the screws of memory.

THESE are some of the barriers any interviewer who wants to work this particular field has to overcome. Beyond them lies a cultural gulf that makes communication between Vietnamese and Americans problematic. At a conference on Vietnam and Central America, one American officer who had been in Saigon during the last days of the war told of a bitter parting between himself and a Saigon government colleague. "At least," said the Vietnamese, "we had something in common with the French. We never had anything in common with you anyway." The American understood the sentiment behind this remark, but still thought it unfair. With 57,000 American dead and a quarter of a million injured there was at least a good deal of blood we had in common.

Of course there was more than the blood. Beyond the national self-interest goals the United States shared with South Vietnam's government and the political values we shared with many educated South Vietnamese (even with quite a few who opposed us), there were personal sympathies, friendships, love affairs, and marriages that bonded Americans to Vietnamese and Vietnamese to Americans. Americans who got to know them found Vietnamese to be an earthy, warm, easygoing, and humorous people. But along with the congeniality were the distinctions.

Behind the interviews that make up this book lie both an ease of rapport and some special difficulties in the interaction between interviewer and respondents. These deserve mention, not only because they are part of the background of the material, but also because they suggest some of the larger problems that plagued American-Vietnamese understanding during the war.

Interviewing Vietnamese is not like interviewing Americans. You don't make your contacts, call for an appointment, and spend an hour or two asking questions, listening, and recording. Americans are like that. Once they decide to talk to you, the chances are good they will speak frankly. They are capable of revealing the most personal experiences, even intimacies, to a stranger. As a writer I've often wondered where that openness comes from, that willingness to expose one's life to others. I suspect it has to do with such cultural themes as the scientific spirit, the psychoanalytical legitimation of self, and hearty individualism.

But wherever it comes from, the Vietnamese don't share it. As open as Americans tend to be, just so secretive are Vietnamese. Their history has taught them not to reveal themselves. Survival requires silence and never letting anyone know where your heart is. They are suspicious of everyone and bestow confidences grudgingly. Vietnam's revolution itself was a collective demonstration of the individual Vietnamese's predilection to hide inner truth behind a facade. The Russian and Chinese Communists made revolution in their own names, but the Vietnamese Communist Party operated behind front organizations, first the Vietminh, then the Vietcong. Ho Chi Minh was so successful at hiding his real motives that even today the argument goes on: Was he primarily a nationalist who used communism to accomplish Vietnamese national objectives, or a Communist who maneuvered nationalism into the service of ideology?

Whatever the truth, Ho's refusal to declare himself was characteristically Vietnamese. Secretiveness is an ingrained trait. The only real way around it is to establish trust, and the only way to do that is through friendship and connections. We spent months finding people through Vietnamese friends, government sources, social agencies, military and intelligence people—anyone who was willing to help locate possible interview subjects and provide introductions. In the end, almost all of our interviews were made possible through personal relationships—friends prevailing on friends to include the "American who was interested in Vietnam" within the circle of trust that determines whom it's safe to talk to.

Once talk did start, another Vietnamese characteristic was likely to surface—the tendency to regard the essence of an event as the only aspect of it worth relating. "Truth" is more likely to be general than specific. By and large, Vietnamese don't have the American's love for hard fact and concrete detail. What did you see, hear, feel, taste, smell are questions that can easily leave them nonplussed. As a people they have a taste for myths, legends, and moral tales; they are more interested in the "why" of things than in the "what," in what events mean, not in what exactly happened.

An American interviewer with his American audience in mind and a Vietnamese respondent tracing his memories with Vietnamese brushstrokes can make an odd couple. QUESTION [to an NVA infantryman who had infiltrated to the South in 1966]: "Can you tell me about your trip down the trail?" ANSWER: "It was very hard." QUESTION: "How did you feel?" ANSWER: "Very tired." QUESTION (after a couple of moments of silence): "Well, what did you have to eat, for example?" ANSWER: "Not much." QUESTION: "I mean, what would you eat for breakfast, in the morning?" ANSWER (silence, then): "Rice."

It wasn't that there was anything necessarily wrong with the questions. It was just that the former *bo doi* couldn't imagine why anyone would be interested in such self-evident and insignificant details.

Of course not all interviews went like this, thank God. But in many cases the natural mode of memory and telling was more general than I would have wished. Close-up, gritty observations—the kind that might flow automatically from an American combat infantryman's lips—didn't come as naturally to his People's Army counterpart. Eventually I learned to circumvent the problem to an extent. One way was simply to explain why I was looking for the kind of details I was. At that point there might be a pause in the interview for a short discussion and a few laughs about different ways of seeing things, maybe even some jokes about Americans and Vietnamese. Then we'd go on.

But I didn't feel altogether comfortable doing this. I suspect that indications from me about the kind of perceptions I was interested in detracted something from the integrity of the experiences I was hearing about. They translated better, but they were just a little bit less the real thing.

These and other problems of interpreting one culture to the other were magnified when it came to interviewing women. In the usual Vietnamese family, men's business is not women's business. Often women will not sit down to dinner with men, especially if the husband has guests. Women will not intrude themselves in a conversation, nor, in a traditional family, will they do anything without their husband's permission. They use the same pronoun in addressing their husbands (*anh*) that they use in addressing older brothers. Their husbands call them *em*, the pronoun for little sisters.

Almost always, wives in the homes I visited took pains to remain in the background. It was only after several visits to a family that I would be able to even broach the subject of an interview. As a result, I wasn't able to do many. It was a shame; those women I did get to talk to were intelligent and tough-minded. There was no question who managed their homes, and there was no doubt that their own lives had demanded emotional resources every bit as sturdy as their men's.

I CAME away from the time I spent with these Vietnamese, both men and women, with an appreciation for why their side triumphed and ours didn't. Utter ruthlessness and massive social manipulation on the part of the Northern-led Party played a large role, of that there's no doubt. The Party controlled information superbly. Because of their success in communicating their own perception of events and excluding others, the Northern leadership was able to excite emotion and guide logic in a way that Southern strongmen could only dream of and that was wholly alien to Americans.

But even more important than the Party's virtuosity was the nature of the human material it had to work with. The psychological landscape of Vietnam, like the political landscape, was full of features unsuspected by Americans when they entered the war. What I thought I glimpsed in talking to its survivors—behind their patience and remarkable stoicism—was a quixotic disregard for the impossible, a quality I came to think of as "ordinary heroism." So many apparently normal human beings had demonstrated in one way or another a damn the consequences approach to life that it began to seem like a national trait. The Assemblyman Nguyen Cong Hoan had left his wife and children behind because he loved the country and had determined on his way of serving it. It was not an extraordinary act, either to him or to them. The Vietcong minister Truong Nhu Tang chose the dangers of pirates, monsoons, and squalid refugee camps over a life of relative comfort. "What was I supposed to do," he said, "resign myself to living and dying like a frightened rodent?" Perhaps a million and a half other Vietnamese threw themselves into the same perils, accepting the terrible risks in exchange for a very distant glimmer of something better. For 30 percent or so, the risks proved fatal.

A man born in the Mekong Delta during the French war remembered his village singing "We Are the Heroes" when he was a child. It was the same song he sang on the way to prison as a man. He had been born into a social matrix that considered self-sacrifice a normal concomitant of the human condition. And that cast of mind could inspire either fatalistic resignation or what Henry Kissinger chose to call "flights of heroism and monomania." It gave the Vietnamese on the other side an advantage over their equally brave, but differently motivated American enemies. When the time came, it helped provide for Vietnamese on both sides the courage to leave.

"It is perhaps terrible to say this," said a U.S. State Department official to a former adversary, now a refugee, "but the great tragedy for your country is a great benefit for ours." He was speaking of the qualities the Vietnamese immigrants have brought along with them. I think he was right.

IMPORTANT DATES AND EVENTS

1945

Mid-August: With the fall of Japan, the Vietnamese independence movement begins in earnest. Vietminh-sponsored demonstrations sweep through Hanoi (starting on August 19) and Saigon (on August 21).

September 2: Ho Chi Minh reads the Declaration of Independence in front of the National Theater in Hanoi.

September 21: Clashes between the Vietminh and French begin. Tension and armed conflict continue as Ho Chi Minh and French negotiator Jean Sainteny attempt to reach a settlement.

1946

March 6: A tentative agreement between the Vietminh and French provides for an independent North Vietnam within the French Union and elections to determine the future of the South.

May–September: Ho Chi Minh is in Paris to conclude the March 6 treaty. But the talks, conducted for the unstable French government by the Colonial Office, break down as French negotiators refuse to confirm that agreement.

September–December: A period of expectant confrontation between French and Vietnamese forces erodes the relative stability of the summer. On November 23 open conflict breaks out in Haiphong, the major North Vietnamese port city.

December 19: Ho Chi Minh issues a nationwide call to arms. By the end of the month French and Vietminh forces are locked in war.

1947–1954

The French war progresses, marked by increasing battlefield casualties in Vietnam and growing public disenchantment in France. By November 1953, French commander General Henri Navarre has decided to turn Dienbienphu in the northwestern mountains into a permanent base.

Early in March 1954, Vietnamese troops commanded by General Vo Nguyen Giap surround the French defenses at Dienbienphu. On March 13 they begin their assault. On May 7 the last French position falls and the Vietminh flag is raised over the French command bunker.

The next day, May 8, the international conference on Indochina opens in Geneva. With domestic public support for the war at a low, the French government agrees to full independence for the northern half of the country under Ho Chi Minh. A nationwide election on reunification is to take place in two years.

With the conclusion of the Geneva Agreements on July 20, 1954, Vietminh forces in the South (below the 17th parallel) begin to regroup North, while the French and their Vietnamese auxiliaries move southward. Geneva also allows for the free movement of civilians across the dividing line. Almost a million Northerners migrate to the South, among them Buddhist monks and anti-Communist Catholic intellectuals and villagers. The monks will revitalize South Vietnam's Buddhist community. The Catholics will provide a base of support for the new Southern prime minister, the American-backed Ngo Dinh Diem. Meanwhile Vietminh fighters from the South steel themselves to wait two years for the election that will let them return home.

1955–1956

Ngo Dinh Diem organizes a referendum in the South that transforms the country from a monarchy to a republic, with Diem himself as the first president. To consolidate his position, Diem institutes an anti-Communist drive aimed at former Vietminh and at the underground organization left behind by the Party. At the same time, he strengthens ties between his family and South Vietnam's Catholics, favoring Catholics for jobs and assistance. As president of the new republic, Diem repudiates the Geneva Agreement's call for elections to reunify North and South.

Meanwhile, under Ho Chi Minh's leadership the North is undergoing a massive land and social reform program. Peasants and townspeople are categorized by class background, land is expropriated and redistributed—later to be collectivized. Those classified as landlords are tried before people's tribunals.

1957–1959

In the South, resistance to the Diem government builds among opposition politicians, Buddhists, and the increasingly effective guerrilla organization. In May 1959, the first military units from North Vietnam are organized to prepare the infiltration of men and matériel down the Ho Chi Minh Trail.

1960

September 5: The Vietnamese Communist Party at its Third Congress makes the liberation of the South a priority.

November 11: An army coup against Ngo Dinh Diem narrowly fails.

December 19–20: The National Liberation Front is formed under Party auspices to provide a political umbrella organization for the Southern opposition to Diem.

1961–1964

Full-scale war develops in the South. Southern "Vietcong" guerrillas are aided by units from the Northern People's Army. The United States provides military advisers, equipment, and economic aid to the Saigon government.

Domestic unrest sharpens in South Vietnam. By May 1963, conflict between the Diem government and militant Buddhists ripens into demonstrations and street clashes. On June 11 a Buddhist monk immolates himself in protest.

November 1, 1963: Ngo Dinh Diem is overthrown and murdered in a military coup. A junta of generals takes his place, but is in turn unseated three months later in a coup led by General Nguyen Khanh.

August 2 and 4, 1964: American destroyers report attacks by North Vietnamese patrol boats in what comes to be known as the Gulf of Tonkin Incident. Congress responds by giving President Lyndon Johnson discretionary power to use military force.

1965

In February and March, U.S. bombers make their first attacks against North Vietnamese territory. On March 9, American Marines land in South Vietnam, signaling the beginning of intervention by American ground forces that by 1968 would total over half a million.

In February, South Vietnamese strongman General Khanh is toppled in an army coup. A civilian government is established and lasts for several months before giving way to a military regime headed by Air Marshal Nguyen Cao Ky and General Nguyen Van Thieu.

1966–1968

American ground strength grows and is countered by increasing infiltration of North Vietnamese troops down the Ho Chi Minh Trail. With their superior mobility and firepower, American forces bloody enemy units in several conventional battles. By 1967, revolutionary forces have gone over to a strategy of guerrilla fighting and attrition.

January 31, 1968: The Tet Offensive begins, with Vietcong and Northern troops attacking major cities and towns throughout the country. When no civilian uprising materializes in support of the offensive, revolutionary forces are caught in the open. Vietcong forces lose almost 50 percent of their fighting manpower, virtually eliminating the Southern guerrillas as an effective military organization. At the same time, news of the widespread attacks, the ferocity of the fighting, and specific revolutionary successes such as the breaching of the U.S. Embassy compound create a swell of public disillusionment in the United States.

March 31, 1968: Lyndon Johnson offers to negotiate with the North Vietnamese and announces he will not seek reelection.

May 1968: Negotiations open in Paris.

November 1968: Richard Nixon is elected President of the United States. A month later he chooses Henry Kissinger as national security adviser.

1969–1971

May 1969: Nixon announces "Vietnamization" of the war and begins withdrawing American troops. The pullback reinvigorates morale among Liberation Army troops, for whom the aftermath of Tet has been a period of retreat and dispersal.

September 3, 1969: Ho Chi Minh dies at the age of seventy-nine.

February 1970: Secret talks between Kissinger and North Vietnamese politburo member Le Duc Tho begin in Paris.

March 18, 1970: Cambodian head of state Prince Sihanouk is overthrown by two of his ministers.

April 30, 1970: American forces strike into Cambodia to eliminate revolutionary bases, sanctuaries, and supply lines.

By late 1970, revolutionary forces are recovering from the crushing defeat of the Tet Offensive and the American thrust into Cambodia. In February 1971, they turn back a South Vietnamese attack into Laos, inflicting heavy losses. Throughout 1971 the Northern military buildup continues, in preparation for a massive new offensive planned for the 1971–1972 dry season.

1972–1973

By the beginning of 1972, American troop strength is down to 140,000 from a high of 540,000. As the withdrawal proceeds, talks in Paris between Kissinger and Le Duc Tho break down. On March 30, 1972, the long-awaited dry season offensive breaks out. At first, North Vietnamese forces make substantial progress against the South Vietnamese army, fighting now without American ground support. In retaliation, Nixon renews bombing of Hanoi and Haiphong, suspended since 1968, and orders Haiphong harbor mined.

By July, U.S. strategic and tactical air power combined with South Vietnamese army resistance has stopped the North Vietnamese offensive and forced a general retreat from territory gained in the initial stages of the battle. On July 13 peace talks resume in Paris.

In October, the last North Vietnamese conquests are recovered. In Paris, Le Duc Tho and Kissinger achieve a breakthrough and Kissinger announces, "Peace is at hand."

November 7, 1972: Richard Nixon is reelected President in a landslide victory over Democratic candidate George McGovern.

December 13, 1972: Paris talks stall over new demands by South Vietnamese President Nguyen Van Thieu. North Vietnamese negotiator Le Duc Tho returns to Hanoi.

December 18–29, 1972: The U.S. Air Force conducts intensive bombing of Hanoi and Haiphong.

January 8–12, 1973: Le Duc Tho and Kissinger resume talks. Several days later President Nixon calls a halt to all offensive operations against North Vietnam.

January 27, 1973: Peace agreement is signed in Paris by representatives of the United States, North Vietnam, South Vietnam, and the National Liberation Front. Within two months the last U.S. troops have left Vietnam.

1974–1975

With U.S. forces gone, South Vietnamese and North Vietnamese resume hostilities. North Vietnamese logistical buildup gives People's Army forces supply and weapons superiority for the first time in the war. Probing attacks by revolutionary forces elicit no response by American air power.

January 8, 1975: North Vietnam initiates major offensive against the South. By the end of March, South Vietnamese resistance has collapsed and the Saigon army is falling back toward the capital.

April 29, 1975: North Vietnamese army begins attack on Saigon.

April 30, 1975: Saigon falls and the Vietnam War ends.

In the immediate postwar period the South is run by the politburo-controlled Military Management Committee, operating as the de facto Southern government. The National Liberation Front of South Vietnam (the Vietcong) and its Provisional Revolutionary Government are progressively isolated from power as plans are formulated for the rapid unification of the country.

1976–1979

In early 1976, elections are held for a National Assembly for the entire country. In July the Assembly meets and the formal unification of North and South is completed, the new nation to be called the Socialist Republic of Vietnam.

In the South, unification brings with it more direct Northern dominance of governmental affairs and a progressive socialization of the economy. These factors, together with a decline in the standard of living and the imposition of totalitarian political controls, give impetus to an exodus from Vietnam that by 1978 is reaching massive proportions. Anti–ethnic Chinese measures, which precede and accompany the 1979 border war with China, increase the flow of refugees into Southeast Asian camps and from there to new homes. As of 1985 some seven hundred thousand Vietnamese and other Indochinese refugees have been resettled in the United States.

A NOTE ON SOURCES

THE VIETNAMESE MATERIAL IN THIS BOOK WAS COMPILED FROM SEVeral sources in addition to personal interviews. Military interrogation reports housed at the Indochina Archives, University of California, Berkeley, furnished the accounts beginning on pages 42, 43, 45, 47, 48, 67, 68, 123, 130, 161, 166, 168, and 171. *Nhan Dan* (*The Party Daily* published in Hanoi) is the source for accounts beginning on pages 130, 146, 147, and 149. Truong Nhu Tang's description of his meeting with Ho Chi Minh (p. 34) is from his autobiography, *A Vietcong Memoir,* published by Harcourt Brace Jovanovich in 1985, while General Tran Van Tra's memoir of Ho (p. 36) and his ode to the battlefield (p. 172) are from his *History of the Bulwark B2 Theatre,* published in Ho Chi Minh City in 1982 and withdrawn from circulation shortly thereafter (JPRS Doc. 82783). The battle of Dong Xoai is excerpted from Vu Hung's *Bong Toi Da Di Qua* (*The Dark Night Past*), published in Saigon, 1972.